175 Essential
Slow Cooker
Classics

175 Essential
Slow Cooker
Classics

Judith Finlayson

Robert
ROSE

For complete cataloguing information, see page 310.

Disclaimer
The recipes in this book have been carefully tested by our kitchen and our tasters. To the best of our knowledge, they are safe and nutritious for ordinary use and users. For those people with food or other allergies, or who have special food requirements or health issues, please read the suggested contents of each recipe carefully and determine whether or not they may create a problem for you. All recipes are used at the risk of the consumer.

We cannot be responsible for any hazards, loss or damage that may occur as a result of any recipe use.

For those with special needs, allergies, requirements or health problems, in the event of any doubt, please contact your medical adviser prior to the use of any recipe.

Design & Production: PageWave Graphics Inc.
Editor: Carol Sherman
Recipe Testers: Jennifer MacKenzie and Audrey King
Copy Editor: Karen Campbell-Sheviak
Photography: Colin Erricson and Mark T. Shapiro
Food Styling: Kate Bush and Kathy Robertson
Prop Styling: Charlene Erricson

Cover image: Country Stew with Fennel (page 74)
Page 2: Lamb with Artichokes (page 142)
Page 5: Easy Vegetable Chili (page 230)
Page 6: Greek Bean Sauce with Feta (page 220)
Page 10: New Mexico Short Ribs (page 92)

We acknowledge the financial support of the Government of Canada through the Book Publishing Industry Development Program (BPIDP) for our publishing activities.

Published by Robert Rose Inc.
120 Eglinton Avenue East, Suite 800, Toronto, Ontario, Canada M4P 1E2
Tel: (416) 322-6552 Fax: (416) 322-6936

Printed in China
1 2 3 4 5 6 7 8 9 RRD 14 13 12 11 10 09 08 07 06

Contents

Acknowledgments

Like all my cookbooks, 175 *Essential Slow Cooker Classics* depends upon many people who work behind the scenes. It takes a team of highly skilled professionals to transform a manuscript of recipes into a beautifully designed book heavily illustrated with photographs. Designers, food and prop stylists, photographers, recipes testers and editors have all contributed to the end result.

Thanks to the group at PageWave Graphics, Andrew Smith, Joseph Gisini, Kevin Cockburn and Daniella Zanchetta, who manage production and the visual aspects of my books, working their alchemy on my plain Word files by converting them into beautifully designed pages; to prop stylist Charlene Erricson, who sets the stage for the photographers; food stylists Kate Bush and Kathy Robertson, and photographers Mark Shapiro and Colin Erricson, who make all my recipes look mouthwatering; recipe testers Jennifer MacKenzie and Audrey King who leave no stone unturned in ensuring recipe accuracy; copy editor Karen Campbell-Sheviak, who catches important little details, which the rest of us miss; and, of course, my editor Carol Sherman, whose unique combination of eagle eyes, a sharp wit and consistent charm makes the editorial process relatively painless. I am extremely appreciative of your combined efforts on my behalf.

I'd also like to thank Bob Dees and Marian Jarkovich at Robert Rose for being consummate publishing professionals. I know they work very hard to ensure the success of my books, for which I am most grateful.

Introduction

Since writing my first slow cooker book more than five years ago, I've become more and more convinced that this simple and easy-to-use appliance can play a significant role in helping families enjoy delicious and nutritious home-cooked food on even the busiest days. Quite simply, the slow cooker is one of the most effective time-management tools any cook can have. It allows you to be in the kitchen when it is most convenient and cooks your meals untended, freeing you up to do all the other things you need to get done in a day.

One great benefit to using a slow cooker is that most dishes can be substantially prepared ahead of time and refrigerated (the Make ahead component of my recipes contains detailed recipe-specific instructions that explain how to do this). When you're ready to cook, you combine the ingredients, drop the stoneware into the casing and turn the appliance on. Then, if other commitments call, you can safely leave the house and, depending how long you are away, arrive home to be greeted by the appetizing aroma of a home-cooked meal.

The list of things you can make in your slow cooker is almost infinite. Mouth-watering soups, chilies, stews, pot roasts — even desserts — cook almost magically on their own. Most savory dishes are cooked with aromatics such as onions and garlic, which bring out their natural flavor and enhance the rich, complex sauces the slow cooker excels at producing. I find that spices, judiciously added, work well in the slow cooker, helping to develop the taste of the final result. Using these recipes, you'll be able to create meals that will soon become family favorites. Better still, producing such outstanding results requires a minimal amount of your attention.

While my slow cooker dishes certainly qualify as nutritious, they are also good for us in other respects. Social scientists tell us that getting families together around the table has benefits that extend beyond nutrition. Among other advantages, when families eat together on a regular basis, children are more likely to do better in school and less likely to become involved in negative behaviors such as smoking or alcohol abuse. At the very least, the kind of dishes the slow cooker excels at producing — hearty soups and stews and comforting old-fashioned desserts — offer a reassuring antidote to the stresses of our fast-paced age.

This book includes many of my favorite recipes from my first two books, as well as more than sixty new ones that have been developed especially for this volume. I hope you will enjoy them and, if you haven't already, will make the slow cooker a regular part of your life.

Judith Finlayson

Using Your Slow Cooker

An Effective Time Manager

In addition to producing great-tasting food, a slow cooker is an extremely effective time-management tool. Where appropriate, I've included Make ahead instructions that explain how to prepare a substantial amount of a recipe prior to cooking it, which enables you to be in the kitchen when it fits your schedule. (Some dishes and ingredients can't be assembled ahead of time for food safety or quality reasons.) Once the ingredients have been assembled in the stoneware and the appliance is turned on, you can forget about it. The slow cooker performs unattended while you carry on with your workaday life. You can be away from the kitchen all day and return to a hot, delicious meal.

Maximize Slow Cooker Convenience

To get the most out of your slow cooker:

- Use Make ahead instructions to partially prepare a dish up to 2 days prior to cooking.
- Do any additional chopping and slicing the night before you intend to cook to keep work to a minimum when it is less convenient.
- Cook a recipe overnight and refrigerate until ready to serve.

A Low-Tech Appliance

Slow cookers are amazingly low tech. The appliance usually consists of a metal casing and a stoneware insert with a tight-fitting lid. For convenience, you should be able to remove the insert from the metal casing. This makes it easier to clean and increases its versatility, not only as a vessel for refrigerating some dishes that have been prepared to the Make ahead stage but also as a serving dish. The casing contains the heat source, electrical coils that usually surround the stoneware insert. These coils do their work on the energy it takes to power a 100-watt light bulb. Because the slow cooker operates on such a small amount of energy, you can safely leave it turned on while you are away from home. However, if you've assembled the dish in the stoneware and refrigerated it overnight (appropriate for some dishes), do not turn the slow cooker on before dropping the stoneware into the casing. The dramatic temperature change could crack the stoneware.

Slow Cooker Basics

Slow cookers are generally round or oval in shape and range in size from 1 to 7 quarts. The small round ones are ideal for dips and fondues, as well as some soups, main courses and desserts. The larger sizes, usually oval in shape, are necessary to cook big batch dishes and those that need to be cooked in a dish or pan, which fits into the stoneware.

Because I use my slow cookers a lot for entertaining, I feel there is a benefit to having two: a smaller (3- to 4-quart size) which is ideal for preparing dips, roasting nuts or making recipes with smaller yields, and a larger (6 quart) oval one, which I use most of the time to cook recipes with large yields as well as for those calling for a baking dish or pan, which is set inside the stoneware. Once you begin using your slow cooker, you will get a sense of what your own needs are.

Some manufacturers sell a "slow cooker" that is actually a multi-cooker. These have a heating element at the bottom and, in my experience, they cook faster than traditional slow cookers. Also, since the heat source is at the bottom, during the long cooking time it is possible that the food will scorch unless it is stirred.

Your slow cooker should come with a booklet that explains how to use the appliance. I recommend that you read this carefully and/or visit the manufacturer's website for specific information on the model you purchased. I've used a variety of slow cookers and have found that cooking times can vary substantially from one to another. Although it may not seem particularly helpful if you're just starting out, the only firm advice I can give is: Know your slow cooker. After trying a few of these recipes, you will get a sense of whether your slow cooker is faster or slower than the ones I use and you will be able to adjust the cooking times accordingly.

Other variables that can affect cooking time are extreme humidity, power fluctuations and high altitudes. Be extra vigilant if any of these circumstances affect you.

Cooking Great-Tasting Food

The slow cooker's less-is-better approach is, in many ways, the secret of its success. The appliance does its work by cooking foods very slowly — from about 200°F (100°C) on the Low setting to 300°F (150°C) on High. This slow, moist cooking environment (remember the tight-fitting lid) enables the appliance to produce mouth-watering pot roasts, briskets, chilies and many other kinds of soups and stews. It also helps to ensure success with delicate puddings and custards, among other dishes. In fact, I'm so pleased with the slow cooker's strengths that there are many dishes I wouldn't cook any other way — for instance, pot roast, beef brisket or short ribs, chilies and many kinds of stew. I also love to make cheesecakes in my slow cooker because they emerge from this damp cocoon, perfectly cooked every time. They don't dry out or crack, which happens all too easily in the oven.

Slow Cooker Tips

Some benefits of long slow cooking:
- breaks down the tough connective tissue of less tender cuts of meat;
- allows the seasoning in complex sauces to intermingle without scorching;
- makes succulent chilies and stews that don't dry out or stick to the bottom of the pot;
- ensures success with delicate dishes such as puddings and custards.

Understanding Your Slow Cooker

Like all appliances, the slow cooker has its unique way of doing things and, as a result, you need to understand how it works and adapt your cooking style accordingly. When friends learned I was writing a slow cooker cookbook, many had a similar response: "Oh, you mean that appliance that allows you to throw the ingredients in and return to a home-cooked meal!"

"Well, sort of," was my response. Over the years, I've learned to think of my slow cooker as an indispensable helpmate, and I can hardly imagine living without its assistance. But I also know that it can't work miracles. Off the top of my head, I can't think of any great dish that results when ingredients are merely "thrown together." Success in the slow cooker, like success in the oven or on top of the stove, depends upon using proper cooking techniques. The slow cooker saves you time because it allows you to forget about the food once it is in the stoneware. But you still must pay attention to the advance preparation. Here are a few tips that will help to ensure slow cooker success.

Brown Meat and Soften Vegetables

Although it requires an extra pan, I am committed to browning most meats and softening vegetables before adding them to the slow cooker. In my experience, this is not the most time-consuming part of preparing a slow cooker dish — it usually takes longer to peel and chop the vegetables, which you have to do anyway. But it dramatically improves the quality of the dish for two reasons. Not only does browning add color, but it also begins the process of caramelization, which breaks down the natural sugars in foods and releases their flavor. It also extracts the fat-soluble components of foods, which further enriches the taste. Moreover, tossing herbs and spices with the softened vegetables helps to produce a sauce in which the flavors are better integrated than they would have been if this step had been skipped.

Reduce the Quantity of Liquid

As you use your slow cooker, one of the first things you will notice is that it generates liquid. Because slow cookers cook at a low heat, tightly covered, liquid doesn't evaporate as it does in the oven or on top of the stove. As a result, food made from traditional recipes will be watery. So the second rule of successful slow cooking is to reduce the amount of liquid. Because you don't want to reduce the flavor, I prefer to cook with stock rather than water.

Cut Root Vegetables into Thin Slices or Small Pieces

Perhaps surprisingly, root vegetables — carrots, parsnips and particularly potatoes — cook even more slowly than meat in the slow cooker. As a result, root vegetables should be thinly sliced or cut into small pieces no larger than 1-inch (2.5 cm) cubes.

Pay Attention to Cooking Temperature

To achieve maximum results, less tender cuts of meat should be cooked as slowly as possible at the Low setting. Expect to cook whole cuts of meat such as roasts for 10 hours on Low and give brisket 12 hours on Low to become truly succulent. If you're short of time and at home during the day, cook whole cuts of meat on High for 1 to 2 hours before switching the temperature to Low. As noted in Food Safety (see page 16) if adding cold ingredients, particularly large cuts of meat, to the slow cooker, set on High for an hour before lowering the temperature.

Many desserts, such as those containing milk, cream or some leavening agents need to be cooked on High. In these recipes, a Low setting is not suggested as an option. For recipes that aren't dependent upon cooking at a particular temperature, the rule of thumb is that 1 hour of cooking on High equals 2 to 2½ hours on Low.

Don't Overcook

Although slow cooking reduces your chances of overcooking food, it is still not a "one size fits all" solution to meal preparation. If you want your slow cooker to cook pork chops or chicken while you are away, you should plan your day carefully. It is very easy to overcook poultry, which shouldn't require more than 6 hours on Low. If cooking white meat, which dries out easily, I recommend leaving the skin on, which helps to maintain precious moisture and flavor. Remove the skin when serving, if desired. Because legs and thighs stand up well in the slow cooker, I remove the skin before cooking to reduce the fat content in the sauce.

Use Ingredients Appropriately

Some ingredients do not respond well to long slow cooking and should be added during the last 30 minutes of cooking, after the temperature has been increased to High. These include: peas, leafy greens, seafood, milk and cream (which will curdle if cooked too long). I love to cook with peppers, but I've learned that most become bitter if cooked for too long. The solution to this problem is to add peppers to recipes during the last 30 minutes of cooking. All the recipes in this book address these concerns in the instructions.

Whole Leaf Herbs and Whole Spices

For best results use whole rather than ground herbs and spices in the slow cooker. Whole spices, such as cinnamon sticks and vanilla beans, and whole leaf herbs, such as dried thyme and oregano leaves, release their flavors slowly throughout the long cooking period, unlike ground spices and herbs, which tend to lose flavor during slow cooking. If you're using fresh herbs, finely chop them and add during the last hour of cooking unless you include the whole stem (this works best with thyme and rosemary).

I recommend the use of cracked black peppercorns rather than ground pepper in most of my recipes because they release flavor slowly during the long cooking process. Cracked pepper can be purchased in the spice sections of supermarkets, but I like to make my own in a mortar with a pestle. A rolling pin or even a heavy can on its side will also break up the peppercorns for use in slow-cooked dishes. If you prefer to use ground black pepper, use one-quarter to one-half the amount of cracked black peppercorns called for in the recipe.

Using Dishes and Pans in the Slow Cooker

Some dishes, notably puddings and custards need to be cooked in an extra dish, which is placed in the slow cooker stoneware. Not only will you need a large oval slow cooker for this purpose, finding a dish or pan that fits into the stoneware can be a challenge. I've found that standard 7-inch (17.5 cm) square, 4-cup (1 L) and 6-cup (1.5 L) ovenproof baking dishes or soufflé dishes are the best all-round dishes for this purpose and I've used them to cook most of the custard-like recipes in this book. A 7-inch (17.5 cm) springform pan, which fits into a large oval slow cooker, is also a useful purchase for making cheesecakes.

Before you decide to make a recipe requiring a baking dish, ensure that you have a container that will fit into your stoneware. I've noted the size and dimensions of the containers used in all relevant recipes. Be aware that varying the size and shape of the dish is likely to affect cooking times.

Food Safety

Food Safety in the Slow Cooker

Because it cooks at a very low temperature for long periods of time, cooking with a slow cooker requires a bit more vigilance about food safety than does cooking at higher temperatures. The slow cooker needs to strike a delicate balance between cooking slowly enough that it doesn't require your attention and fast enough to ensure that food reaches temperatures that are appropriate to inhibit bacterial growth. Bacteria grow rapidly at temperatures higher than 40°F (4°C) and lower than 140°F (60°C). Once the temperature reaches 165°F (74°C) bacteria are killed. That's why it is so important to leave the lid on when you're slow cooking, particularly during the early stages. This helps to ensure that bacteria-killing temperatures are reached in the appropriate amount of time.

Slow cooker manufacturers have designed the appliance to ensure that bacterial growth is not a concern. So long as the lid is left on and the food is cooked for the appropriate length of time, that temperature will be reached quickly enough to ensure food safety. Unless you have made part of the recipe ahead and refrigerated it, most of the ingredients in my recipes are warm when added to the slow cooker (the meat has been browned and the sauce has been thickened on the stovetop), which adds a cushion of comfort to any potential concerns about food safety.

The following tips will help to ensure that utmost food safety standards are met:

- Keep food refrigerated until you are ready to cook. Bacteria multiply quickly at room temperature. Do not allow ingredients to rise to room temperature before cooking.
- Do not partially cook meat or poultry and refrigerate for subsequent cooking. If you're browning meat before adding it to the slow cooker, do so just before placing it in the slow cooker. When cooking meat try to get it to a high temperature as quickly as possible.
- If cooking a large cut of meat, such as a pot roast, which has been added to the stoneware without being browned, set the temperature at High for at least an hour to accelerate the cooking process.
- If preparing ingredients in advance of cooking, refrigerate precooked meat, such as ground beef or sausage, and vegetables in separate containers and assemble when ready to cook.

- Pay attention to the Make ahead instructions for those recipes that can be partially prepared in advance of cooking because they have been developed to address food safety issues.
- Do not put frozen meat, fish or poultry into a slow cooker. Unless otherwise instructed, thaw frozen food before adding to the slow cooker. Frozen fruits and vegetables should usually be thawed under cold running water to separate before being added to recipes.
- Don't lift the lid while food is cooking. Each time the lid is removed it takes approximately 20 minutes to recover the lost heat. This increases the time it takes for the food to reach the "safe zone."
- If you are away and the power goes out, discard the food if it has not finished cooking. If the food has cooked completely, it should be safe for up to 2 hours.
- Refrigerate leftovers as quickly as possible.
- Do not reheat food in the slow cooker.

Testing for Safety

If you are concerned that your slow cooker isn't cooking quickly enough to ensure food safety try this simple test. Fill the stoneware insert with 8 cups (2 L) of cold water. Set temperature to Low for 8 hours. Using an accurate thermometer, and checking quickly because the temperature drops when the lid is removed, check to ensure that the temperature is 185°F (85°C). If it has not reached that temperature, it's not heating food fast enough to avoid food safety problems. If the temperature is significantly higher than that, the appliance is not cooking slowly enough to be used as a slow cooker.

Leftovers

Cooked food can be kept warm in the slow cooker for up to 2 hours. At that point it should be transferred to small containers so it cools as rapidly as possible and refrigerated or frozen. Because the appliance heats up so slowly, food should never be reheated in a slow cooker.

Crab Timbale with Spinach Sauce (page 37)

Appetizers, Fondues and Savories

Chilly Dilly Eggplant

**MAKES ABOUT
4 CUPS (1 L)**

This is a versatile recipe, delicious as a dip with raw vegetables or on pita triangles, as well as a sandwich spread on crusty French bread. It also makes a wonderful addition to a mezes or tapas-style meal. Although it is tasty warm, the flavor dramatically improves if it is thoroughly chilled before serving.

Make ahead

You'll achieve the best results if you make this a day ahead and chill thoroughly before serving, or cook overnight, purée in the morning and chill.

• **Works best in a small (maximum 3½ quart) slow cooker**

2	large eggplants, peeled, cut into 1-inch (2.5 cm) cubes and drained of excess moisture (see Tip, below)	2
2 to 3 tbsp	olive oil	25 to 45 mL
2	onions, chopped	2
4	cloves garlic, chopped	4
1 tsp	dried oregano leaves	5 mL
1 tsp	salt	5 mL
½ tsp	freshly ground black pepper	2 mL
1 tbsp	balsamic or red wine vinegar	15 mL
½ cup	chopped fresh dill	125 mL
	Dill sprigs, optional	
	Finely chopped black olives, optional	

1. In a skillet, heat 2 tbsp (25 mL) of the oil over medium-high heat for 30 seconds. Add eggplant, in batches, and cook, stirring and tossing, until it begins to brown, about 3 minutes per batch. Transfer to slow cooker stoneware.

2. Reduce heat to medium. Add more oil, if necessary and cook onions, stirring, until softened, about 3 minutes. Add garlic, oregano, salt and pepper and cook, stirring, for 1 minute. Transfer to slow cooker stoneware and stir to combine thoroughly. Cover and cook on Low for 7 to 8 hours or on High for 4 hours, until eggplant is tender.

3. Transfer contents of slow cooker (in batches, if necessary) to a blender or food processor. Add vinegar and dill and process until smooth, scraping down sides of bowl at halfway point. Taste for seasoning and adjust. Spoon into a small serving bowl and chill thoroughly. Garnish with sprigs of dill and chopped black olives, if using.

TIP

• Although eggplant is delicious when properly cooked, some varieties tend to be bitter. Since the bitterness is concentrated under the skin, I peel eggplant before using. Sprinkling the pieces with salt and leaving them to "sweat" for an hour or two also draws out the bitter juice. If time is short, blanch the pieces for a minute or two in heavily salted water. In either case, rinse thoroughly in fresh cold water and, using your hands, squeeze out the excess moisture. Pat dry with paper towels and it's ready for cooking.

Sumptuous Spinach and Artichoke Dip

SERVES 6 TO 8

Although spinach and artichoke dip has become a North American classic, its roots lie in Provençal cuisine, in which the vegetables are usually baked with cheese and served as a gratin. This chunky dip, simplicity itself, always draws rave reviews and disappears to the last drop.

- **Works best in a small (maximum 3½ quart) slow cooker**

1 cup	shredded mozzarella cheese	250 mL
8 oz	cream cheese, cubed	250 g
¼ cup	grated Parmesan cheese	50 mL
1	clove garlic, minced	1
¼ tsp	freshly ground black pepper	1 mL
1	can (14 oz/398 mL) artichokes, drained and finely chopped	1
1 lb	fresh spinach, stems removed, or 1 package (10 oz/300 g) spinach leaves, thawed if frozen (see Tips, below)	500 g
	Tostadas or tortilla chips	

1. In slow cooker stoneware, combine cheese, cream cheese, Parmesan, garlic, pepper, artichokes and spinach. Cover and cook on High for 2 hours, until hot and bubbly. Stir well and serve with tostadas or other tortilla chips.

TIPS
- If you are using fresh spinach leaves in this recipe, take care to wash them thoroughly, as they can be quite gritty. To wash spinach: Fill a clean sink with lukewarm water. Remove the tough stems and submerge the tender leaves in the water, swishing to remove the grit. Rinse thoroughly in a colander under cold running water, checking carefully to ensure that no sand remains. If you are using frozen spinach in this recipe, thaw and squeeze the excess moisture out before adding to the slow cooker.
- If you prefer a smoother dip, place spinach and artichokes in a food processor, in separate batches, and pulse until desired degree of fineness is achieved. Then combine with remaining ingredients in slow cooker stoneware.

Black Bean and Salsa Dip

**MAKES ABOUT
3 CUPS (750 ML)**

This tasty Cuban-inspired dip can be made from ingredients you're likely to have on hand. Nutritious and flavorful, it's a welcome treat, any time of the day. Serve with tortilla chips, tostadas, crisp crackers or crudités.

● **Works best in a small (maximum 3½ quart) slow cooker**

2 cups	cooked dried or canned black beans, drained and rinsed (see Tips, below)	500 mL
8 oz	cream cheese, cubed	250 g
½ cup	tomato salsa	125 mL
¼ cup	sour cream	50 mL
2 tsp	cumin seeds, toasted and ground (see Tip, page 59)	10 mL
1 tsp	chili powder	5 mL
1 tsp	cracked black peppercorns	5 mL
1	jalapeño pepper, finely chopped, optional (see Tips, below)	1
1	roasted red bell pepper, finely chopped, optional (see Tips, below)	1
	Finely chopped green onion, optional	
	Finely chopped cilantro, optional	

1. In slow cooker stoneware, combine beans, cream cheese, salsa, sour cream, cumin, chili powder, peppercorns, jalapeño pepper and roasted red pepper, if using. Cover and cook on High for 1 hour. Stir again and cook on High for an additional 30 minutes, until mixture is hot and bubbly. Serve immediately or set temperature at Low until ready to serve. Garnish with green onion and/or cilantro, if desired.

TIPS
- You can use 1 can (14 to 19 oz/398 to 540 mL) black beans to make this recipe.
- For a smoother dip, purée the beans in a food processor or mash with a potato masher before adding to stoneware.
- If you use a five-alarm salsa in this dip, you may find it too spicy with the addition of jalapeño pepper.
- If you don't have time to roast your own pepper, use a bottled roasted red pepper.
- To roast peppers: Preheat oven to 400°F (200°C). Place pepper(s) on a baking sheet and roast, turning two or three times, until the skin on all sides is blackened. (This will take about 25 minutes.) Transfer pepper(s) to a heatproof bowl. Cover with a plate and let stand until cool. Remove and, using a sharp knife, lift off skins. Discard skins, stem and core and slice according to recipe instructions.

Artichoke, Sun-Dried Tomato and Goat Cheese Spread

SERVES 6

Serve this sophisticated spread on leaves of Belgian endive, topped with toasted pine nuts for added flair. Or spoon it into a pottery bowl and surround with pieces of flatbread for a more informal presentation.

• **Works best in a small (maximum 3½ quart) slow cooker**

1	can (14 oz/398 mL) artichokes, drained and finely chopped	1
4	sun-dried tomatoes, packed in olive oil, drained and finely chopped	4
2	cloves garlic, crushed	2
¼ tsp	salt	1 mL
¼ tsp	freshly ground black pepper	1 mL
8 oz	soft goat cheese, crumbled	250 g
	Belgian endive, optional	
¼ cup	toasted pine nuts, optional	50 mL

1. In slow cooker stoneware, combine artichokes, sun-dried tomatoes, garlic, salt and pepper. Cover and cook on High for 1 hour.

2. Add goat cheese and stir to combine. Cover and cook on High for 1 hour, until hot and bubbly. Stir well. Spoon into a bowl or spread on leaves of Belgian endive and top with toasted pine nuts, if using.

TIP

• To toast pine nuts: Place pine nuts in a dry skillet over medium heat. Cook, stirring constantly, until they begin to turn light gold, 3 to 4 minutes. Remove from heat and immediately transfer to a small bowl. Once they begin to brown, they can burn very quickly.

Caponata

**MAKES ABOUT
4 CUPS (1 L)**

*This robust spread
is a treat from Sicily.
Serve it on crostini
or with crackers, pita
bread or crudités
such as celery sticks.
It keeps, covered, in
the refrigerator for
up to one week.*

Make ahead

You'll achieve the best
results if you make the
caponata a day ahead
and chill overnight in
the refrigerator.

• *Works best in a small (maximum 3½ quart) slow cooker*

1	medium eggplant, peeled, cut into 1-inch (2.5 cm) cubes and drained of excess moisture (see Tip, page 20)	1
2 tbsp	balsamic vinegar	25 mL
1 tsp	packed brown sugar	5 mL
2 to 3 tbsp	olive oil	25 to 45 mL
1	onion, finely chopped	1
2	stalks celery, finely chopped	2
4	cloves garlic, minced	4
1 tsp	dried oregano leaves	5 mL
½ tsp	cracked black peppercorns	2 mL
1	can (14 oz/398 mL) diced tomatoes, including juice	1
	Salt, optional	
½ cup	chopped pitted black olives	125 mL
1 tbsp	drained capers	15 mL
2 tbsp	toasted pine nuts	25 mL
2 tbsp	chiffonade of basil leaves, optional	25 mL

1. In a small bowl, combine vinegar and brown sugar. Stir until sugar dissolves. Set aside.

2. In a skillet, heat 2 tbsp (25 mL) of the oil over medium-high heat for 30 seconds. Add eggplant, in batches, and cook, stirring and tossing, until it begins to brown, about 3 minutes per batch. Transfer to slow cooker stoneware.

3. In same skillet over medium heat, adding more oil if necessary, cook onion and celery, stirring, until softened, about 5 minutes. Add garlic, oregano and peppercorns and cook, stirring, for I minute. Add tomatoes with juice and balsamic mixture and bring to a boil. Boil for I minute to reduce liquid. Season to taste with salt, if using. Transfer to stoneware and stir thoroughly.

4. Cover and cook on Low for 7 to 8 hours or on High for 4 hours, until eggplant is tender. Stir in olives and capers. Transfer to a serving bowl. Cover and refrigerate for 2 hours or overnight. Garnish with pine nuts and basil, if using.

TIP

• To cut the basil into chiffonade, stack the leaves, 4 at a time, roll them into a cigar shape and slice as thinly as you can.

Hot Roasted Nuts

SERVES 6 TO 8

When entertaining in winter, I like to light a fire and place small bowls full of these tasty nibblers around the living room. I recommend using a small slow cooker for these recipes, as the nuts are less likely to burn. If you use a large slow cooker (5 or 6 quarts), watch carefully and stir every 15 minutes, as the nuts will cook quite quickly (just over an hour).

Everyone loves these hot buttery peanuts — even me, and I'm usually not a fan of this Southern legume. Use peanuts with skins on or buy them peeled, depending upon your preference. Both work well in this recipe.

Variation
Curried Buttery Peanuts
In a small bowl, combine sea salt with 2 tsp (10 mL) curry powder and a pinch of cayenne pepper. Substitute for plain salt.

- **These recipes work best in a small (maximum 3½ quart) slow cooker**

Salty Almonds with Thyme

2 cups	unblanched almonds	500 mL
½ tsp	ground white pepper	2 mL
1 tbsp	fine sea salt, or more to taste	15 mL
2 tbsp	extra virgin olive oil	25 mL
2 tbsp	fresh thyme leaves	25 mL

1. In slow cooker stoneware, combine almonds and white pepper. Cover and cook on High for 1½ hours, stirring every 30 minutes, until nuts are nicely toasted.

2. In a mixing bowl, combine salt, olive oil and thyme. Add to hot almonds in stoneware and stir thoroughly to combine. Spoon mixture into a small serving bowl and serve hot or allow to cool.

Buttery Peanuts

2 cups	raw peanuts	500 mL
¼ cup	melted butter or butter substitute	50 mL
2 tsp	fine sea salt (see Tip, right)	10 mL

1. In slow cooker stoneware, combine peanuts and butter. Cover and cook on High for 2 to 2½ hours, stirring occasionally, until peanuts are nicely roasted. Drain on paper towels. Place in a bowl, sprinkle with salt and stir to combine.

Orange-Spiced Pecans

2 cups	pecan halves	500 mL
1 tbsp	grated orange zest	15 mL
2 tbsp	orange juice	25 mL
1/4 cup	granulated sugar	50 mL
1/2 tsp	ground cinnamon	2 mL
1/4 tsp	freshly grated nutmeg	1 mL
Pinch	fine sea salt (see Tip, below)	Pinch

1. In slow cooker stoneware, combine pecans and orange juice. Cover and cook on High for 1 hour or until nuts release their aroma and are nicely toasted. Transfer to a serving bowl.

2. In a small bowl, combine sugar, orange zest, cinnamon, nutmeg and salt. Pour over hot nuts and toss to combine. Serve warm.

TIP
- Sea salt is available in most supermarkets. It is much sweeter than table salt and is essential for these recipes as table salt would impart an unpleasant acrid taste to the nuts. Be sure to buy sea salt without additives, such as iodine or anti-caking agents.

Variation
Sweet and Spicy Cashews
Substitute 1 tbsp (15 mL) butter for the olive oil and add along with 2 tbsp (25 mL) brown sugar.

Spicy Cashews

2 cups	raw cashews	500 mL
1 tsp	chili powder	5 mL
1/2 tsp	cayenne pepper	2 mL
1/4 tsp	ground cinnamon	1 mL
2 tsp	fine sea salt	10 mL
1 tbsp	extra virgin olive oil	15 mL

1. In slow cooker stoneware, combine cashews, chili powder, cayenne and cinnamon. Stir to combine thoroughly. Cover and cook on High for 1 1/2 hours, stirring every 30 minutes, until nuts are nicely toasted.

2. In a small bowl, combine sea salt and olive oil. Add to nuts in slow cooker and stir to thoroughly combine. Transfer mixture to a serving bowl. Serve hot or cool.

Nippy Cheddar Rabbit

SERVES 6

When I was growing up, my mother's Welsh rarebit (the English term for this dish) was one of my favorite treats. Now that I'm a mother myself, I still think it's yummy, and so does my family. Made with beer, this slightly adult version is a great predinner nibbler for guests. It also doubles as a light luncheon dish served, like Mom's, over hot toast.

- **Works best in a small (maximum 3½ quart) slow cooker**
- **Fondue forks**

8 oz	old Cheddar cheese, shredded	250 g
1 cup	beer	250 mL
2	egg yolks, beaten	2
¼ tsp	dry mustard	1 mL
1 tsp	Worcestershire sauce	5 mL
1 tsp	packed brown sugar	5 mL
Pinch	cayenne pepper	Pinch
	White bread, crusts removed, cut into 1-inch (2.5 cm) cubes and lightly toasted under broiler.	

1. In slow cooker stoneware, combine cheese and beer. Cover and cook on Low for 30 minutes, or until cheese melts.

2. In a bowl, whisk together egg yolks, mustard, Worcestershire sauce, brown sugar and cayenne. Pour mixture into slow cooker stoneware and stir until thickened.

3. Spear toasted bread with fondue forks and dip in cheese, ensuring that guests have napkins or plates to catch any dripping sauce.

TIP
- I always keep a bottle of Worcestershire sauce in the pantry as just a spoonful of this venerable concoction (it was created over a century and a half ago) adds welcome zest to many dishes.

Spicy Spinach Dip

SERVES 6

Here's a great dip with a bit of punch. If you are a heat seeker, add the extra jalapeño pepper and use extra hot salsa.

• **Works best in a small (maximum 3½ quart) slow cooker**

1 lb	fresh spinach, stems removed, or 1 package (10 oz/300 g) spinach leaves, thawed if frozen (see Tip, below)	500 g
2 cups	shredded Monterey Jack cheese	500 mL
½ cup	tomato salsa	125 mL
¼ cup	sour cream	50 mL
4	green onions, white part only, finely chopped	4
1 to 2	jalapeño peppers, seeds removed and finely chopped	1 to 2
¼ tsp	freshly ground black pepper	1 mL
	Tostadas or tortilla chips	

1. In slow cooker stoneware, combine spinach, cheese, salsa, sour cream, green onions, jalapeño peppers and black pepper. Cover and cook on High for 2 hours, until hot and bubbly. Stir well and serve with tostadas or other tortilla chips.

TIP

• If you are using fresh spinach leaves in this recipe, take care to wash them thoroughly, as they can be quite gritty. To wash spinach: Fill a clean sink with lukewarm water. Remove the tough stems and submerge the tender leaves in the water, swishing to remove the grit. Rinse thoroughly in a colander under cold running water, checking carefully to ensure that no sand remains. If you are using frozen spinach in this recipe, thaw and squeeze the excess moisture out before adding to the slow cooker. Dry thoroughly before adding to the slow cooker. If excess moisture is not removed from the dip it will be quite runny — but still delicious!

Classic Swiss Fondue

**SERVES 6 TO 8
AS AN APPETIZER**

This is the mother of all fondues — thick and luscious cheese with an intriguing hint of kirsch, an aromatic cherry eau de vie. It's wonderfully welcoming after a day in the cold. If you live in an area that receives lots of snow, think about initiating a tradition of serving fondue on the day of the first snowfall, as some of our friends do.

- **Works best in a small (maximum 3½ quart) slow cooker**
- **Fondue forks**

1	clove garlic, split	1
1 lb	Swiss Emmenthal cheese, shredded	500 g
2 tbsp	all-purpose flour	25 mL
2 cups	dry white wine	500 mL
¼ cup	kirsch	50 mL
	Freshly grated nutmeg	
	Sliced baguette	

1. Rub slow cooker stoneware with garlic. Cover and turn heat to High.

2. On a large plate or platter, combine cheese and flour, using your hands to ensure that flour is distributed as evenly as possible. Set aside.

3. In a saucepan over medium heat, bring wine to a rapid boil (see Tip, below). Pour into slow cooker stoneware. Add cheese mixture in handfuls, stirring to thoroughly combine after each addition. When all the cheese has been added, cover and cook on High for 30 minutes, until cheese is melted and mixture is hot. Add kirsch and stir to combine. Grate fresh nutmeg over mixture and turn heat to Low.

4. Break baguette slices into halves or quarters and, using fondue forks, dip into the hot cheese.

TIP
- One secret to getting a Swiss fondue to work in a slow cooker is to ensure that the wine is boiling before you add the cheese. Benefits to making a fondue in the slow cooker are that it keeps the mixture at the right temperature and eliminates concern about keeping a flame lit, often a problem with traditional fondue pots.

Kids' Favorite Fondue

Thanks to my dear friend, Marilyn Linton, writer, editor and volunteer extraordinaire, for this oh-so-easy "fondue." Creamy and delicious, it is a great hit with adults as well as kids. Give everyone their own fondue fork and serve with thick slices of French baguette, quartered, celery sticks or slices of green pepper.

- **Works best in a small (maximum 3 ¹/₂ quart) slow cooker**
- **Fondue forks**

1	large can (28 oz/796 mL) tomatoes, including juice (see Tips, below)	1
1 tsp	dried oregano leaves	5 mL
1 tsp	salt	5 mL
¹/₄ tsp	freshly ground black pepper	1 mL
3 cups	shredded Cheddar cheese	750 mL
	Sliced baguette	
	Celery sticks	
	Sliced green pepper	

1. In a food processor or blender, process tomatoes with juice until relatively smooth. Transfer to slow cooker stoneware. Add oregano, salt and pepper and cook on High for 1 hour, until tomatoes are hot and bubbly.

2. Add cheese to slow cooker in handfuls, stirring to combine after each addition. Reduce heat to Low and serve, or cover and keep on Low until ready to serve. Using fondue forks, dip bread or vegetables into fondue.

TIPS

- If you're in a hurry, bring the tomatoes to a boil on top of the stove after they have been processed. Then transfer to the slow cooker.
- Large cans of tomatoes come in 28 oz (796 mL) and 35 oz (980 mL) sizes. For convenience, I've called for the 28 oz (796 mL) size in my recipes. If you're using the 35 oz (980 mL) size, drain off 1 cup (250 mL) liquid before adding to the recipe.

Creamy Italian Fondue

SERVES 6 TO 8

Although Swiss Fondue has become the standard against which others are measured, other countries have their own techniques for making delicious dips with hot melted cheese. One of my favorites is Fonduta, a particularly rich and creamy fondue that comes from the region of Piedmont in Italy. I like to serve this with chunks of focaccia, a crusty Italian bread, but any crusty white bread will do. Since the sauce is runny — part of its unctuous charm — pass napkins or small plates to catch drips. You can also serve this as a sauce over slices of grilled polenta, which turns it into a plated appetizer eaten with forks.

- **Works best in a small (maximum 3½ quart) slow cooker**
- **Fondue forks**

3 cups	shredded Fontina cheese	750 mL
¾ cup	half-and-half (10%) cream	175 mL
1 tbsp	unsalted butter, melted	15 mL
½	small clove garlic, put through a press or finely grated (see Tip, below)	½
2	egg yolks	2
2 tbsp	hot milk	25 mL
¼ tsp	freshly ground black pepper	1 mL
	Chunks of crusty bread	

1. In slow cooker stoneware, combine cheese and cream. Cover and cook on Low for 1 hour. Increase heat to High.

2. In a small bowl, combine melted butter and garlic. Pour mixture into cheese mixture, stirring well until thoroughly combined and the cheese is completely melted.

3. In a bowl, beat egg yolks with hot milk. Add to cheese mixture, stirring thoroughly to combine. Add pepper and stir. Reduce heat to Low.

4. Using fondue forks, dip bread in sauce, ensuring that guests have napkins or plates to catch any dripping sauce.

TIP

- Because this fondue doesn't cook for a long time, I prefer to put the garlic through a press or to grate it using a fine grater, such as a Microplane, rather than mincing to ensure that the flavor is fully integrated into the cheese mixture. If you don't have either of these tools, a fine mince will do.

Crab Timbale with Spinach Sauce

SERVES 4 TO 6

This is a versatile dish — delicious as a starter to an elegant meal, for lunch, a light dinner or as part of a buffet table. For a light family dinner, make a big salad and try the timbale without the Spinach Sauce — it's great on its own with a few drops of hot pepper sauce and makes a nice alternative to scrambled eggs or an omelet.

Make ahead

Both the timbale and the sauce can be made ahead and refrigerated until you're ready to serve. They reheat very well in the microwave.

- **Works best in a large (minimum 5 quart) slow cooker**
- **Lightly greased 4-cup (1 L) baking dish**

Crab Timbale

2 cups	table (18%) cream	500 mL
2	eggs	2
2	egg yolks	2
1 tsp	each paprika and salt	5 mL
¼ tsp	cayenne pepper	1 mL
¼ tsp	ground white pepper	1 mL
2	cans (each 6 oz/170 g) crabmeat, drained	2

Spinach Sauce

1 lb	fresh spinach, stems removed, or 1 package (10 oz/300 g) spinach leaves, thawed if frozen (see Tips, page 22)	500 g
¼ cup	chicken or vegetable stock or water	50 mL
¼ cup	freshly grated Parmesan cheese	50 mL
1 tsp	Dijon mustard	5 mL
¼ tsp	salt	1 mL
Pinch	freshly ground black pepper	Pinch
Pinch	dried tarragon	Pinch

1. In a bowl, whisk cream with eggs and egg yolks until well integrated. Whisk in paprika, salt, cayenne and white pepper. Stir in crab. Transfer to prepared dish. Cover with foil and tie with string. Place in slow cooker stoneware and pour in enough boiling water to reach 1 inch (2.5 cm) up the sides of dish. Cover and cook on High for 3 hours, or until a knife inserted in timbale comes out clean.

2. *Spinach Sauce:* In a large heavy pot with a tight-fitting lid, combine spinach with stock or water. Cover. Bring to a boil and cook until wilted.

3. Transfer spinach and cooking liquid to a blender or food processor. Add Parmesan, mustard, salt, pepper and tarragon and process until smooth.

4. When ready to serve, remove foil from dish. Run a sharp knife around the outside of the dish and invert onto a serving plate. Spoon Spinach Sauce over timbale and serve immediately.

Chili Cheesecake

SERVES 6

This savory cheesecake is different and delicious. Although it is tasty on crackers, I like to spread it on tortilla chips.

Make ahead

You'll achieve best results if you make this cheesecake the day before you intend to serve it and chill it overnight.

- **Works best in a large (minimum 5 quart) oval slow cooker**
- **7-inch (17.5 cm) 6-cup (1.5 L) soufflé dish, lined with greased heavy-duty foil, or 7-inch (17.5 cm) well-greased springform pan (see Tip, page 42)**

Crust

1 cup	ground tortilla chips, preferably corn	250 mL
2 tbsp	melted butter	25 mL

Cheesecake

1	package (8 oz/250 g) cream cheese, softened	1
2	eggs	2
1 tsp	ground cumin	5 mL
1 tsp	dried oregano leaves	5 mL
1 tsp	chili powder, preferably ancho or New Mexico	5 mL
¼ tsp	freshly ground black pepper	1 mL
1 cup	shredded Monterey Jack or Cheddar cheese	250 mL
2 tbsp	diced red bell pepper	25 mL
1	chile pepper, such as cayenne or jalapeño, seeded and diced	1
1	can (4½ oz/127 mL) diced mild green chiles, drained	1
	Salsa	

1. *Crust:* In a bowl, combine tortilla chips and melted butter. Press mixture into the bottom of prepared dish. Place in freezer until ready to use.

2. *Cheesecake:* In a food processor fitted with a metal blade, combine cream cheese and eggs and process until smooth. Add cumin, oregano, chili powder, black pepper and cheese and pulse until blended. Stir in bell pepper, chile pepper and green chiles. Pour mixture over crust. Cover dish tightly with foil and secure with string. (If using a springform pan, see Tip, page 42.) Place dish in slow cooker stoneware and pour in enough boiling water to come 1 inch (2.5 cm) up the sides.

3. Cover and cook on High for 2½ hours, or until edges are set and center is slightly jiggly. Remove from slow cooker and chill thoroughly, preferably overnight. Spread cake with a layer of salsa, just before serving.

Cheese Loaves with Mushroom Tomato Sauce

SERVES 6 AS A STARTER OR 4 AS A LIGHT MEAL

This is a versatile and delicious dish. Serve it as a starter to an elegant meal or as the centerpiece of a light dinner or lunch. If using canned tomatoes, use good-quality Italian tomatoes, such as San Marzano, for the sauce.

- **Works best in a large (minimum 6 quart) slow cooker**
- **2 mini loaf pans (each 6 by 3 inches/15 by 7.5 cm), lightly greased**

Cheese Loaves

2 cups	table (18%) cream	500 mL
2	eggs	2
2	egg yolks	2
½ tsp	paprika	2 mL
½ tsp	salt	2 mL
¼ tsp	freshly ground black pepper	1 mL
¾ cup	freshly grated Parmesan cheese	175 mL

Mushroom Tomato Sauce

2 tbsp	butter	25 mL
8 oz	cremini mushrooms, sliced	250 g
½ tsp	salt	2 mL
¼ tsp	freshly ground black pepper	1 mL
¼ tsp	dried oregano leaves	1 mL
4	green onions, white part only, finely chopped	4
2 cups	diced, peeled tomatoes or 1 can (28 oz/796 mL) tomatoes, drained and chopped	500 mL

1. *Cheese Loaves:* In a bowl, whisk cream with eggs and egg yolks until well integrated. Whisk in paprika, salt and pepper. Stir in Parmesan cheese. Divide mixture equally between prepared pans. Cover with foil and tie with string. Place in slow cooker stoneware and pour in enough boiling water to come 1 inch (2.5 cm) up the sides. Cover and cook on High for 3 hours, or until a knife inserted in loaf comes out clean.

2. *Mushroom Tomato Sauce:* In a skillet, melt butter over medium heat. Add mushrooms and cook, stirring, until they release their liquid. Add salt, pepper and oregano and cook, stirring, for 1 minute. Add onions and tomatoes and cook, stirring often, until thickened.

3. When ready to serve, remove foil from loaf pans, run a sharp knife around the loaves and invert onto a large platter. Spoon Mushroom Tomato Sauce over loaves and serve immediately.

TIP

- Many supermarkets stock mini loaf pans among their selection of foil baking pans.

Savory Bread Pudding

SERVES ABOUT 6

What could be more inviting than this mouth-watering combination of tomatoes, cheese and milk with hints of mustard and onion? It makes a delicious supper or brunch dish, served with a simple green salad. As a bonus, it's a great way to use up day-old bread.

- **Works best in a large (minimum 6 quart) slow cooker**
- **Lightly greased slow cooker stoneware**

1 tbsp	vegetable oil	15 mL
1	onion, halved and thinly sliced on the vertical	1
4	cloves garlic, thinly sliced	4
2 tsp	dried Italian seasoning	10 mL
1 tsp	salt	5 mL
½ tsp	cracked black peppercorns	2 mL
1	can (28 oz/796 mL) tomatoes, including juice, coarsely chopped	1
4	eggs, beaten	4
1 tbsp	Dijon mustard	15 mL
2 cups	evaporated milk	500 mL
8 cups	cubed (½ inch/1 cm) country-style bread (about half a large Calabrese loaf)	2 L
2 cups	shredded Fontina cheese	500 mL

1. In a skillet, heat oil over medium heat for 30 seconds. Add onion and cook, stirring, until softened, about 3 minutes. Add garlic, Italian seasoning, salt and peppercorns and cook, stirring, for 1 minute. Add tomatoes with juice and bring to a boil. Remove from heat and set aside.

2. In a bowl, combine eggs and mustard. Beat to blend. Add evaporated milk and beat well. Set aside.

3. In prepared stoneware, spoon one-third of the tomato mixture. Spread half the bread evenly over top and sprinkle bread evenly with half of the cheese. Repeat, finishing with final third of tomato mixture. Pour milk mixture evenly over top.

4. Place two clean tea towels, each folded in half (so you will have four layers), over top of stoneware to absorb the moisture (see Tip, below). Cover and cook on Low for 6 hours or High for 3 hours, until pudding is set and edges are browning.

TIP
- Tea towels prevent accumulated moisture from dripping on the bread by absorbing the liquid generated during cooking.

Sun-Dried Tomato and Dill Cheesecake

SERVES 6

When biting into this tasty cheesecake, you'll be hit with an appealing burst of sun-dried tomato flavor. All it needs is simple crackers. It's also delicious on celery sticks.

Make ahead

You'll achieve best results if you make this cheesecake the day before you intend to serve it and chill it overnight.

- **Works best in a large (minimum 5 quart) oval slow cooker**
- **7-inch (17.5 cm) 6-cup (1.5 L) soufflé dish, lined with greased heavy-duty foil, or 7-inch (17.5 cm) well-greased springform pan (see Tip, below)**

Crust		
1 cup	cracker crumbs, such as wheat thins	250 mL
2 tbsp	melted butter	25 mL
Cheesecake		
1	package (8 oz/250 g) cream cheese, softened	1
2	eggs	2
½ cup	coarsely chopped dill	125 mL
¼ cup	chopped sun-dried tomatoes, packed in olive oil, drained	50 mL
2 tbsp	finely chopped green onion or chives	25 mL
	Salt	
	Freshly ground black pepper	
¾ cup	shredded Emmenthal or Swiss cheese	175 mL

1. *Crust:* In a bowl, combine cracker crumbs and melted butter. Press mixture into the bottom of prepared dish. Place in freezer until ready to use.

2. *Cheesecake:* In a food processor fitted with a metal blade, combine cream cheese and eggs. Process until smooth. Add dill, sun-dried tomatoes and green onion. Season to taste with salt and pepper. Pulse until blended (do not overmix). Add cheese and pulse just until blended. Pour mixture over crust. Cover dish tightly with foil and secure with a string. (If using a springform pan, see Tip, below.) Place dish in slow cooker stoneware and pour in enough boiling water to come 1 inch (2.5 cm) up the sides.

3. Cover and cook on High for 3 hours, or until edges are set and center is slightly jiggly. Remove from slow cooker and chill thoroughly, preferably overnight.

TIP

- If using a springform pan, ensure that water doesn't seep into the cheesecake by wrapping the bottom of the pan in one large seamless piece of foil that extends up the sides and over the top. Cover the top with a single piece of foil that extends down the sides and secure with a string.

Ribollita (page 62)

Soups

Butternut Apple Soup with Swiss Cheese

SERVES 6 TO 8

Topped with melted cheese, this creamy and delicious soup is an ideal antidote to a blustery day. Serve it as a light main course, accompanied by a green salad and whole grain bread or as a starter to a more substantial meal.

Make ahead

This soup can be partially prepared the night before it is cooked. Complete Step 1. Cover and refrigerate for up to 2 days. When you're ready to cook, continue with the recipe.

- **Works best in a large (minimum 5 quart) slow cooker**

1 tbsp	olive oil	15 mL
2	onions, chopped	2
4	cloves garlic, minced	4
2 tsp	dried rosemary leaves, crumbled, or 1 tbsp (15 mL) chopped fresh rosemary leaves	10 mL
½ tsp	cracked black peppercorns	2 mL
5 cups	vegetable or chicken stock	1.25 L
1	butternut squash, peeled, seeded and cut into 1-inch (2.5 cm) cubes (about 2½ lbs/1.25 kg)	1
2	tart apples, such as Granny Smith, cored, peeled and coarsely chopped	2
	Salt, optional	
1 cup	shredded Swiss cheese	250 mL
½ cup	finely chopped walnuts, optional	125 mL

1. In a skillet, heat oil over medium heat for 30 seconds. Add onions and cook, stirring, until softened, about 3 minutes. Add garlic, rosemary and peppercorns and cook, stirring, for 1 minute. Transfer to slow cooker stoneware. Add stock.

2. Stir in squash and apples. Cover and cook on Low for 8 hours or on High for 4 hours, until squash is tender.

3. Preheat broiler. Working in batches, purée soup in a food processor or blender. (You can also do this in the stoneware using an immersion blender.) Season to taste with salt, if using. Ladle soup into ovenproof bowls. Sprinkle with cheese and broil until cheese melts, about 2 minutes. (You can also do this in a microwave oven, in batches, on High, about 1 minute per batch.) Sprinkle with walnuts, if using.

Pumpkin Soup with Shrimp and Lime

Although pumpkin is normally associated with Thanksgiving pie, in many other cultures it is used more innovatively as a vegetable or in richly flavored sauces. This soup, which is delicious hot or cold, has its origins in both French provincial and Latin American cuisine. If pumpkin is unavailable, substitute any orange-fleshed squash, such as acorn or butternut.

Make ahead

This soup can be made a day ahead, refrigerated overnight and served cold or reheated. It can also be cooked overnight, puréed and chilled. To serve hot: Refrigerate puréed soup until ready to serve. In a pot, bring to a boil on the stovetop and simmer for 5 to 10 minutes. Add lime zest and juice, cayenne, cream and shrimp and cook until heated through. Continue with Step 4. To serve cold: Add lime zest and juice, cayenne, cream and shrimp after the mixture is puréed and refrigerate. When ready to serve, complete Step 4.

- **Works best in a large (minimum 5 quart) slow cooker**

6 cups	peeled pie pumpkin, cut into 2-inch (5 cm) cubes	1.25 L
3	leeks, white part only, cleaned and coarsely chopped (see Tips, page 66)	3
4 cups	chicken or vegetable stock	1 L
1 tsp	salt	5 mL
1/4 tsp	freshly ground black pepper	1 mL
	Grated zest and juice of 1 lime	
Pinch	cayenne pepper	Pinch
1 cup	whipping (35%) cream	250 mL
8 oz	cooked salad shrimp or 2 cans (3¾ oz/106 g) shrimp, rinsed and drained	250 g
6 to 8	cherry tomatoes, halved	6 to 8
2 tbsp	toasted pumpkin seeds, optional (see Tip, below)	25 mL
	Finely chopped chives or cilantro	

1. In slow cooker stoneware, combine pumpkin, leeks, stock, salt and pepper. Cover and cook on Low for 8 to 10 hours or on High for 4 to 6 hours, until pumpkin is tender.

2. Working in batches, purée soup in a food processor or blender. (You can also do this in the stoneware using an immersion blender.)

3. If serving hot, return soup to slow cooker, add lime zest and juice, cayenne, cream and shrimp and cook on High for 20 minutes, or until shrimp are heated through. If serving cold, combine ingredients in a large bowl and chill thoroughly.

4. When ready to serve, ladle soup into individual bowls and garnish with cherry tomatoes, pumpkin seeds, if using, and chives.

TIP

- If using pumpkin seeds, pan-fry in a dry, hot skillet over medium heat until they are lightly browned and puffed. When purchasing pumpkin seeds, taste first, as they tend to go rancid quickly. Store in the freezer until ready to use.

Soup à la Crécy

SERVES 8

In French cooking, crécy is a term for certain dishes containing carrots. In my books, this soup, which may be thickened with potatoes or rice, is one of the tastiest. This classic soup makes a nice centerpiece for a light soup and salad dinner accompanied with dark rye bread. It also makes an elegant first course for a more sophisticated meal.

Make ahead

This dish can be partially prepared before it is cooked. Complete Step 1. Cover and refrigerate for up to 2 days. When you're ready to cook, continue with the recipe.

- **Works best in a large (minimum 5 quart) slow cooker**

1 tbsp	olive oil	15 mL
2	leeks, white part with just a bit of green, cleaned and thinly sliced (see Tips, page 66)	2
4 cups	thinly sliced, peeled carrots (about 1 lb/500 g)	1 L
2 tsp	dried thyme leaves, crumbled	10 mL
1 tsp	cracked black peppercorns	5 mL
2	bay leaves	2
6 cups	vegetable or chicken stock	1.5 L
½ cup	brown rice (see Tip, below)	125 mL
	Salt, optional	
	Whipping (35%) cream, optional	
½ cup	finely chopped parsley or snipped chives	125 mL
½ cup	garlic croutons	125 mL

1. In a large skillet, heat oil over medium heat for 30 seconds. Add leeks and carrots and cook, stirring, until carrots are softened, about 7 minutes. Add thyme, peppercorns and bay leaves and cook, stirring, for 1 minute. Transfer to slow cooker stoneware. Add stock and stir well.

2. Stir in rice. Cover and cook on Low for 8 hours or on High for 4 hours, until carrots are tender. Discard bay leaves.

3. Working in batches, purée soup in a food processor or blender. (You can also do this in the stoneware using an immersion blender.) Season to taste with salt, if using. Ladle into individual serving bowls and drizzle with cream, if using. Garnish with parsley and croutons. Serve hot.

TIP

- Store brown rice in the refrigerator or use it within a few weeks of purchase. The bran layer contains oil, which although healthy, becomes rancid when kept at room temperature for a long period.

Split Green Pea Soup with Mint Cream

SERVES 6 TO 8

Not only is this soup delicious and elegant, it's extremely easy to make. If you grow mint in your garden, or on your windowsill, it can be made from pantry ingredients. The addition of Mint Cream provides a nice finish, and if you prefer a richer soup, you can add additional cream, to taste, before serving.

Make ahead

This soup can be partially prepared before it is cooked. Complete Step 1. Cover and refrigerate for up to 2 days. When you're ready to cook, continue with the recipe, reducing the cooking time to 8 to 10 hours on Low or 4 to 5 hours on High.

Variation

Split Green Pea Soup with Tarragon Cream
Substitute fresh tarragon for the mint.

• *Works best in a large (minimum 5 quart) slow cooker*

1 cup	dried split green peas, soaked, rinsed and drained (see page 219)	250 mL
1 tbsp	vegetable oil	15 mL
1	large onion, chopped	1
3	stalks celery, thinly sliced	3
2	cloves garlic, chopped	2
4	sprigs mint	4
1 tsp	salt	5 mL
½ tsp	cracked black peppercorns	2 mL
6 cups	vegetable or chicken stock	1.5 L
Mint Cream		
¼ cup	whipping (35%) cream	50 mL
¼ cup	sour cream	50 mL
2 tbsp	finely chopped mint	25 mL
1½ cups	hot cooked green peas	375 mL

1. In a skillet, heat oil over medium heat for 30 seconds. Add onion and celery and cook, stirring, until celery is softened, about 5 minutes. Add garlic, mint, salt and peppercorns and cook, stirring, for 1 minute. Transfer to slow cooker stoneware. Stir in soaked split green peas and stock.

2. Cover and cook on Low for 10 to 12 hours or on High for 5 to 6 hours, until peas are tender.

3. Meanwhile, make *Mint Cream*: In a bowl, whisk cream until thick. Add sour cream and mint and blend well. Refrigerate until ready to use.

4. Working in batches, purée soup in a food processor or blender. (You can also do this in the stoneware using an immersion blender.) Stir in cooked green peas. Ladle soup into individual bowls and garnish with Mint Cream.

Mediterranean Lentil Soup with Spinach

SERVES 6 TO 8

This delicious soup, delicately flavored with lemon and cumin, reminds me of hot, languid days under the Mediterranean sun. Serve it as a starter or add a green salad and warm country-style bread for a refreshing and nutritious light meal.

Make ahead

This soup can be partially prepared before it is cooked. Complete Step 1. Cover and refrigerate for up to 2 days. When you're ready to cook, continue with the recipe.

- *Works best in a large (minimum 5 quart) slow cooker*

1 tbsp	vegetable oil	15 mL
2	onions, chopped	2
2	stalks celery, chopped	2
2	large carrots, peeled and chopped	2
1	clove garlic, minced	1
1 tsp	cumin seeds, toasted and ground (see Tip, page 59)	5 mL
1 tsp	grated lemon zest	5 mL
6 cups	vegetable or chicken stock	1.5 L
1	potato, peeled and grated	1
1 cup	green or brown lentils, rinsed	250 mL
2 tbsp	freshly squeezed lemon juice	25 mL
1/2 tsp	cayenne pepper, optional (see Tips, below)	2 mL
1 lb	fresh spinach, stems removed, or 1 package (10 oz/300 g) spinach leaves, thawed if frozen (see Tips, below)	500 g

1. In a skillet, heat oil over medium heat for 30 seconds. Add onions, celery and carrots and cook, stirring, until carrots are softened, about 7 minutes. Add garlic, toasted cumin and lemon zest and cook, stirring, for 1 minute. Transfer to slow cooker stoneware. Add stock.

2. Stir in potato and lentils. Cover and cook on Low for 8 to 10 hours or on High for 4 to 6 hours, until vegetables are tender. Add lemon juice and cayenne, if using, and stir. Add spinach. Cover and cook on High for 20 minutes, until spinach is cooked and mixture is hot and bubbly.

TIPS

- If you're using cayenne pepper, dissolve it in the lemon juice before adding to the slow cooker.
- If you are using fresh spinach leaves in this recipe, take care to wash them thoroughly, as they can be quite gritty. To wash spinach: Fill a clean sink with lukewarm water. Remove the tough stems and submerge the tender leaves in the water, swishing to remove the grit. Rinse thoroughly in a colander under cold running water, checking carefully to ensure that no sand remains. If you are using frozen spinach in this recipe, thaw and squeeze the excess moisture out before adding to the slow cooker.

Creamy Onion Soup with Kale

SERVES 6

There is no cream in this delicious soup — unless you decide to drizzle a bit over individual servings. The creaminess is achieved with the addition of potatoes, which are puréed into the soup, providing it with a velvety texture.

Make ahead

This soup can be partially prepared before it is cooked. Complete Steps 1 and 2. Cover and refrigerate for up to 2 days. When you're ready to cook, continue with the recipe.

● **Works best in a large (minimum 5 quart) slow cooker**

4	slices bacon, optional (see Tips, below)	4
4	onions, thinly sliced	4
2	cloves garlic, minced	2
1 tsp	grated lemon zest	5 mL
½ tsp	cracked black peppercorns	2 mL
1	bay leaf	1
4	whole allspice	4
4 cups	vegetable or chicken stock	1 L
3	medium potatoes, peeled and diced	3
1 tsp	paprika, dissolved in 2 tbsp (25 mL) lemon juice (see Tips, below)	5 mL
4 cups	chopped kale	1 L

1. In a skillet, cook bacon, if using, over medium-high heat until crisp. Drain on paper towel and crumble. Cover and refrigerate until ready to use. Drain all but 2 tbsp (25 mL) fat from pan.

2. Reduce heat to medium. Add onions to pan and cook, stirring, until softened, about 5 minutes. Add lemon zest, garlic, peppercorns, bay leaf and allspice and cook, stirring, for 1 minute. Transfer to slow cooker stoneware. Add stock and stir well.

3. Stir in potatoes. Cover and cook on Low for 8 hours or on High for 4 hours, until potatoes are tender. Discard bay leaf and allspice. Stir in paprika solution, kale and reserved bacon, if using. Cover and cook on High for 20 minutes, until kale is tender. Working in batches, purée soup in a food processor or blender. (You can also do this in the stoneware using an immersion blender.) Serve immediately.

TIPS
● If you are making this soup for vegetarians, omit the bacon and heat 1 tbsp (15 mL) vegetable oil in a skillet over medium heat for 30 seconds. Add the onions and continue with the recipe.
● You can use any kind of paprika in this recipe: Regular, hot, which produces a nicely peppery version, or smoked, which adds a delicious note of smokiness to the soup. If you have regular paprika and would like a bit a heat, dissolve ¼ tsp (1 mL) cayenne pepper in the lemon juice along with the paprika.

Southwestern Corn and Roasted Red Pepper Soup

SERVES 6

Although the roots of this soup lie deep in the heart of Tex-Mex cuisine, it is elegant enough for even the most gracious occasion. Serve it as a starter or add canned crab (see Variation, below) for a deliciously different meal-in-a-bowl. Hot sourdough bread makes a perfect accompaniment.

Make ahead

This soup can be partially prepared before it is cooked. Complete Step 1. Cover and refrigerate for up to 2 days. When you're ready to cook, continue with the recipe.

Variation

Corn and Roasted Red Pepper Soup with Crab

For a more substantial soup, add 2 cans (each 6 oz/170 g) drained crabmeat along with the corn and pepper.

• *Works best in a large (minimum 5 quart) slow cooker*

1 tbsp	vegetable oil	15 mL
1	large onion, finely chopped	1
6	cloves garlic, minced	6
1 tbsp	cumin seeds, toasted and ground (see Tip, page 59)	15 mL
1 tbsp	chopped fresh rosemary leaves or dried rosemary, crumbled	15 mL
1	bay leaf	1
1 tsp	salt	5 mL
½ tsp	cracked black peppercorns	2 mL
6 cups	vegetable or chicken stock	1.5 L
1	dried New Mexico, ancho or guajillo chile pepper	1
1 cup	boiling water	250 mL
1	jalapeño pepper, seeded and coarsely chopped, optional	1
4 cups	corn kernels, thawed if frozen	1 L
2	red bell peppers, roasted and cut into ½-inch (1 cm) cubes (see Tips, page 24)	2
½ cup	whipping (35%) cream	125 mL
	Finely chopped parsley or cilantro	

1. In a skillet, heat oil over medium heat for 30 seconds. Add onion and cook, stirring, until softened, about 3 minutes. Add garlic, toasted cumin, rosemary, bay leaf, salt and peppercorns and cook, stirring, for 1 minute. Transfer to slow cooker stoneware. Add stock and stir well.

2. Cover and cook on Low for 6 to 8 hours or on High for 3 to 4 hours, until flavors meld.

3. Half an hour before soup has finished cooking, in a heatproof bowl, soak dried chile pepper in boiling water for 30 minutes, weighing down with a cup to ensure it remains submerged. Drain, discarding soaking liquid and stem, and chop coarsely. Transfer to a blender. Add 1 cup (250 mL) of stock from the soup, the jalapeño pepper, if using, and purée. Add to slow cooker and stir well. Add corn, roasted red pepper and whipping cream. Cover and cook on High for 30 minutes, until corn is tender. Discard bay leaf. Spoon into individual bowls and garnish with parsley.

Creamy Corn Chowder

Here's a comfort food classic that never goes out of style. In addition to adding nutrients and substance to the soup, the potatoes thicken and add flavor to the broth. If you like a bit of spice, add the jalapeño pepper.

Make ahead

This soup can be partially prepared the night before it is cooked. Complete Steps 1 and 2. Cover and refrigerate for up to 2 days. When you're ready to cook, continue with the recipe.

Variations

Creamy Corn Chowder with Scallops

In a skillet over medium heat, melt 2 tbsp (25 mL) butter. Add 8 oz (250 g) scallops, lightly seasoned with salt and freshly ground black pepper and cook, stirring, until scallops are browned on both sides and cooked through, about 2 minutes. Add to hot soup just before serving.

Smoked Salmon and Corn Chowder

Add chopped smoked salmon, to taste, to hot soup just before serving.

- **Works best in a large (minimum 5 quart) slow cooker**

2	slices bacon	2
2	onions, finely chopped	2
2	stalks celery, thinly sliced	2
2	carrots, peeled and diced	2
1 tsp	salt	5 mL
½ tsp	poultry seasoning (see Tips, below)	2 mL
½ tsp	cracked black peppercorns	2 mL
1	bay leaf	1
3½ cups	vegetable or chicken stock	875 mL
2	potatoes, peeled and grated (about 2 cups/500 mL)	2
2	cans (each 19 oz/540 mL) cream-style corn	2
1	green bell pepper, seeded and finely chopped	1
1	jalapeño pepper, finely chopped, optional	1

1. In a skillet, cook bacon over medium-high heat until crisp. Drain thoroughly on paper towel and crumble. Cover and refrigerate until ready to use. Drain all but 1 tbsp (15 mL) fat from pan.

2. Reduce heat to medium. Add onions, celery and carrots to pan and cook, stirring, until vegetables are softened, about 7 minutes. Add salt, poultry seasoning, peppercorns and bay leaf and cook, stirring, for 1 minute. Add stock and bring to a boil. Transfer mixture to slow cooker stoneware.

3. Stir in potatoes. Cover and cook on Low for 8 hours or on High for 4 hours, until vegetables are tender. Add corn, green pepper, jalapeño pepper, if using, and reserved bacon. Stir well. Cover and cook on High for 30 minutes, until soup is hot and bubbly. Discard bay leaf.

TIPS
- If you don't have poultry seasoning, use dried thyme leaves instead.
- If you are partially preparing the soup as in the Make ahead, peel and shred the potatoes just before cooking to prevent them from browning.

Mulligatawny Soup

SERVES 8

Mulligatawny, which means "pepper water" in Tamil, is an Anglo-Indian soup, imported to England by seafaring merchants. It is usually made with chicken, but a vegetarian version was documented by the great English cook Eliza Acton in her book Modern Cookery, published in 1845. This is a hearty and tasty soup that is suitable for many occasions, either as a first course or the focal point of a light meal.

Make ahead

This soup can be partially prepared the night before it is cooked. Complete Step 1. Cover and refrigerate for up to 2 days. When you're ready to cook, continue with recipe.

Variation

Chicken Mulligatawny Soup

This is a great way to use up leftover chicken. Use chicken stock instead of vegetable stock and stir in 8 oz (250 g) cooked chicken (shredded or diced) along with, or instead of, the cauliflower.

- • **Works best in a large (minimum 5 quart) slow cooker**

1 tbsp	vegetable oil	15 mL
2	onions, finely chopped	2
2	carrots, peeled and thinly sliced	2
4	stalks celery, thinly sliced	4
4	cloves garlic, minced	4
1 tsp	cumin seeds, toasted and ground (see Tip, below)	5 mL
1 tsp	salt	5 mL
½ tsp	cracked black peppercorns	2 mL
5 cups	vegetable or chicken stock	1.25 L
2	medium potatoes, peeled and diced	2
1 tbsp	curry powder	15 mL
1 cup	whipping (35%) cream or plain yogurt, divided	250 mL
2 cups	cooked cauliflower florets, optional	500 mL
	Finely chopped cilantro or parsley	

1. In a large skillet, heat oil over medium heat for 30 seconds. Add onions, carrots and celery and cook, stirring, until vegetables are softened, about 7 minutes. Add garlic, toasted cumin, salt and peppercorns and cook, stirring, for 1 minute. Transfer to slow cooker stoneware. Add stock and stir to combine.

2. Stir in potatoes. Cover and cook on Low for 8 to 10 hours or on High for 4 to 5 hours, until vegetables are tender. Working in batches, purée soup in a food processor or blender and return to slow cooker. (You can also do this in the stoneware using an immersion blender.)

3. In a small bowl, place curry powder. Gradually add ¼ cup (50 mL) of the cream, beating until smooth. Add to stoneware along with remaining cream and cauliflower, if using. Cover and cook on High for 30 minutes, until flavors meld. When ready to serve, ladle into bowls and garnish with cilantro.

TIP

- • To toast cumin seeds: Place seeds in a dry skillet over medium heat, stirring, until fragrant, about 3 minutes. Immediately transfer to a mortar or a spice grinder and grind. If you prefer to use ground cumin, substitute half of the quantity called for.

Curried Butternut and Chestnut Soup

SERVES 8 TO 10

This soup is absolutely delicious, but very rich; a little goes a long way as a unique taste sensation. Serve small bowls as the first course to a special dinner or make it a cold-weather treat. Like chestnuts roasting on an open fire, it's an ideal antidote to a winter freeze. Ladle steaming hot soup into pottery mugs and hand them to brave souls returning from the slopes or other bracing outdoor excursions.

Make ahead

This soup can be partially prepared before it is cooked. Complete Step 1. Cover and refrigerate for up to 2 days. When you're ready to cook, continue with the recipe.

- **Works best in a large (minimum 5 quart) slow cooker**

1 tbsp	vegetable oil	15 mL
3	leeks, cleaned and chopped (see Tips, page 66)	3
2	cloves garlic, chopped	2
1 tbsp	minced gingerroot	15 mL
½ tsp	cracked black peppercorns	2 mL
1	whole star anise	1
5 cups	vegetable or chicken stock	1.25 L
3 cups	cubed (1 inch/2.5 cm) peeled butternut squash (about 1 lb/500 g)	750 mL
1 tbsp	curry powder, preferably Madras	15 mL
½ cup	whipping (35%) cream or soy creamer, divided	125 mL
1	can (15 oz/435 g) unsweetened chestnut purée, removed from can and cut into 1-inch (2.5 cm) cubes	1

1. In a skillet, heat oil over medium heat for 30 seconds. Add leeks and cook, stirring, until softened, about 5 minutes. Add garlic, gingerroot, peppercorns and star anise and cook, stirring, for 1 minute. Add stock and bring to a boil. Transfer to slow cooker stoneware.

2. Stir in squash. Cover and cook on Low for 6 to 8 hours or on High for 3 to 4 hours, until squash is very tender.

3. In a small bowl, place curry powder. Gradually add ¼ cup (50 mL) of the whipping cream, beating until smooth. Set aside for 2 minutes to allow curry to absorb the cream. Stir into stoneware. Add chestnut purée and stir well, mashing purée into soup as best you can. Cover and cook on High for 30 minutes, until flavors meld. Discard star anise. Working in batches, purée soup in a food processor or blender. (You can also do this in the stoneware using an immersion blender.) Ladle into bowls and drizzle with remaining cream.

TIP

- Straight from the can, chestnut purée is very congealed. Cutting it into small cubes before adding it to the soup, helps it to integrate into the stock. Use a wooden spoon to mash it up a bit and be aware that once the soup is puréed, if not before, it will be completely integrated.

Ribollita

SERVES 6 AS A MAIN
COURSE OR 8 AS
A STARTER

*Originally intended
as a method for using
up leftover minestrone
— hence the name
ribollita, which means
"twice cooked" — this
hearty Italian soup has
acquired an illustrious
reputation of its own.
The distinguishing
ingredient is country-
style bread, which is
added to the soup and
cooked in the broth.
Drizzled with olive oil
and sprinkled with
grated Parmesan
cheese, this makes a
satisfying light meal
or tasty starter to an
Italian-themed dinner.*

Make ahead

Cook this soup overnight
or the day before you
intend to serve it. Refrigerate
until you are ready to
serve, then reheat in the
oven. Ladle the soup into
ovenproof bowls, drizzle
with olive oil and sprinkle
with Parmesan. Bake
in a preheated oven
(350°F/180°C) for about
30 minutes, until the top
is lightly browned.

• **Works best in a large (minimum 5 quart) slow cooker**

2 cups	cooked dried or canned white kidney beans, drained and rinsed	500 mL
5 cups	vegetable or chicken stock, divided	1.25 L
1 tbsp	vegetable oil	15 mL
2	onions, finely chopped	2
2	carrots, peeled and diced	2
2	stalks celery, diced	2
4	cloves garlic, minced	4
¼ cup	finely chopped parsley	50 mL
1 tbsp	grated lemon zest	15 mL
1 tsp	finely chopped fresh rosemary leaves or dried rosemary leaves, crumbled	5 mL
1 tsp	salt	5 mL
½ tsp	cracked black peppercorns	2 mL
2	potatoes, peeled and grated	2
4 cups	packed torn Swiss chard leaves (about 1 bunch) (see Tip, below)	1 L
1	long red chile pepper, minced, optional	1
3	thick slices day-old country-style bread	3
	Extra virgin olive oil	
	Freshly grated Parmesan cheese	

1. In a food processor, combine beans with 1 cup (250 mL) of the stock and purée until smooth. Set aside.

2. In a skillet, heat oil over medium heat. Add onions, carrots and celery and cook, stirring, until carrots are softened, about 7 minutes. Add garlic, parsley, lemon zest, rosemary, salt and peppercorns and cook, stirring, for 1 minute. Add bean mixture and bring to a boil. Transfer mixture to stoneware.

3. Stir in potatoes and remaining 4 cups (1 L) stock. Cover and cook on Low for 8 to 10 hours or on High for 4 to 5 hours, until vegetables are tender. Stir in Swiss chard, chile pepper, if using, and bread. Cover and cook on High for 30 minutes, until chard is cooked.

4. When ready to serve, ladle into bowls, breaking bread into pieces. Drizzle with extra virgin olive oil and sprinkle with Parmesan.

TIP

• If you can't find Swiss chard, use an equal quantity of spinach. Be sure to wash Swiss chard thoroughly like spinach (see Tips, page 22).

South American Black Bean Soup

SERVES 4 TO 6 AS
A MAIN COURSE OR
6 TO 8 AS A STARTER

This mouth-watering combination of black beans, lime juice and cilantro with just a hint of hot pepper is one of my favorite one-dish meals. To jack up the heat, add a chopped jalapeño along with the cayenne. The flavor of this soup actually improves if it is allowed to sit overnight and then reheated. Garnish with finely chopped cilantro, sour cream or salsa.

Make ahead

This soup can be partially prepared before it is cooked. Complete Steps 1 and 2. Cover and refrigerate for up to 2 days. When you're ready to cook, continue with the recipe.

● **Works best in a large (minimum 5 quart) slow cooker**

6	slices bacon, chopped	6
2	onions, finely chopped	2
2	stalks celery, finely chopped	2
2	carrots, peeled and finely chopped	2
2	cloves garlic, minced	2
2 tbsp	cumin seeds, toasted and ground	25 mL
1 tbsp	dried oregano leaves	15 mL
1 tsp	dried thyme leaves	5 mL
1 tsp	salt	5 mL
1 tsp	cracked black peppercorns	5 mL
2 tbsp	tomato paste	25 mL
6 cups	chicken stock	1.5 L
4 cups	cooked dried or canned black beans, drained and rinsed (see Tip, below)	1 L
1/3 cup	freshly squeezed lime juice	75 mL
1/4 tsp	cayenne pepper	1 mL
1	jalapeño pepper, chopped, optional	1

1. In a skillet, cook bacon over medium-high heat until crisp. Drain thoroughly on paper towel. Cover and refrigerate until ready to use. Drain all but 1 tbsp (15 mL) fat from pan.

2. Reduce heat to medium. Add onions, celery and carrots and cook, stirring, until vegetables are softened, about 7 minutes. Add garlic, toasted cumin, oregano, thyme, salt and peppercorns and cook, stirring, for 1 minute. Add tomato paste and stir to combine thoroughly. Transfer to stoneware. Stir in stock.

3. Add beans and reserved bacon and stir well. Cover and cook on Low for 8 to 10 hours or on High for 4 to 6 hours, until vegetables are tender. Stir in lime juice, cayenne and jalapeño, if using. Cover and cook on High for 10 minutes, until heated through. Working in batches, purée soup in a food processor or blender. (You can also do this in the stoneware using an immersion blender.) Spoon into bowls and garnish.

> **TIP**
> ● You can use cooked dried beans or canned beans interchangeably in these recipes. One cup (250 mL) dried beans, cooked, is about 2 cups (500 mL) canned beans or a standard-size can.

Red Lentil and Carrot Soup with Coconut

SERVES 8 TO 10 AS A STARTER OR 4 TO 6 AS A MAIN COURSE

I love the combination of flavors in this unusual soup. The red lentils partially dissolve while cooking, creating a creamy texture without adding fat. The carrots enhance color as well as taste, and the coconut milk creates an intriguing, almost nutty note. The combination is mouth-watering. Serve as a starter or add an Indian bread such as naan, and a green salad for a delicious light meal.

Make ahead

This soup can be partially prepared before it is cooked. Complete Step 1. Cover and refrigerate for up to 2 days. When you're ready to cook, continue with the recipe.

* **Works best in a large (minimum 5 quart) slow cooker**

1 tbsp	vegetable oil	15 mL
2	onions, finely chopped	2
4	cloves garlic, minced	4
2 tsp	turmeric	10 mL
2 tsp	cumin seeds, toasted and ground (see Tip, page 59)	10 mL
1 tsp	salt	5 mL
½ tsp	cracked black peppercorns	2 mL
1	can (28 oz/796 mL) tomatoes, including juice	1
2	large carrots, peeled, cut in half lengthwise and thinly sliced	2
2 cups	red lentils, rinsed	500 mL
1 tbsp	freshly squeezed lemon juice	15 mL
6 cups	vegetable or chicken stock	1.5 L
1	can (14 oz/398 mL) coconut milk	1
1	long red chile pepper or 2 Thai chiles, finely chopped (see Tip, below)	1
	Thin slices lemon, optional	
	Finely chopped cilantro, optional	

1. In a large skillet, heat oil over medium heat for 30 seconds. Add onions and cook, stirring, until softened, about 3 minutes. Add garlic, turmeric, toasted cumin, salt and peppercorns and cook, stirring, for 1 minute. Add tomatoes with juice and bring to a boil, breaking up with the back of a spoon. Transfer to slow cooker stoneware.

2. Stir in carrots, lentils, lemon juice and stock. Cover and cook on Low for 8 to 10 hours or on High for 4 to 5 hours, until lentils are tender and mixture is bubbly. Stir in coconut milk and chile pepper and cook on High for 20 to 30 minutes, until heated through.

3. When ready to serve, ladle into bowls and top with lemon slices and cilantro, if using.

TIP

* If you don't have fresh chile peppers, stir in your favorite hot pepper sauce, to taste, just before serving.

Creamy Leek Soup with Stilton

SERVES 6 TO 8

This English version of a classic French soup is a quintessential winter dish. In summer transform it into Vichyssoise.

Make ahead

To serve hot, complete Step 1 and refrigerate overnight. The next morning, continue with the recipe. To serve cold, see Vichyssoise, below. Purée in the morning and chill until ready to serve, for up to 1 day.

Variations

Vichyssoise

Omit Stilton. Reduce the quantity of leeks to 3 cups (750 mL) and increase the quantity of potatoes to 5 cups (1.25 L). After the soup is puréed, transfer to a large bowl and chill thoroughly. Before serving, stir in cream. Spoon into individual soup bowls and garnish with finely chopped chives.

Watercress Vichyssoise

Omit Stilton. Add one bunch watercress to mixture when puréeing. Serve soup garnished with chopped watercress.

- **Works best in a large (minimum 5 quart) slow cooker**

2 tbsp	melted butter	15 mL
6 cups	leeks, white part with about 2 inches (5 cm) green, about 5 medium leeks, cleaned and coarsely chopped (see Tips, below)	1.5 L
1 cup	chopped onion	250 mL
2 tbsp	finely chopped garlic	25 mL
1 tsp	salt	5 mL
1/4 tsp	freshly ground black pepper	1 mL
6 cups	vegetable or chicken stock	1.5 L
3 cups	cubed (1/2 inch/1 cm) peeled potatoes	750 mL
1 cup	whipping (35%) cream	250 mL
8 oz	Stilton cheese, crumbled	250 g

1. In slow cooker stoneware, combine melted butter, leeks, onion, garlic, salt and pepper. Stir to coat vegetables thoroughly. Cover and cook on High for 30 minutes to 1 hour, until vegetables are softened. Add stock and stir to combine.

2. Add potatoes and stir well. Cover and cook on Low for 8 to 10 hours or on High for 4 to 6 hours, until vegetables are tender.

3. Working in batches, purée soup in a food processor or blender. (You can also do this in the stoneware using an immersion blender.) Ladle into bowls. Drizzle with whipping cream and top each serving with about 2 heaping tbsp (25 mL) Stilton. Serve immediately.

TIPS

- To clean leeks: Fill sink full of lukewarm water. Split leeks in half lengthwise and submerge in water, swishing them around to remove all traces of dirt. Transfer to a colander and rinse under cold water.
- If you're in a hurry, you can soften the leeks and onion in a skillet over medium heat. Melt the butter and cook, stirring, until softened, about 4 minutes. Stir in garlic, salt and pepper. Transfer to slow cooker and continue as directed.

Santa Fe Sweet Potato Soup

SERVES 6 TO 8

Here's a flavorful, rib-sticking soup with lots of pizzazz and universal appeal. New Mexico chiles add an enticing, slightly smoky flavor, but ancho or guajillo chiles also work well. The lime, roasted red pepper and cilantro finish provides a nice balance to the sweet potatoes. If you are a heat seeker, add the jalapeño pepper.

Make ahead

This soup can be partially prepared before it is cooked. Complete Step 1. Cover and refrigerate for up to 2 days. When you're ready to cook, continue with the recipe.

● **Works best in a large (minimum 5 quart) slow cooker**

1 tbsp	vegetable oil	15 mL
2	onions, finely chopped	2
4	cloves garlic, minced	4
1 tsp	salt	5 mL
1 tsp	dried oregano leaves	5 mL
6 cups	vegetable or chicken stock	1.5 L
4 cups	cubed (about ½ inch/1 cm) peeled sweet potatoes	1 L
2	dried New Mexico, ancho or guajillo chile peppers	2
2 cups	boiling water	500 mL
1	jalapeño pepper, finely chopped, optional	1
2 cups	corn kernels, thawed if frozen	500 mL
1 tsp	grated lime zest	5 mL
2 tbsp	freshly squeezed lime juice	25 mL
2	roasted red peppers, cut into thin strips (see Tips, page 24)	2
	Finely chopped cilantro	

1. In a skillet, heat oil over medium heat for 30 seconds. Add onions and cook, stirring, until softened, about 3 minutes. Add garlic, salt and oregano and cook, stirring, for 1 minute. Transfer to slow cooker stoneware. Add stock and stir to combine.

2. Add sweet potatoes and stir to combine. Cover and cook on Low for 8 to 10 hours or on High for 4 to 6 hours, until sweet potatoes are tender.

3. Half an hour before soup has finished cooking, in a heatproof bowl, soak dried chile peppers in boiling water for 30 minutes, weighing down with a cup to ensure they remain submerged. Drain, discarding soaking liquid and stems. Pat dry, chop coarsely and add to stoneware, along with the jalapeño pepper, if using. Working in batches, purée soup in a food processor or blender and return to slow cooker. (You can also do this in the stoneware using an immersion blender.) Add corn, lime zest and juice. Cover and cook on High for 30 minutes, until corn is tender. When ready to serve, ladle soup into individual bowls and garnish with red pepper strips and cilantro.

New Mexico Short Ribs (page 92)

Beef and Veal

Moroccan-Spiced Beef with Couscous

SERVES 6 TO 8

Here's a stew that is every bit as delicious as it is unusual. I love the hint of sweetness provided by the parsnips and the way the cumin, coriander, cinnamon, black peppercorns and cayenne combine to create the richly flavored broth. Accompanied by a bowl of steaming couscous, this makes a perfect meal for any occasion.

Make ahead

This dish can be partially prepared before it is cooked. Complete Step 2, heating 1 tbsp (15 mL) oil in pan before softening the vegetables. Cover and refrigerate mixture overnight. The next morning, brown beef (Step 1), or if you're pressed for time, omit this step and add meat directly to stoneware. Continue cooking as directed in Step 3. Alternatively, cook stew overnight, but do not add the parsley. Cover and refrigerate for the day. When you're ready to serve, bring to a boil in a Dutch oven and simmer for 10 minutes, until meat is heated through and sauce is bubbly. Stir in the parsley and serve.

- **Large (minimum 5 quart) slow cooker**

1 tbsp	vegetable oil (approx.)	15 mL
2 lbs	stewing beef, trimmed of fat and cut into 1-inch (2.5 cm) cubes and patted dry	1 kg
2	onions, chopped	2
4	large carrots, peeled and chopped (about 1 lb/500 g)	4
4	large parsnips, peeled and chopped (about 1 lb/500 g)	4
4	cloves garlic, minced	4
1 tsp	cracked black peppercorns	5 mL
1	cinnamon stick piece (6 inches/15 cm)	1
2 tbsp	cumin seeds, toasted and ground (see Tips, page 216)	25 mL
2 tsp	coriander seeds, toasted and ground (see Tips, page 216)	10 mL
2 tbsp	all-purpose flour	25 mL
1	can (28 oz/796 mL) tomatoes, drained and chopped	1
1 tbsp	tomato paste	15 mL
1 cup	beef stock	250 mL
1/2 cup	dry red wine	125 mL
	Salt	
1/2 tsp	cayenne pepper	2 mL
1 tbsp	freshly squeezed lemon juice	15 mL
	Finely chopped parsley	
	Cooked couscous	

1. In a skillet, heat oil over medium-high heat for 30 seconds. Add beef, in batches, and cook, stirring, adding a bit more oil if necessary, until lightly browned, about 4 minutes per batch. Using a slotted spoon, transfer to slow cooker stoneware.

2. Reduce heat to medium. Add onions, carrots and parsnips to pan and cook, stirring, until carrots are softened, about 7 minutes. Add garlic, peppercorns, cinnamon stick and toasted seeds and cook, stirring, for 1 minute. Add flour and cook, stirring, for 1 minute. Add tomatoes, tomato paste, stock and red wine and bring to a boil, stirring. Add salt to taste.

3. Transfer to slow cooker stoneware. Cover and cook on Low for 8 hours or on High for 4 hours, until vegetables are tender. Dissolve cayenne in lemon juice and stir into mixture. Garnish liberally with parsley before serving. Serve with couscous.

Country Stew with Fennel

Full of character, this robust beef stew, which is rooted in French country cooking, is the perfect antidote to a bone-chilling night. Don't worry if you're not a fan of anchovies — they add depth to the sauce and their taste is negligible in the finished dish. I like to serve this over quinoa or whole wheat couscous, liberally garnished with parsley, but mashed potatoes work well, too.

Make ahead

This dish can be partially prepared before it is cooked. Complete Step 1. Complete Step 3, heating 1 tbsp (15 mL) oil in pan before softening onions. Cover and refrigerate for up to 2 days. When you're ready to cook, either brown the beef as outlined in Step 2 or add it to the stoneware without browning. Stir well and continue with Step 4.

- **Large (minimum 5 quart) slow cooker**

½ tsp	fennel seeds	2 mL
1 tbsp	olive oil (approx.)	15 mL
1½ lbs	stewing beef, trimmed of fat and cut into 1-inch (2.5 cm) cubes and patted dry	750 g
2	onions, finely chopped	2
4	stalks celery, thinly sliced	4
1	bulb fennel, trimmed, cored and thinly sliced on the vertical	1
4	cloves garlic, minced	4
4	anchovy fillets, minced	4
1 tsp	dried thyme leaves	5 mL
½ tsp	salt	2 mL
½ tsp	cracked black peppercorns	2 mL
1 tbsp	all-purpose flour	15 mL
1	can (28 oz/796 mL) tomatoes, including juice, coarsely chopped	1
2	bay leaves	2
½ cup	chopped pitted black olives	125 mL

1. In a dry skillet over medium heat, toast fennel seeds, stirring, until fragrant, about 3 minutes. Immediately transfer to a mortar or a spice grinder and grind. (Or place the seeds on a cutting board and crush, using the bottom of a bottle or cup.) Set aside.

2. In same skillet, heat oil over medium-high heat for 30 seconds. Add beef, in batches, and cook, stirring, adding a bit more oil if necessary, until lightly browned, about 4 minutes per batch. Using a slotted spoon, transfer to slow cooker stoneware.

3. Reduce heat to medium. Add onions, celery and bulb fennel to pan and cook, stirring, until celery is softened, about 5 minutes. Add garlic, anchovies, thyme, salt, peppercorns and reserved fennel seeds and cook, stirring, for 1 minute. Add flour and cook, stirring, for 1 minute. Add tomatoes with juice and bring to a boil. Cook, stirring, just until mixture begins to thicken, about 2 minutes. Add bay leaves and stir well.

4. Transfer to slow cooker stoneware. Cover and cook on Low for 8 hours or on High for 4 hours, until beef is tender. Discard bay leaves. Stir in olives and serve.

Greek Beef Stew with Onions and Feta

This robust stew, known as Stiffado in Greece, is different and delicious. The feta and vinegar add tartness, which is nicely balanced by a tiny bit of sugar, along with cinnamon and allspice. Use only good-quality tomato sauce and serve as the Greeks do, with long strands of hot buttered macaroni, often known as bucatini (not the usual broken or stubby variety) or fluffy mashed potatoes.

Make ahead

This dish can be partially prepared before it is cooked. Complete Step 2, heating 1 tbsp (15 mL) oil in pan before softening onions. Cover and refrigerate mixture for up to 2 days. When you're ready to cook, brown beef (Step 1), or if you're pressed for time, omit this step and add meat directly to stoneware. Continue cooking as directed in Steps 3 and 4.

• **Large (minimum 5 quart) slow cooker**

1 tbsp	vegetable oil (approx.)	15 mL
2 lbs	stewing beef, trimmed of fat and cut into 1-inch (2.5 cm) cubes and patted dry	1 kg
3	large onions, finely chopped, or 2 lbs (1 kg) pearl onions (see Tip, below)	3
4	cloves garlic, minced	4
1/2 tsp	ground cinnamon	2 mL
1/2 tsp	ground allspice	2 mL
1 1/2 cups	tomato sauce	375 mL
3 tbsp	red wine vinegar	45 mL
1 tsp	granulated sugar	5 mL
1	bay leaf	1
1 cup	crumbled feta cheese	250 mL
	Macaroni, noodles or mashed potatoes	

1. In a skillet, heat oil over medium-high heat for 30 seconds. Add beef, in batches, and cook, stirring, adding a bit more oil if necessary, until lightly browned, about 4 minutes per batch. Using a slotted spoon, transfer to slow cooker stoneware.

2. Reduce heat to medium. Add onions and cook, stirring, until softened, about 3 minutes. Add garlic, cinnamon and allspice and cook, stirring, for 1 minute. Add tomato sauce, vinegar, sugar and bay leaf and stir to combine.

3. Pour mixture over meat and cook on Low for 8 to 10 hours or on High for 4 to 5 hours, until beef is tender.

4. Add feta cheese and cook on High for 10 minutes. Discard bay leaf. Spoon over hot buttered macaroni, noodles or mashed potatoes.

TIP

• To peel pearl onions, cut a small "x" in the bottom and drop in a pot of boiling water for 1 minute. Drain and rinse under cold running water. The skins will come off easily with a paring knife.

Beef Stew with Sauerkraut and Sausage

SERVES 6

I can't think of a better way to conclude an active day in the chilly outdoors than to be greeted by a steaming plate of this robust stew. Serve with plenty of mashed potatoes to soak up the tasty sauce, and pass dark rye bread and sour cream at the table.

Make ahead

This dish can be partially prepared before it is cooked. Complete Steps 1 and 3. Cover and refrigerate for up to 2 days. When you're ready to cook, brown meat (Step 2), or if you're pressed for time, omit this step and place beef directly in stoneware. Continue with Step 4.

• **Large (minimum 5 quart) slow cooker**

4	slices bacon	4
2 lbs	stewing beef, trimmed of fat and cut into 1-inch (2.5 cm) cubes and patted dry	1 kg
2	onions, finely chopped	2
4	cloves garlic, minced	4
1 tbsp	caraway seeds	15 mL
1 tsp	salt	5 mL
1/2 tsp	cracked black peppercorns	2 mL
4	juniper berries or 2 tbsp (25 mL) gin	4
1 tbsp	all-purpose flour	15 mL
1 cup	dry white wine	250 mL
1/2 cup	beef stock	125 mL
4 cups	sauerkraut, drained and rinsed (see Tip, page 268)	1 L
1 lb	kielbasa sausage, cut into 1/4-inch (0.5 cm) slices	500 g
	Sour cream	

1. In a skillet, cook bacon over medium-high heat until crisp. Drain thoroughly on paper towel and crumble. Cover and refrigerate until ready to use. Drain all but 2 tbsp (25 mL) fat from pan.

2. Add beef, in batches, and cook, stirring, adding bacon fat if necessary, until lightly browned, about 4 minutes per batch. Using a slotted spoon, transfer to slow cooker stoneware.

3. Reduce heat to medium. Add onions and cook, stirring, until softened, about 3 minutes. Add garlic, caraway seeds, salt, peppercorns and juniper berries. Cook, stirring, for 1 minute. Sprinkle flour over mixture and cook, stirring, for 1 minute. Add wine and stock, bring to a boil and cook, stirring, until mixture thickens. Stir in sauerkraut.

4. Add mixture to slow cooker stoneware. Stir to combine. Cover and cook on Low for 8 hours or on High for 4 hours, until beef is very tender. Stir in sausage and reserved bacon. Cover and cook on High for 15 minutes, until sausage is heated through. Pass the sour cream at the table.

TIP

• Juniper is the predominant aroma in gin, which makes the spirit an acceptable substitute in this stew. Add along with the wine.

Classic Beef Stew

Here's an old-fashioned stew that is delicious as is and spectacular with Madeira mushrooms.

Make ahead

This stew can be partially prepared before it is cooked. Complete Step 2, heating 1 tbsp (15 mL) oil in skillet before softening the vegetables. Cover and refrigerate for up to 2 days. When you're ready to cook, brown the meat (Step 1) or if you're pressed for time, omit this step and place the meat directly in the stoneware. Continue with the recipe.

Variations

Classic Beef Stew with Madeira Mushrooms
In a skillet, melt 2 tbsp (25 mL) butter over medium heat. Add 12 oz (375 g) sliced button mushrooms and cook until mushrooms release their liquid. Season to taste, then sprinkle with 1 tbsp (15 mL) all-purpose flour. Cook, stirring, for 1 minute. Add ¼ cup (50 mL) Madeira or port wine and stir until thickened. Just before serving, stir into stew, then garnish with parsley.

- **Large (minimum 5 quart) slow cooker**

1 tbsp	vegetable oil (approx.)	15 mL
2 lbs	stewing beef, trimmed of fat and cut into 1-inch (2.5 cm) cubes and patted dry	1 kg
2	large onions, finely chopped	2
4	stalks celery, diced	4
2	large carrots, peeled and diced	2
2	cloves garlic, minced	2
1 tsp	dried thyme leaves	5 mL
1 tsp	salt	5 mL
½ tsp	cracked black peppercorns	2 mL
¼ cup	all-purpose flour	50 mL
1 cup	beef stock	250 mL
½ cup	dry red wine or additional beef stock	125 mL
2	bay leaves	2
	Finely chopped fresh parsley	

1. In a skillet, heat oil over medium-high heat for 30 seconds. Add beef, in batches, and cook, stirring, adding a bit more oil if necessary, until lightly browned, about 4 minutes per batch. Using a slotted spoon, transfer to slow cooker stoneware.

2. Reduce heat to medium. Add onions, celery and carrots and cook, stirring, until vegetables are softened, about 7 minutes. Add garlic, thyme, salt and peppercorns and cook, stirring, for 1 minute. Add flour and cook, stirring, for 1 minute. Add stock and wine and cook, stirring, until thickened. Add bay leaves.

3. Transfer mixture to slow cooker stoneware and stir thoroughly to combine ingredients. Cover and cook on Low for 8 to 10 hours or on High for 4 to 5 hours, until beef is very tender. Discard bay leaves. Just before serving, garnish liberally with parsley.

The Best Beef Daube

With its robust Provençal flavors, daube is French comfort food, and this one is particularly delicious. Although it takes a long time to make, it is really a series of small steps completed over the course of three days. I love the addition of short ribs, which add fabulous flavor to the dish, but they also add fat. As a result, it makes sense to let the cooked daube sit overnight in the refrigerator. When you're ready to serve, the fat can be easily skimmed off before reheating in the oven. Hot orzo, tossed with freshly grated Parmesan cheese and some of the cooking juices, makes a superb accompaniment, but daube is also delicious over noodles or mashed potatoes.

Variation

Garnished Daube

In a small bowl, combine $\frac{1}{2}$ cup (125 mL) pitted finely chopped black olives and $\frac{1}{4}$ cup (50 mL) finely chopped parsley leaves. Pass at the table.

- **Large (minimum 5 quart) slow cooker**

3 lbs	beef chuck, cut into thin slices, about $\frac{1}{4}$ inch (0.5 cm), patted dry	1.5 kg
2½ to 3 lbs	beef short ribs	1.25 to 1.5 kg
2	onions, thinly sliced	2
2	carrots, peeled and diced	2
4	cloves garlic, minced	4
3	sprigs fresh thyme or $\frac{1}{2}$ tsp (2 mL) dried thyme leaves	3
2	bay leaves	2
4	whole cloves	4
$\frac{1}{2}$ tsp	cracked black peppercorns	2 mL
1	750 mL bottle robust red wine	1
4	slices bacon	4
	Coarse sea salt	
2 tbsp	tomato paste	25 mL

1. In a large bowl, combine beef chuck, short ribs, onions, carrots, garlic, thyme, bay leaves, cloves, peppercorns and wine. Cover and refrigerate overnight or for up to 2 days. Drain, reserving vegetables, meat and liquid separately.

2. In a skillet, cook bacon over medium-high heat until crisp. Drain on paper towel. Crumble and set aside. Drain all but 2 tbsp (25 mL) fat from pan.

3. Reduce heat to medium. Add reserved vegetables to pan and cook, stirring, until softened, about 7 minutes. Transfer to slow cooker stoneware. Increase heat to medium-high. Add meat in batches, and brown on both sides, about 5 minutes per batch. Using a slotted spoon, transfer to stoneware as completed. Sprinkle bacon and sea salt over each layer as completed. Add tomato paste and reserved liquid to skillet and heat, just until the boiling point, scraping up any brown bits stuck to pan. Add to slow cooker stoneware. Cover and cook on Low for 8 to 10 hours or on High for 4 to 5 hours, until short ribs are falling off the bone. Transfer to a large bowl. Cool, cover and refrigerate overnight.

4. Thirty minutes before you're ready to serve the daube, preheat oven to 350°F (180°C). Skim the fat off the daube and discard. Transfer the meat, with sauce, to a large oven-to-table serving dish. Cover loosely with foil and heat for 30 minutes.

Home-Style Pot Roast

SERVES 6 TO 8

I love this recipe — it is so delicious and easy to make. The secret ingredient is a flavorful steak sauce. I prefer HP Sauce, a British brand, but any well-loved variety will do. Be sure to include mounds of steamy mashed potatoes to soak up the mouth-watering sauce.

Make ahead

This dish can be partially prepared before it is cooked. Complete Step 2, heating 1 tbsp (15 mL) oil in pan before softening vegetables. Cover and refrigerate for up to 2 days. When you're ready to cook, brown the roast (Step 1), or if you're pressed for time, omit this step and place meat directly in stoneware. Continue cooking as directed in Step 3, cooking on High for at least the first two hours if the vegetable mixture has been refrigerated and the meat has not been browned.

- **Large (minimum 5 quart) slow cooker**

1 tbsp	vegetable oil	15 mL
1	beef pot roast, about 3 to 4 lbs (1.5 to 2 kg), patted dry	1
2	onions, thinly sliced	2
4	stalks celery, thinly sliced	4
2	cloves garlic, minced	2
1/2 tsp	dried thyme leaves	2 mL
1 tsp	salt	5 mL
1/2 tsp	cracked black peppercorns	2 mL
1/4 cup	all-purpose flour	50 mL
1 cup	beef stock	250 mL
1	bay leaf	1
1 to 2	green bell peppers, seeded and finely chopped	1 to 2
3 tbsp	steak sauce	45 mL

1. In a skillet, heat oil over medium-high heat for 30 seconds. Add roast and cook, turning, until brown on all sides, about 8 minutes. Transfer to slow cooker stoneware.

2. Reduce heat to medium. Add onions and celery and cook, stirring, until softened, about 5 minutes. Add garlic, thyme, salt and peppercorns and cook, stirring, for 1 minute. Add flour and cook, stirring, for 1 minute. Add stock and bay leaf and cook, stirring, until mixture thickens.

3. Pour mixture over roast. Cover and cook on Low for 10 to 12 hours or on High for 5 to 6 hours, until meat is tender. Stir green peppers and steak sauce into gravy. Cover and cook on High for 30 minutes, until peppers are soft. To serve, discard bay leaf, place roast on a deep platter and spoon sauce over top.

TIP

- If you feel the gravy is not thick enough after the roast has finished cooking, add a flour thickener. Transfer the meat to a deep platter and keep warm. Pour the sauce into a saucepan and heat slowly. Meanwhile, in a small mixing bowl, place 2 tbsp (25 mL) all-purpose flour. Add some of the sauce, a tablespoonful (15 mL) at a time, stirring after each addition, until mixture is smooth. When you have about 1/2 cup (125 mL), add the mixture to the saucepan and bring to a boil over medium-low heat, stirring constantly, until the sauce thickens. Pour over roast and serve.

Italian-Style Pot Roast with Polenta

SERVES 6 TO 8

Although pot roast is not a dish I automatically associate with Italian cuisine, there are many regional Italian recipes that involve braising less tender cuts of beef in copious quantities of a local red wine. This delicious roast falls into that tradition. Serve the luscious sauce over hot polenta.

Make ahead

This dish can be partially prepared before it is cooked. Complete Step 2, heating 1 tbsp (15 mL) oil in pan before softening onions. Cover and refrigerate for up to 2 days. When you're ready to cook, brown roast (Step 1), or if you're pressed for time, omit this step and place meat directly in stoneware. Continue cooking as directed in Step 3, cooking on High for at least the first two hours if the vegetable mixture has been refrigerated and the meat has not been browned.

- **Large (minimum 5 quart) slow cooker**

1 tbsp	vegetable oil	15 mL
1	beef pot roast, about 3 to 4 lbs (1.5 to 2 kg), patted dry	1
2 oz	pancetta or sliced bacon	60 g
2	onions, finely chopped	2
2	carrots, peeled and thinly sliced	2
2	stalks celery, thinly sliced	2
2	cloves garlic, minced	2
1 tsp	salt	5 mL
½ tsp	cracked black peppercorns	2 mL
4	whole cloves	4
2	bay leaves	2
1	cinnamon stick piece (2 inches/5 cm)	1
2 tbsp	tomato paste	25 mL
1 cup	dry red wine	250 mL
½ cup	small black olives, pitted	125 mL
	Slow-Cooked Polenta (see recipe, page 264)	

1. In a skillet, heat oil over medium-high heat for 30 seconds. Add roast and cook, turning, until brown on all sides, about 8 minutes. Transfer to slow cooker stoneware.

2. Reduce heat to medium. Add pancetta, onions, carrots and celery to pan and cook, stirring, until vegetables are softened, about 7 minutes. (If you are using bacon in this recipe, I recommend that you spoon off most of the fat from the pan before adding the tomato paste and wine.) Add garlic, salt, peppercorns, cloves, bay leaves and cinnamon stick and cook, stirring, for 1 minute. Stir in tomato paste and wine and bring to a boil.

3. Pour mixture over roast, making sure that it thoroughly coats the meat. Cover and cook on Low for 10 to 12 hours or on High for 5 to 6 hours, until meat is very tender. Remove roast from slow cooker and keep warm. Pour cooking liquid into a saucepan and simmer on medium heat until reduced by one-third. Taste and adjust seasoning. Add olives and heat through. Discard bay leaves and cinnamon stick.

4. Meanwhile, spread polenta over bottom of a deep platter. Slice roast and layer slices over top of polenta. Pour sauce over meat and serve any extra in a separate sauceboat. Serve piping hot.

Easy Pot Roast with Rich Tomato Gravy

There's no substitute for an old-fashioned pot roast. Its appetizing aromas, wafting through the house, are every bit as good as the meal itself. This easy-to-make version uses a can of tomato soup to create a rich sumptuous gravy. The brown sugar and vinegar finish creates a subtle sweet-and-sour taste, but the gravy is delicious without this addition. Serve this with plenty of mashed potatoes to soak up the sauce.

Make ahead

This dish can be partially prepared before it is cooked. Complete Step 2, heating 1 tbsp (15 mL) oil in pan before softening vegetables. Cover and refrigerate for up to 2 days. When you're ready to cook, brown roast (Step 1), or if you're pressed for time, omit this step and place roast directly in stoneware. Continue cooking as directed in Step 3, cooking on High for at least the first two hours if the vegetable mixture has been refrigerated and the meat has not been browned.

- **Large (minimum 5 quart) slow cooker**

1 tbsp	vegetable oil	15 mL
1	beef pot roast, cross rib or rump, about 3 to 4 lbs (1.5 to 2 kg), patted dry	1
2	onions, thinly sliced	2
3	stalks celery, thinly sliced	3
3	large carrots, peeled and cut into ½-inch (1 cm) cubes	3
2	cloves garlic, minced	2
1 tsp	dry mustard	5 mL
½ tsp	dried thyme leaves	2 mL
1 tsp	salt	5 mL
¼ to ½ tsp	cracked black peppercorns	1 to 2 mL
2 tbsp	all-purpose flour	25 mL
1	can (10 oz/284 mL) condensed tomato soup	1
½ cup	beef stock	125 mL
1 tbsp	Worcestershire sauce	15 mL
2 tbsp	packed brown sugar, optional	25 mL
2 tbsp	balsamic or red wine vinegar, optional	25 mL

1. In a skillet, heat oil over medium-high heat for 30 seconds. Add roast and cook, turning, until brown on all sides, about 8 minutes. Transfer to slow cooker stoneware.

2. Reduce heat to medium. Add onions, celery and carrots to pan and cook, stirring, until vegetables are softened, about 7 minutes. Add garlic, mustard, thyme, salt and peppercorns and cook, stirring, for 1 minute. Sprinkle mixture with flour and stir. Add tomato soup and stock and cook, stirring, until thickened. Stir in Worcestershire sauce.

3. Pour mixture over roast, cover and cook on Low for 10 to 12 hours or on High for 5 to 6 hours, until meat is very tender. Remove roast from slow cooker and place on serving platter. Stir in brown sugar and vinegar, if using, to pan juices. Pour sauce over roast or serve in a separate sauceboat. Serve piping hot.

Braised Beef Curry with Fragrant Spices

SERVES 6

In this Indian-inspired dish, chunks of beef cook in their own juices, seasoned with spices. Using whole spices such as cloves and coriander seeds and cinnamon sticks, rather than ground versions, improves the result since they release their flavor slowly as the curry cooks. Serve with lots of fluffy white rice and Indian bread such as naan to soak up the delicious sauce.

Make ahead

This dish can be partially prepared before it is cooked. Complete Step 2, heating 1 tbsp (15 mL) oil in pan before softening onions. Cover and refrigerate for up to 2 days. When you're ready to cook, brown beef (Step 1), or omit this step and place meat directly in stoneware. Continue cooking as directed in Step 3.

- **Works in slow cookers from 3½ to 5 quarts**

1 tbsp	vegetable oil (approx.)	15 mL
2 lbs	stewing beef, trimmed of fat and cut into 1-inch (2.5 cm) cubes and patted dry	1 kg
2	onions, finely chopped	2
4	cloves garlic, minced	4
1 tbsp	minced gingerroot	15 mL
1 tbsp	coriander seeds	15 mL
1 tsp	turmeric	5 mL
1	cinnamon stick piece (2 inches/5 cm)	1
4	whole cloves	4
1 tsp	salt	5 mL
1 tsp	cracked black peppercorns	5 mL
½ tsp	fennel seeds	2 mL
¼ cup	beef stock	50 mL
2	long red or green chiles, finely chopped (see Tip, below)	2

1. In a skillet, heat oil over medium-high heat for 30 seconds. Add beef, in batches, and cook, stirring, adding a bit more oil if necessary, until nicely browned, about 4 minutes per batch. Using a slotted spoon, transfer to slow cooker stoneware.

2. Reduce heat to medium. Add onions to pan and cook, stirring, until softened, about 3 minutes. Add garlic, gingerroot, coriander seeds, turmeric, cinnamon stick, cloves, salt, peppercorns and fennel seeds and cook, stirring, for 1 minute. Add stock and bring to a boil.

3. Pour mixture over beef. Cover and cook on Low for 8 to 10 hours or on High for 4 to 5 hours, until beef is tender. Stir in chiles. Cover and cook on High for 10 minutes. Serve immediately.

> **TIP**
> - Chile nomenclature can be confusing. Long red or green chiles are usually used in Indian cooking and can be found in Asian markets. They are sometimes called cayenne or serrano chiles, not to be confused with Mexican serrano chiles, which are different.

Brisket in Tomatillo Sauce

SERVES 6 TO 8

If you've never cooked brisket in the slow cooker, try this recipe. I absolutely love the combination of slightly tart tomatillos, robust meat and the finish of cilantro and chipotle peppers in adobo sauce. It's delicious any time, but I particularly like to serve it as the centerpiece of a casual Friday night dinner with friends (see Tips, page 89). Serve over fluffy mashed potatoes, hot onion buns or, to continue the Mexican theme, a pot full of beans and rice. Yum!

Make ahead

For best results, cook the brisket the day before you intend to serve it. Not only is brisket easiest to slice when it is cold, this allows you to spoon off the accumulated fat, which congeals on top of the dish. Thirty minutes before you're ready to serve, purée the chiles and cilantro, reheat the meat and prepare the accompaniments.

- **Large (minimum 5 quart) slow cooker**

1 tbsp	vegetable oil	15 mL
4 to 5 lbs	double beef brisket, trimmed	2 to 2.5 kg
2	onions, thinly sliced on the vertical	2
4	cloves garlic, minced	4
1 tbsp	cumin seeds, toasted and ground (see Tip, page 59)	15 mL
1 tsp	dried oregano leaves	5 mL
1 tsp	salt	5 mL
1 tsp	cracked black peppercorns	5 mL
1	can (28 oz/796 mL) tomatillos, drained	1
1 cup	beef stock	250 mL
2	chipotle chiles in adobo sauce	2
1 cup	coarsely chopped cilantro, stems and leaves	250 mL

1. In a skillet, heat oil over medium-high heat for 30 seconds. Add brisket and brown well on both sides. Transfer to stoneware (see Tips, below).

2. Reduce heat to medium. Add onions to pan and cook, stirring, until softened, about 3 minutes. Add garlic, toasted cumin, oregano, salt and peppercorns and cook, stirring, for 1 minute. Add tomatillos and stock and bring to a boil. Transfer to stoneware. Cover and cook on Low for 12 hours, until beef is very tender. Cool, cover and refrigerate until meat is thoroughly chilled.

3. When you're ready to serve, preheat the oven to 350°F (180°C). Skim the fat off the brisket sauce and discard. Transfer the meat to a cutting board. Slice it very thinly and place in a Dutch oven or large baking dish. In a blender, combine chipotle chiles in adobo sauce, cilantro and approximately ½ cup (125 mL) of the brisket sauce and purée. Pour over brisket. Add remaining sauce. Cover and cook until hot and bubbly and flavors have melded, about 30 minutes.

TIPS
- If the whole piece of brisket won't fit in your slow cooker, cut it in half and lay the two pieces on top of each other.
- This quantity of chiles produces a nicely spicy result. If you're a heat seeker, increase the quantity.

Brisket of Beef with Dilled Onion Gravy

Don't let the simplicity of this recipe fool you. This is one of those yummy comfort food dishes your family will remember and request time and again. I like to add sour cream to the gravy just before serving, although this isn't essential. Serve with plenty of fluffy mashed potatoes and a green vegetable, such as fresh green beans.

Make ahead

For best results, cook the brisket the day before you intend to serve it. Not only is brisket easiest to slice when it is cold, but this also allows you to spoon off the accumulated fat, which congeals on top of the dish.

- **Large (minimum 5 quart) slow cooker**

1 tbsp	vegetable oil	15 mL
4 to 5 lbs	double beef brisket, trimmed	2 to 2.5 kg
4	onions, thinly sliced	4
6	cloves garlic, minced	6
1 tsp	salt	5 mL
1 tbsp	cracked black peppercorns	15 mL
1 cup	beef stock	250 mL
½ cup	tomato-based chili sauce (see Tips, below)	125 mL
1 cup	chopped dill	250 mL
	Sour cream, to taste, optional	

1. In a skillet, heat oil over medium-high heat for 30 seconds. Add brisket and brown well on both sides. Transfer to slow cooker stoneware (see Tips, below).

2. Reduce heat to medium. Add onions to pan and cook, stirring, until softened, about 3 minutes. Add garlic, salt and peppercorns and cook, stirring, for 1 minute. Add stock and chili sauce and bring to a boil. Pour mixture over brisket.

3. Cover and cook on Low for 12 hours, until beef is very tender. Cool, cover and refrigerate until meat is thoroughly chilled. When you're ready to serve, preheat the oven to 350°F (180°C). Skim the fat off the sauce and discard. Transfer the meat to a cutting board. Slice it very thinly and place in a Dutch oven or a large baking dish. Add remaining sauce. Cover and cook until hot and bubbly, about 30 minutes. Remove from heat and stir in dill and sour cream, if using.

TIPS

- If the whole piece of brisket won't fit in your slow cooker, cut it in half and lay the two pieces on top of each other.
- Slow cooked brisket is a perfect Friday night dinner because brisket is much easier to slice after it's been thoroughly chilled. I put the brisket in the slow cooker Thursday night and when it is cooked on Friday morning, cover and refrigerate the meat in the sauce during the day. Just before my guests arrive, I slice the meat, add the remaining ingredients to the sauce and reheat the dish in the oven.
- Tomato-based chili sauce is the kind I grew up with — at our house we always had a bottle of Heinz 57 in the fridge and it's still good enough for me. Nowadays, with so many sauces made from chili peppers widely available, I like to specify the kind of chili sauce called for in a recipe to avoid potential confusion.

Southwestern Brisket

I've never met anyone, except vegetarians, who didn't enjoy a properly cooked brisket. Juicy and full of flavor, brisket is tender and delicious and lends itself to a wide variety of sauces and seasonings. This version, which relies on New Mexico chiles for its rich, tangy taste, is mildly piquant and can be enjoyed by all family members. If you prefer a spicier version, add 1 to 2 finely chopped jalapeño peppers, along with the green bell peppers. I like to serve this over piping hot mashed potatoes.

Make ahead

Brisket responds very well to moist slow cooking. For best results, cook overnight on Low heat for 12 hours. Once cooked, cover and refrigerate immediately. When meat is cool, slice thinly. Place in a Dutch oven, cover with sauce and reheat on stovetop over medium-low heat, until hot and bubbly. Serve immediately.

• **Large (minimum 5 quart) slow cooker**

1 tbsp	vegetable oil	15 mL
4 lbs	double beef brisket, trimmed	2 kg
2	onions, thinly sliced	2
6	stalks celery, thinly sliced	6
6	cloves garlic, minced	6
1 tbsp	dry mustard	15 mL
1 tbsp	dried oregano leaves	15 mL
1 tbsp	cracked black peppercorns	15 mL
2 tsp	cumin seeds, toasted and ground (see Tip, page 59)	10 mL
1 tsp	salt	5 mL
¼ cup	all-purpose flour	50 mL
1	can (28 oz/796 mL) diced tomatoes, drained	1
½ cup	beef stock	125 mL
¼ cup	red wine vinegar	50 mL
½ cup	packed brown sugar	125 mL
4	bay leaves	4
2	dried New Mexico chile peppers	2
2 cups	boiling water	500 mL
2	green bell peppers, thinly sliced	2
½ cup	finely chopped parsley	125 mL

1. In a skillet, heat oil over medium-high heat for 30 seconds. Add brisket and brown well. Transfer to stoneware (see Tips, page 89).

2. Reduce heat to medium. Add onions and celery to pan and cook, stirring, until vegetables are softened, about 5 minutes. Add garlic, mustard, oregano, peppercorns, toasted cumin and salt and cook, stirring, for 1 minute. Sprinkle with flour and cook, stirring, for 1 minute.

3. Add tomatoes, stock and vinegar and cook, stirring, until thickened. Stir in brown sugar and bay leaves and pour over brisket. Cover and cook on Low for 12 hours, until brisket is very tender.

4. Half an hour before serving, in a heatproof bowl, soak New Mexico chiles in boiling water for 30 minutes, weighing down with a cup to ensure they remain submerged. Drain, discarding soaking liquid and stems. Transfer to a blender and add approximately 1 cup (250 mL) of the brisket cooking liquid. Purée. Add to brisket along with the green bell peppers. Cover and cook on High for 30 minutes, until peppers are soft. Discard bay leaf. To serve, slice brisket thinly and place on a deep platter. Spoon sauce over top and garnish with parsley.

New Mexico Short Ribs

These flavorful short ribs are meaty, spicy and delicious. All they really need is a bowl of steaming rice, but they really pop over garlic mashed potatoes or red beans and rice. If you prefer a spicier mixture, add $1/2$ to 1 jalapeño pepper to the blender mixture and use 4 dried chiles.

Make ahead

This dish can be partially prepared before it is cooked. Complete Steps 2 and 4. Cover and refrigerate onion mixture and chile mixture separately for up to 2 days, being aware that the chile mixture will lose some of its vibrancy if held for this long. (For best results, rehydrate chiles while the ribs are cooking or no sooner than the night before you plan to cook.) When you're ready to cook, brown the ribs (Step 1) and continue with the recipe.

- **Large (minimum 5 quart) slow cooker**
- **Preheat broiler**

4 to 5 lbs	beef short ribs	2 to 2.5 kg
1 tbsp	vegetable oil	15 mL
2	onions, thinly sliced on the vertical	2
4	cloves garlic, minced	4
1 tbsp	cumin seeds, toasted and ground (see Tip, page 59)	15 mL
2 tsp	dried oregano leaves	10 mL
1 tsp	salt	5 mL
1 tsp	cracked black peppercorns	5 mL
1	cinnamon stick piece (4 inches/10 cm)	1
1	can (14 oz/398 mL) diced tomatoes, including juice	1
1 cup	beef stock, divided	250 mL
2 to 4	dried New Mexico, ancho or guajillo chiles	2 to 4
2 cups	boiling water	500 mL
$1/2$ cup	coarsely chopped cilantro, stems and leaves	125 mL

1. Position broiler rack 6 inches (15 cm) from heat source. Broil ribs on both sides, turning once, until browned, about 10 minutes per side. Drain on paper towels. Separate ribs if in strips and place in slow cooker stoneware.

2. In a skillet, heat oil over medium heat for 30 seconds. Add onions and cook, stirring, until softened, about 3 minutes. Add garlic, toasted cumin, oregano, salt, peppercorns and cinnamon stick and cook, stirring, for 1 minute. Add tomatoes with juice and $1/2$ cup (125 mL) of the stock and bring to a boil.

3. Transfer to stoneware. Cover and cook on Low for 10 to 12 hours or on High for 5 to 6 hours, until ribs are tender and falling off the bone.

4. Half an hour before the recipe is finished cooking, in a heatproof bowl, soak dried chiles in boiling water for 30 minutes, weighing down with a cup to ensure they remain submerged. Drain, discarding soaking liquid and stems and chop coarsely. Transfer to a blender. Add cilantro and remaining $1/2$ cup (125 mL) of the stock. Purée.

5. Add puréed chiles to stoneware and stir well. Cover and cook on High for 30 minutes, until flavors meld.

Short Ribs Braised in Spicy Black Bean Sauce

SERVES 4 TO 6

This terrific Chinese-inspired recipe for cooking short ribs is easy and so delicious you won't be able to resist seconds. I like to serve this with plain steamed rice and puréed spinach or Swiss chard (see Tips, right).

Make ahead

This dish can be partially prepared before it is cooked. Complete Step 2. Cover and refrigerate mixture for up to 2 days. When you're ready to cook, brown ribs (Step 1) and continue with the recipe.

- **Large (minimum 5 quart) slow cooker**
- **Preheat broiler**

4 to 5 lbs	beef short ribs	2 to 2.5 kg
¼ cup	finely chopped shallots	50 mL
3 tbsp	black bean sauce with garlic (see Tips, below)	45 mL
2 tbsp	sake or vodka	25 mL
1 tsp	minced gingerroot	5 mL
½ tsp	cracked black peppercorns	2 mL
	Grated zest and juice of 1 orange	
1 to 2	long red chile peppers, minced (see Tips, below)	1 to 2
	Finely chopped green onion	

1. Position broiler rack 6 inches (15 cm) from heat source. Broil ribs on both sides, turning once, until well browned, about 10 minutes per side. Drain on paper towels. Separate ribs if in strips and place in slow cooker stoneware.

2. In a bowl, combine shallots, black bean sauce, sake, gingerroot, peppercorns and orange zest and juice.

3. Spoon sauce mixture over short ribs and toss to combine. Cover and cook on Low for 10 to 12 hours or on High for 5 to 6 hours, until ribs are tender and falling off the bone. Stir in chile peppers. Transfer to a warm platter and garnish with green onions.

TIPS

- Black bean sauce with garlic is a prepared sauce that comes in a jar and is widely available. Look for it in the Asian foods section of supermarkets or in specialty stores.
- If your guests like plenty of heat, use the second chile pepper; otherwise, stick with one.
- Serve this with puréed spinach or Swiss chard. For 1 lb (500 g) cooked spinach, use the white part of 2 green onions, half a clove of garlic, 1 tsp (5 mL) Dijon mustard, 2 tsp (10 mL) butter, and salt and freshly ground black pepper to taste. Combine in a food processor and process until smooth.

Short Ribs with Orange Gremolata

SERVES 4 TO 6

These delicious Italian-inspired ribs are classy enough for the most discriminating guest yet homey enough for a family dinner. Serve with creamy polenta and steamed broccoli spears or rapini for a scrumptious Italian-themed meal.

Make ahead

This dish can be partially prepared before it is cooked. Complete Step 2. Cover and refrigerate for up to 2 days. When you're ready to cook, brown the ribs (Step 1) and continue with the recipe.

- **Large (minimum 5 quart) slow cooker**
- **Preheat broiler**

4 to 5 lbs	beef short ribs	2 to 2.5 kg
1 tbsp	vegetable oil	15 mL
2	onions, finely chopped	2
2	large carrots, peeled and thinly sliced	2
4	stalks celery, thinly sliced	4
4	cloves garlic, minced	4
1 tsp	salt	5 mL
1 tsp	cracked black peppercorns	5 mL
2	whole sprigs fresh thyme or 1/2 tsp (2 mL) dried thyme leaves	2
2 tbsp	all-purpose flour	25 mL
1 tbsp	tomato paste	15 mL
1/2 cup	beef stock	125 mL
1/2 cup	dry red wine	125 mL

Orange Gremolata

1/2 cup	flat-leaf parsley, finely chopped	125 mL
1	clove garlic, minced	1
	Zest of 1 orange, finely chopped	

1. Position broiler rack 6 inches (15 cm) from heat source. Broil ribs on both sides, turning once, until well browned, about 10 minutes per side. Drain on paper towels. Separate ribs if in strips and place in slow cooker stoneware.

2. In a skillet, heat oil over medium heat for 30 seconds. Add onions, carrots and celery and cook, stirring, until softened, about 7 minutes. Add garlic, salt, peppercorns and thyme and cook, stirring, for 1 minute. Sprinkle flour over mixture and cook, stirring, for 1 minute. Add tomato paste, stock and wine and bring to a boil.

3. Pour sauce mixture over ribs and stir to combine. Cover and cook on Low for 10 to 12 hours or on High for 5 to 6 hours, until ribs are tender and falling off the bone.

4. *Orange Gremolata:* Combine parsley, garlic and orange zest in a small bowl just before serving and pass at the table.

TIP

- I love short ribs but they are very fatty. Browning them under the broiler before cooking renders much of the fat.

Savory Short Ribs

These robust short ribs are delicious and make a great casual dinner with friends. I like to serve them with hot orzo tossed with extra virgin olive oil and sprinkled with Parmesan. Add a tossed green salad, crusty rolls and some robust red wine to finish the meal.

Make ahead

After refrigerating the ribs to marinate, complete Step 3. Cover and refrigerate mixture overnight. The next morning, complete the recipe, but don't add the olives. Cover and refrigerate the cooked ribs for up to 2 days. Thirty minutes before you're ready to serve the ribs, preheat oven to 350°F (180°C). Skim the fat off the ribs and discard. Transfer meat and sauce to a large oven-to-table serving dish. Cover loosely with foil and heat for 20 minutes. Stir in olives. Return to oven and continue heating until sauce is hot and bubbly, about 10 minutes.

● *Large (minimum 5 quart) slow cooker*

1 tbsp	cracked black peppercorns	15 mL
1 tbsp	dried thyme leaves	15 mL
1 tbsp	fennel seeds, toasted and ground	15 mL
2 tbsp	extra virgin olive oil	25 mL
4 to 5 lbs	beef short ribs	2 to 2.5 kg
4 oz	bacon, diced	125 g
2	onions, finely chopped	2
2	carrots, peeled and finely chopped	2
4	cloves garlic, minced	4
4	anchovy fillets, finely chopped	4
1 tsp	salt	5 mL
½ tsp	cracked black peppercorns	2 mL
1 tbsp	red wine vinegar	15 mL
1 cup	robust red wine	250 mL
1	can (28 oz/796 mL) diced tomatoes, including juice	1
1	bouquet garni	1
1 cup	chopped pitted black olives	250 mL

1. In a baking dish large enough to accommodate the short ribs, combine peppercorns, thyme, toasted fennel and oil. Add ribs, in batches, turning until evenly coated. Cover and refrigerate overnight.

2. Preheat broiler and position broiler rack 6 inches (15 cm) from the heat source. Broil ribs on both sides, turning once, until well browned, about 10 minutes per side. Drain on paper towels. Separate ribs if in strips and place in slow cooker stoneware.

3. In a skillet, cook bacon over medium-high heat, stirring, until brown on all sides. Using a slotted spoon, transfer to slow cooker stoneware. Drain all but 1 tbsp (15 mL) fat from pan. Reduce heat to medium. Add onions and carrots and cook, stirring, until carrots are softened, about 7 minutes. Add garlic, anchovies, salt and ½ tsp (2 mL) peppercorns and cook, stirring, for 1 minute. Add vinegar and wine and cook, stirring, for 2 minutes. Add tomatoes with juice and bouquet garni and transfer to slow cooker stoneware.

4. Cover and cook on Low for 10 to 12 hours or on High for 5 to 6 hours, until ribs are tender and falling off the bone. Stir in olives.

Ranch House Chicken Fried Steak

SERVES 6

There's no chicken in it, so where did this classic cowboy dish get its name? Frankly, who cares? Making it in the slow cooker eliminates the traditional tasks of pounding the meat and watching the frying pan. It also produces melt-in-your-mouth results. The rich, spicy pan gravy served over mashed potatoes is a marriage made in heaven. To turn up the heat, increase the quantity of jalapeño pepper.

Make ahead

This dish can be partially prepared before it is cooked. Complete Step 2, heating 1 tbsp (15 mL) oil in pan before softening onions. Cover and refrigerate mixture for up to 2 days. When you're ready to cook, brown steak (Step 1), or omit this step and place meat directly in stoneware. Continue with the recipe.

• **Large (minimum 5 quart) slow cooker**

1 tbsp	vegetable oil	15 mL
2 lbs	round steak or "simmering" steak (see Tip, below)	1 kg
2	onions, thinly sliced	2
3	cloves garlic, minced	3
1 tsp	salt	5 mL
1 tsp	cracked black peppercorns	5 mL
¼ cup	all-purpose flour	50 mL
¾ cup	chicken stock	175 mL
1 tsp	paprika	5 mL
¼ tsp	cayenne pepper	1 mL
¼ cup	whipping (35%) cream	50 mL
1 to 2	jalapeño peppers, finely chopped	1 to 2
	Hot fluffy mashed potatoes	

1. In a skillet, heat oil over medium-high heat for 30 seconds. Add steak, in pieces, if necessary, and brown on both sides. Transfer to slow cooker stoneware.

2. Reduce heat to medium. Add onions to skillet and cook, stirring, until softened, about 3 minutes. Add garlic, salt and peppercorns and cook, stirring, for 1 minute. Sprinkle flour over mixture and cook, stirring, for 1 minute. Add stock and cook, stirring, until thickened. (Sauce will be very thick.)

3. Spoon sauce over meat in slow cooker, cover and cook on Low for 8 hours or on High for 4 hours, until meat is tender.

4. In a small bowl, combine paprika and cayenne. Gradually add cream, mixing until blended. Add to stoneware along with jalapeño pepper. Cover and cook on High for 15 minutes, until flavors meld. Serve with hot, fluffy mashed potatoes.

TIP
• While round steak is traditionally used for this dish, an equally successful version can be made with "simmering steak." This is cut from the blade or cross rib and is available at many supermarkets.

Mom's Meat Loaf

Here's a meat loaf that reminds me of the kind my mother used to make. Its simple, old-fashioned flavors are perfectly paired with a bubbly dish of scalloped potatoes or a big bowl of fluffy mashed potatoes to soak up the tasty juices.

- **Large (minimum 5 quart) slow cooker**

2 lbs	lean ground beef	1 kg
1	can (10 oz/284 mL) condensed tomato soup	1
2	onions, finely chopped	2
2	stalks celery, finely diced	2
2	cloves garlic, minced	2
¼ cup	finely chopped flat-leaf parsley	50 mL
1 tsp	salt	5 mL
½ tsp	cracked black peppercorns	2 mL
3	eggs, lightly beaten	3
1½ cups	fine dry bread crumbs	375 mL

1. Fold a 2-foot (60 cm) piece of foil in half lengthwise. Place on bottom and up sides of slow cooker stoneware overlapping the top.

2. In a large bowl, combine beef, tomato soup, onions, celery, garlic, parsley, salt, peppercorns, eggs and bread crumbs and mix well. Shape into a loaf and place in middle of foil strip on bottom of slow cooker stoneware. Cover and cook on Low for 8 to 10 hours or on High for 4 to 5 hours, until juices run clear when meat loaf is pieced with a fork or a meat thermometer reads 160°F (71°C). Lift out loaf using foil strip and transfer to a warm platter. Pour juices into a sauceboat and serve alongside sliced loaf.

Beef Noodle Casserole

This comfort food dish is a favorite with kids and adults. There's something about the combination of well-seasoned beef, soft bland noodles and creamy cheese that is irresistible. I like to serve this with a big tossed salad — plenty of tomatoes, lots of Boston lettuce and a handful of mesclun greens in a robust vinaigrette.

Make ahead

This dish can be partially prepared before it is cooked. Complete Steps 1 and 2, chilling cooked meat and onion mixture separately. Refrigerate for up to 2 days. When you're ready to cook, continue cooking as directed in the recipe. If the tomato mixture has thickened with chilling, heat it gently until it is a spreadable consistency. To facilitate preparation, the night before you plan to cook this casserole, shred Cheddar cheese, cover and refrigerate.

- **Large (minimum 5 quart) oval slow cooker**
- **Lightly greased slow cooker stoneware**

2 tbsp	vegetable oil, divided	25 mL
1 lb	lean ground beef	500 g
2	onions, finely chopped	2
4	stalks celery, thinly sliced	4
4	cloves garlic, minced	4
2 tsp	dried oregano leaves	10 mL
1 tsp	salt	5 mL
1 tsp	cracked black peppercorns	5 mL
1 cup	beef stock	250 mL
1 cup	tomato sauce	250 mL
4 oz	cream cheese, softened and cubed	125 g
8 oz	egg noodles, cooked and drained	250 g

Cheddar-Crumb Topping

1 cup	dry bread crumbs	250 mL
2 tbsp	melted butter	25 mL
1 cup	shredded Cheddar cheese	250 mL

1. In a skillet, heat 1 tbsp (15 mL) of the oil over medium-high heat for 30 seconds. Add beef and cook, stirring and breaking up with the back of a spoon, until no longer pink, about 5 minutes. Remove with a slotted spoon and set aside. Drain off liquid in pan.

2. Reduce heat to medium and add remaining oil to pan. Add onions and celery and cook, stirring, until softened, about 5 minutes. Add garlic, oregano, salt and peppercorns and cook, stirring, for 1 minute. Add stock, tomato sauce and cream cheese and cook, stirring, until cheese is melted.

3. *To assemble casserole:* Spoon 1/2 cup (125 mL) tomato-sauce mixture in bottom of slow cooker stoneware. Cover with half of the meat, then half of the noodles. Repeat layers of meat and noodles. Finish with a layer of sauce. Cover and cook on Low for 5 to 6 hours or on High for 2 1/2 to 3 hours, until mixture is hot and bubbly.

4. *Cheddar-Crumb Topping:* In a bowl, combine bread crumbs and butter. Add cheese and stir well. Spread over casserole and cook on High for 30 minutes, until cheese is melted and top is bubbly.

Beef Collops with Barley

SERVES 6 TO 8

Collops is a Scottish term for a dish made from scallops of meat or minced meat, stewed with onion and a sauce. I've updated this version to include dried mushrooms for enhanced flavor and added barley for nutrition, transforming it into a casserole. With its flavorful gravy and soothing grain base, this is the ultimate comfort food dish and is perfect for those evenings when everyone is coming and going at different times. Just leave it in the slow cooker on Warm and people can help themselves. Leave the fixin's for salad and whole grain rolls to complete the meal.

Make ahead

This dish can be partially prepared before it is cooked. Complete Steps 1 and 2. Cover and refrigerate overnight. The next morning, continue with the recipe.

- **Large (minimum 5 quart) slow cooker**

2 tbsp	dried wild mushrooms, crumbled (see Tips, below)	25 mL
½ cup	hot water	125 mL
1 tbsp	olive oil	15 mL
1 lb	lean ground beef	500 g
2	onions, finely chopped	2
4	cloves garlic, minced	4
1 tbsp	fresh rosemary leaves, finely chopped, or 2 tsp (10 mL) dried rosemary, crumbled	15 mL
½ tsp	cracked black peppercorns	2 mL
12 oz	cremini mushrooms, sliced	375 g
1	can (28 oz/796 mL) tomatoes, drained and coarsely chopped	1
2 cups	beef stock	500 mL
	Salt, optional	
1 cup	barley, rinsed (see Tips, below)	250 mL
2 cups	corn kernels, thawed if frozen, optional	500 mL

1. In a heatproof bowl, combine dried mushrooms and hot water. Stir well and let stand for 30 minutes. Strain through a fine sieve, reserving mushrooms and liquid separately. Set aside.

2. In a skillet, heat oil over medium heat for 30 seconds. Add beef and onions and cook, stirring and breaking beef up with a spoon, until beef is no longer pink, about 5 minutes. Add garlic, rosemary, peppercorns and reserved soaked mushrooms and cook, stirring, for 1 minute. Add cremini mushrooms and stir well. Add tomatoes, stock and reserved mushroom liquid and bring to a boil. Season to taste with salt, if using.

3. Transfer to slow cooker stoneware. Stir in barley. Cover and cook on Low for 6 to 8 hours or on High for 3 to 4 hours, until barley is tender. Add corn, if using. Cover and cook on High for 15 to 20 minutes, until corn is tender.

TIPS
- This quantity of dried mushrooms equates to half of a ½ oz (14 g) package. Crumbling them with your fingers before soaking eliminates the need to chop them, and the powdery texture works well.
- Use whole, pot or pearl barley in this recipe.

Cuban Picadillo with Pimento-Stuffed Olives

SERVES 6

This easy and delicious dish can best be described as a Cuban version of hash. We like to eat it topped with a fried egg and accompanied by Fried Plantains.

Make ahead

This dish can be partially prepared before it is cooked. Complete Steps 1 and 2. Cover and refrigerate meat and tomato mixtures separately for up to 2 days. When you're ready to cook, combine in slow cooker stoneware and continue with the recipe.

Variation

Picadillo with Chili-Almond Garnish

This recipe is great as is, but if you want to dress it up for friends, add a chili-almond garnish. Melt 2 tbsp (25 mL) butter in a small saucepan over low heat. Add 1 tsp (5 mL) chili powder and cook for 1 minute. Add ¼ cup (50 mL) slivered almonds and cook, stirring, until they begin to turn brown. Spoon over the Picadillo.

• **Large (minimum 5 quart) slow cooker**

2 tbsp	vegetable oil, divided	25 mL
2 lbs	lean ground beef	1 kg
4	cloves garlic, minced	4
2 tsp	dried oregano leaves	10 mL
1 tsp	salt	5 mL
½ tsp	cracked black peppercorns	2 mL
¼ tsp	ground cinnamon	1 mL
2	whole cloves	2
1	bay leaf	1
1	can (5½ oz/156 mL) tomato paste	1
2 tbsp	red wine vinegar	25 mL
1	jalapeño pepper, finely chopped	1
12	large pimento-stuffed olives, sliced	12

Fried Plantains, optional

2 tbsp	butter	25 mL
4	plantains, thinly sliced	4
2 tbsp	freshly squeezed lemon or lime juice	25 mL

1. In a skillet, heat 1 tbsp (15 mL) of the oil over medium-high heat for 30 seconds. Add beef and cook, stirring and breaking up with a spoon, until no longer pink, about 10 minutes. Using a slotted spoon, transfer to slow cooker stoneware. Drain off liquid from pan.

2. Reduce heat to medium. Add remaining oil to pan. Add garlic, oregano, salt, peppercorns, cinnamon, cloves and bay leaf and cook, stirring, for 1 minute. Stir in tomato paste and red wine vinegar and bring mixture to a boil.

3. Pour mixture over meat and stir well. Cover and cook on Low for 8 hours or on High for 4 hours, until mixture is hot and bubbly.

4. Stir in jalapeño pepper and olives. Cover and cook on High for 20 minutes, until heated through. Serve immediately.

5. *Fried Plantains*: In a skillet, melt butter over medium heat. Add plantains and cook, turning once, until brown. Pour lemon or lime juice over top and serve hot.

Best-Ever Meatballs in Tomato Sauce

SERVES 8

I love the flavor of these savory meatballs, which are seasoned with cumin and oregano. A hint of cinnamon in the simple tomato sauce adds an intriguing note. Although they are delicious over spaghetti, the traditional combination, I also like to serve these tasty nuggets over steaming hot couscous or baked potatoes, cut into quarters.

Make ahead

This dish can be partially prepared before it is cooked. Complete Step 3, adding 1 tbsp (15 mL) oil to pan before softening onions. Cover and refrigerate for up to 2 days. When you're ready to cook, make the meatballs (Step 1) and continue with the recipe.

● **Large (minimum 5 quart) slow cooker**

Meatballs

¼ cup	long-grain parboiled rice	50 mL
2 lbs	lean ground beef (see Tip, page 107)	1 kg
2	eggs, beaten	2
1	onion, grated	1
2	cloves garlic, minced	2
1 tsp	dried oregano leaves	5 mL
1 tsp	ground cumin	5 mL
½ tsp	salt	2 mL
¼ tsp	freshly ground black pepper	1 mL
2 tbsp	vegetable oil	25 mL

Tomato Sauce

2	onions, finely chopped	2
4	cloves garlic, minced	4
2 tsp	dried oregano leaves	10 mL
1 tsp	salt	5 mL
½ tsp	cracked black peppercorns	2 mL
1	cinnamon stick piece (2 inches/5 cm)	1
1	can (28 oz/796 mL) tomatoes, including juice	1
2 tbsp	freshly squeezed lemon juice	25 mL

1. *Meatballs:* In a bowl, stir rice into 4 cups (1 L) boiling water. Set aside for 30 minutes to soak. Drain well. Return rice to bowl. Add beef, eggs, onion, garlic, oregano, cumin, salt and pepper and mix well. Form into 16 balls, each approximately 2 inches (5 cm) in diameter.

2. In a skillet, heat oil over medium-high heat. Add meatballs, in batches, and brown on all sides. Transfer to slow cooker stoneware. Drain all but 1 tbsp (15 mL) fat from pan.

3. *Tomato Sauce:* Reduce heat to medium. Add onions to pan and cook, stirring, until softened, about 3 minutes. Add garlic, oregano, salt, peppercorns and cinnamon stick and cook, stirring, for 1 minute. Stir in tomatoes with juice and lemon juice and bring to a boil, breaking up tomatoes with a spoon as they cook.

4. Pour sauce over meatballs. Cover and cook on Low for 8 hours or on High for 4 hours, until meatballs are no longer pink inside. Discard cinnamon stick.

Beef and Rigatoni Bake

This is a nice weekday meal. It is particularly suitable for those evenings when everyone is coming and going at different times. You can leave the fixings for salad out, set the slow cooker to Warm and let people help themselves.

Make ahead

This dish can be partially prepared before it is cooked. Complete Steps 1 and 2. Cover and refrigerate meat and vegetable mixtures separately for up to 2 days. When you're ready to cook, combine in slow cooker stoneware and continue with the recipe.

• **Large (minimum 5 quart) slow cooker**

2 tbsp	vegetable oil, divided	25 mL
2 lbs	lean ground beef (see Tip, below)	1 kg
2	onions, finely chopped	2
4	stalks celery, thinly sliced	4
4	cloves garlic, minced	4
½ tsp	dried thyme leaves	2 mL
½ tsp	salt	2 mL
½ tsp	cracked black peppercorns	2 mL
1	can (10 oz/284 mL) condensed tomato soup	1
1 cup	tomato juice, beef stock or water	250 mL
2 tbsp	Worcestershire sauce	25 mL
4 cups	rigatoni, cooked until barely tender (about 7 minutes) and drained	1 L
2 cups	shredded Cheddar cheese	500 mL
1	green bell pepper, finely chopped, optional	1
1	fresh hot chile pepper, minced, optional	1

1. In a skillet, heat 1 tbsp (15 mL) of the oil over medium-high heat for 30 seconds. Add beef and cook, breaking up with a wooden spoon, until no longer pink, about 10 minutes. Using a slotted spoon, transfer to slow cooker stoneware. Drain liquid from pan.

2. Reduce heat to medium. Add remaining oil to pan. Add onions and celery and cook, stirring, until softened, about 5 minutes. Add garlic, thyme, salt and peppercorns and cook, stirring, for 1 minute. Stir in tomato soup, juice and Worcestershire sauce. Transfer to slow cooker stoneware.

3. Add cooked rigatoni and stir well. Cover and cook on Low for 6 hours or on High for 3 hours, until hot and bubbly. Stir in cheese, green pepper and chile pepper, if using. Cover and cook on High for 20 minutes, until cheese is melted and pepper is heated through.

TIP
• If you used extra-lean ground beef, you may have to add extra oil when browning meatballs or to cook onions.

Butternut Chili

I love this chili. The combination of beef, butternut squash, ancho chiles and cilantro is a real winner. Don't be afraid to make extra because it's great reheated.

Make ahead

This dish can be partially prepared before it is cooked. Complete Steps 1 and 3. Cover and refrigerate tomato and chile mixtures separately overnight. The next morning, continue with the recipe.

- **Large (minimum 5 quart) slow cooker**

1 tbsp	vegetable oil	15 mL
1 lb	lean ground beef	500 g
2	onions, finely chopped	2
4	cloves garlic, minced	4
1 tbsp	cumin seeds, toasted and ground	15 mL
2 tsp	dried oregano leaves	10 mL
1 tsp	salt	5 mL
½ tsp	cracked black peppercorns	2 mL
1	cinnamon stick piece (2 inches/5 cm)	1
1	can (28 oz/796 mL) diced tomatoes, including juice	1
3 cups	cubed (1 inch/2.5 cm) peeled butternut squash	750 mL
2 cups	cooked dried or canned kidney beans, drained and rinsed	500 mL
2	dried New Mexico, ancho or guajillo chiles	2
2 cups	boiling water	500 mL
½ cup	coarsely chopped cilantro	125 mL

1. In a skillet, heat oil over medium-high heat for 30 seconds. Add beef and onions and cook, stirring, until beef is no longer pink, about 5 minutes. Add garlic, toasted cumin, oregano, salt, peppercorns and cinnamon stick and cook, stirring, for 1 minute. Add diced tomatoes with juice and bring to a boil.

2. Place squash and beans in slow cooker stoneware and cover with sauce. Cover and cook on Low for 6 to 8 hours or on High for 3 to 4 hours, until squash is tender.

3. Half an hour before recipe is finished cooking, in a heatproof bowl, soak dried chile peppers in boiling water for 30 minutes, weighing down with a cup to ensure they are submerged. Drain, reserving ½ cup (125 mL) of the soaking liquid. Discard stems and chop coarsely. In a blender, combine rehydrated chiles, cilantro and reserved soaking liquid. Purée. Add to stoneware and stir well. Cover and Cook on High for 30 minutes, until hot and bubbly and flavors meld.

TIP

- If you prefer, you can soak and purée the chiles while preparing the chili and refrigerate until you're ready to add them to the recipe.

Chunky Black Bean Chili

Here is a great-tasting, stick-to-the-ribs chili that is perfect for a family dinner or casual evening with friends. The combination of milder New Mexico and ancho chili peppers gives the mix unique flavoring, and the optional fresh chili peppers will satisfy any heat seekers in your group. Serve this with crusty country bread, a big green salad and robust red wine or ice cold beer.

Make ahead

This dish can be partially prepared before it is cooked. Complete Steps 2 and 4, heating 1 tbsp (15 mL) oil in pan before softening the onions. Cover and refrigerate tomato and chile mixtures separately for up to 2 days, being aware that chile mixture will lose some of its vibrancy if held for this long. (For best results, rehydrate chiles while the chili is cooking or no sooner than the night before you plan to cook.) When you're ready to cook, brown the beef, or if you're pressed for time, omit this step. Continue with the recipe.

- **Large (minimum 5 quart) slow cooker**

1 tbsp	vegetable oil (approx.)	15 mL
2 lbs	stewing beef, trimmed of fat and cut into 1-inch (2.5 cm) cubes and patted dry	1 kg
2	onions, finely chopped	2
4	cloves garlic, minced	4
1 tbsp	cumin seeds, toasted and ground	15 mL
1 tbsp	dried oregano leaves, crumbled	15 mL
1 tsp	each cracked black peppercorns and salt	5 mL
1	can (28 oz/796 mL) diced tomatoes, including juice	1
1½ cups	flat beer or beef stock, divided	375 mL
4 cups	cooked black beans, drained and rinsed	1 L
2	each dried ancho and New Mexico chile peppers	2
1 cup	coarsely chopped cilantro, leaves and stems	250 mL
1 to 2	jalapeño peppers, chopped, optional	1 to 2
	Sour cream, finely chopped red or green onion, shredded Monterey Jack cheese and salsa, optional	

1. In a skillet, heat oil over medium-high heat for 30 seconds. Add beef, in batches, and cook, stirring, adding a bit more oil if necessary, until lightly browned, about 4 minutes per batch. Using a slotted spoon, transfer to slow cooker stoneware.

2. Reduce heat to medium. Add onions and cook, stirring, until softened. Add garlic, cumin, oregano, peppercorns and salt and cook, stirring, for 1 minute. Add tomatoes with juice and cook, breaking up with the back of a spoon, until desired consistency is achieved. Add 1 cup (250 mL) of the beer and bring to a boil.

3. Pour mixture over beef. Add beans and stir well. Cover and cook on Low for 8 to 10 hours or on High for 4 to 5 hours, until beef is tender.

4. Half an hour before recipe is finished cooking, in a heatproof bowl, soak ancho and New Mexico chiles in 4 cups (1 L) boiling water for 30 minutes, weighing down with a cup to ensure they remain submerged. Drain, discarding soaking liquid and stems and chop coarsely. Transfer to a blender. Add cilantro, jalapeño, if using, and remaining beer. Purée.

5. Add chile mixture to stoneware and stir well. Cover and cook on High for 30 minutes until mixture is hot and bubbly and flavors meld. To serve, ladle into bowls and garnish.

Blue Plate Chili

Here's a good, basic chili recipe — just like the chili my mother used to make or that we ate for lunch at local restaurants when, as a preschooler, I accompanied her on household errands. I have fond memories of those "blue plate specials" of chili and toast, and judging by my own family's response to this version, it remains a popular dish. I still serve it with toast — it wouldn't be the same without it.

Make ahead

This recipe can be partially prepared before it is cooked. Complete Steps 1 and 2. Cover and refrigerate cooked meat and onion mixture separately for up to 2 days. Chop green pepper and cover. When you're ready to cook, combine in slow cooker stoneware and continue with the recipe.

• **Large (minimum 5 quart) slow cooker**

1 tbsp	vegetable oil	15 mL
1 lb	lean ground beef	500 g
1	onion, finely chopped	1
3	stalks celery, thinly sliced	3
2	cloves garlic, minced	2
1 tsp	caraway seeds	5 mL
1 tsp	salt	5 mL
1 tsp	cracked black peppercorns	5 mL
1	can (28 oz/796 mL) tomatoes, drained and coarsely chopped	1
½ cup	beef stock	125 mL
2 cups	cooked dried or canned red kidney beans, drained and rinsed	500 mL
1 tbsp	chili powder	15 mL
1	green bell pepper, chopped	1
1	jalapeño pepper, finely chopped, optional	1

1. In a skillet, heat oil over medium-high heat. Add beef and cook, breaking up with a spoon, stirring, until no longer pink, about 5 minutes. Using a slotted spoon, transfer to slow cooker stoneware.

2. Reduce heat to medium. Add onion and celery to pan and cook, stirring, until softened, about 5 minutes. Add garlic, caraway seeds, salt and peppercorns and cook, stirring, for 1 minute. Stir in tomatoes and stock and bring to a boil.

3. Transfer to slow cooker stoneware. Stir in beans. Cover and cook on Low for 8 to 10 hours or on High for 4 to 5 hours. Stir in chili powder, green pepper and jalapeño pepper, if using. Cover and cook on High for 20 minutes, until peppers are tender and flavors meld.

Dilled Veal Stew

SERVES 6 TO 8

This is a streamlined and lower fat version of a Veal Blanquette I've been making for many years from The Silver Palate Cookbook. My husband likes to increase the quantity of nutmeg and cream, so feel free to do so, if that appeals to your taste buds. All variations are delicious. I like to serve this for Sunday dinner, over hot buttered noodles.

Make ahead

This dish can be partially prepared before it is cooked. Complete Step 3. Cover and refrigerate for up to 2 days. When you're ready to cook, continue with the recipe.

• **Large (minimum 5 quart) slow cooker**

2 tbsp	all-purpose flour	25 mL
1 tbsp	paprika	15 mL
1/4 tsp	ground nutmeg	1 mL
1 tsp	salt	5 mL
1/2 tsp	freshly ground black pepper	2 mL
3 tbsp	butter, divided	45 mL
2 lbs	stewing veal, cut into 1-inch (2.5 cm) cubes and patted dry	1 kg
2	onions, thinly sliced	2
2	large carrots, peeled, cut into quarters lengthwise and very thinly sliced	2
4	stalks celery, thinly sliced	4
1 cup	chicken stock	250 mL
1/2 cup	dry vermouth or white wine	125 mL
1/2 cup	whipping (35%) cream	125 mL
1/2 cup	finely chopped dill	125 mL
	Hot buttered noodles, optional	

1. In a bowl, combine flour, paprika, nutmeg, salt and pepper. Set aside.

2. In a skillet, melt 2 tbsp (25 mL) of the butter over medium heat. Add veal and cook, stirring, for 3 to 4 minutes without browning. Sprinkle flour mixture over meat, stir to combine and using a slotted spoon, transfer to slow cooker stoneware.

3. Add remaining butter to pan. Add onions, carrots and celery and cook, stirring, until vegetables are softened, about 7 minutes. Add stock and dry vermouth and bring to a boil.

4. Pour mixture over veal, cover and cook on Low for 8 to 10 hours or on High for 4 to 5 hours, until stew is hot and bubbly. Stir in cream and dill and serve over noodles, if desired.

Wine-Braised Veal with Rosemary

SERVES 6

This is a delicious Italian-inspired stew that is both simple and elegant. Serve over hot Slow-Cooked Polenta (see recipe, page 264) and accompany with steamed broccoli or rapini.

Make ahead

This dish can be partially prepared before it is cooked. Complete Steps 1 and 3, refrigerating mixture for up to 2 days. When you're ready to cook, place veal in slow cooker (don't bother with browning) and continue with Step 4.

- **Large (minimum 5 quart) slow cooker**

1 tbsp	olive oil (approx.)	15 mL
3 oz	pancetta or bacon, cut into ¼-inch (0.5 cm) dice (see Tips, below)	90 g
2 lbs	stewing veal, cut into 1-inch (2.5 cm) cubes and patted dry	1 kg
3	leeks, white part only, cleaned and coarsely chopped	3
3	large carrots, peeled and diced	3
2	stalks celery, diced	2
2	cloves garlic, minced	2
1½ tbsp	chopped fresh rosemary leaves or dried rosemary leaves, crumbled (see Tips, below)	22 mL
1 tsp	salt	5 mL
½ tsp	cracked black peppercorns	2 mL
2 tbsp	all-purpose flour	25 mL
½ cup	dry red wine	125 mL
½ cup	chicken stock	125 mL
	Fresh rosemary sprigs, optional	

1. In a skillet, heat oil over medium heat for 30 seconds. Add pancetta and cook, stirring, until browned. Using a slotted spoon, transfer to a bowl and set aside.

2. Add veal to pan, in batches, and cook, stirring, adding a bit more oil if necessary, just until it begins to brown, about 4 minutes. Using a slotted spoon, transfer to slow cooker stoneware.

3. Add leeks, carrots and celery to pan and cook, stirring, until softened, about 7 minutes. Add garlic, rosemary, salt, peppercorns and reserved pancetta and cook, stirring, for 1 minute. Sprinkle flour over mixture and cook, stirring, for 1 minute. Add wine and stock and cook, stirring, until mixture thickens.

4. Pour mixture over meat and stir to combine. Cover and cook on Low for 8 to 10 hours or on High for 4 to 6 hours, until meat is tender. Garnish with rosemary sprigs, if using, and serve.

TIPS
- If you are using bacon in this recipe, drain all but 1 tbsp (15 mL) of the fat before proceeding with Step 2.
- If you are using fresh rosemary and prefer a more pronounced flavor, bury a whole sprig in the meat before adding the sauce. Remove before serving.

Saucy Swiss Steak

SERVES 6

Here's a dish that many people will remember from the 1950s. Back then it required a fair bit of muscle to pound the steak with a mallet. Today, you can avoid all that dreary work by using the slow cooker. This is so good, you'll want seconds. Serve with garlic mashed potatoes and a plain green vegetable.

Make ahead

This dish can be partially prepared before it is cooked. Complete Step 2, heating 1 tbsp (15 mL) oil in pan before softening onions, carrots and celery. Cover and refrigerate mixture for up to 2 days. When you're ready to cook, brown steak (Step 1), or omit this step and place steak directly in stoneware. Continue cooking as directed. Alternatively, cook steak overnight, cover and refrigerate. When ready to serve, bring to a boil in a large skillet and simmer for 10 minutes, until meat is heated through and sauce is hot and bubbly.

- **Large (minimum 5 quart) slow cooker**

1 tbsp	vegetable oil	15 mL
2 lbs	round steak or "simmering" steak (see Tip, below)	1 kg
2	onions, finely chopped	2
1	carrot, peeled and thinly sliced	1
I	stalk celery, thinly sliced	1
½ tsp	salt	2 mL
¼ tsp	cracked black peppercorns	1 mL
2 tbsp	all-purpose flour	25 mL
1	can (28 oz/796 mL) tomatoes, drained and chopped, ½ cup (125 mL) juice reserved	1
1 tbsp	Worcestershire sauce	15 mL
1	bay leaf	1

1. In a skillet, heat oil over medium-high heat for 30 seconds. Add steak, in pieces, if necessary, and brown on both sides. Transfer to slow cooker stoneware.

2. Reduce heat to medium-low. Add onions, carrot, celery, salt and peppercorns to pan. Cover and cook until carrots are softened, about 7 minutes. Sprinkle flour over vegetables and cook, stirring, for I minute. Add tomatoes, reserved juice and Worcestershire sauce. Bring to a boil, stirring until slightly thickened. Add bay leaf.

3. Pour tomato mixture over steak. Cover and cook on Low for 8 hours or on for High 4 hours, until meat is tender. Discard bay leaf.

> **TIP**
> - While round steak is traditionally used for this dish, an equally successful version can be made with "simmering steak." This is cut from the blade or cross rib and is available at many supermarkets.

Shepherd's Pie with Creamy Corn Filling

Shepherd's Pie is home cooking at its most basic. This is a great dish for those evenings when everyone is coming and going at different times. Just leave the slow cooker on Low or Warm and let people help themselves. Serve with a big tossed salad.

Make ahead

This dish can be partially prepared the night before it is cooked. Make mashed potatoes, cover and refrigerate. Complete Steps 1 and 2, chilling cooked meat and onion mixtures separately. Refrigerate overnight. The next morning, continue with the recipe.

- **Large (minimum 5 quart) slow cooker**

1 tbsp	vegetable oil	15 mL
1 lb	lean ground beef	500 g
2	onions, finely chopped	2
4	cloves garlic, minced	4
1 tsp	dried thyme leaves	5 mL
1 tsp	salt	5 mL
½ tsp	cracked black peppercorns	2 mL
2 tbsp	all-purpose flour	25 mL
1 cup	beef stock	250 mL
2 tbsp	tomato paste	25 mL
1	can (19 oz/540 mL) cream-style corn	1
4 cups	mashed potatoes, seasoned with 1 tbsp (15 mL) butter, ½ tsp (2 mL) salt and ¼ tsp (1 mL) freshly ground black pepper (see Tip, below)	1 L
¼ cup	shredded Cheddar cheese	50 mL

1. In a skillet, heat oil over medium-high heat for 30 seconds. Add beef and cook, stirring and breaking up with the back of a spoon, until meat is no longer pink, about 5 minutes. Using a slotted spoon, transfer to slow cooker stoneware. Drain off liquid.

2. Reduce heat to medium. Add onions to pan and cook, stirring, until softened, about 3 minutes. Add garlic, thyme, salt and peppercorns and cook, stirring, for 1 minute. Sprinkle flour over mixture and cook, stirring, for 1 minute. Add stock and tomato paste, stir to combine and cook, stirring, until thickened.

3. Transfer mixture to slow cooker stoneware and stir well. Spread corn evenly over mixture. Cover and cook on Low for 4 to 6 hours or on High for 2 to 3 hours, until hot and bubbly. Spread mashed potatoes over top of mixture and sprinkle with cheese. Cover and cook on High for 30 minutes, until potatoes are heated through.

> **TIP**
> - For perfect mashed potatoes, invest in a ricer, a handy gadget resembling a large garlic press, which eliminates those pesky lumps.

Osso Buco with Lemon Gremolata

SERVES 6 TO 8

This is probably my all-time favorite veal dish. I love the wine-flavored sauce and the succulent meat, enhanced with just a soupçon of gremolata, pungent with fresh garlic and lemon zest. But best of all, I adore eating the marrow from the bones, a rare and delicious treat. Pass coffee spoons to ensure that every mouth-watering morsel is extracted from the bone.

Make ahead

This dish can be partially prepared before it is cooked. Complete Steps 1 and 4, heating 1 tbsp (15 mL) olive oil in pan before softening leeks, carrots and celery. Cover sauce and refrigerate for up to 2 days. When you're ready to cook, continue with the recipe. Alternatively, Osso Buco can be cooked overnight in slow cooker, covered and refrigerated for up to 2 days. When ready to serve, spoon off congealed fat, and transfer to a Dutch oven. Bring to a boil and simmer for 10 minutes, until meat is heated through and sauce is bubbly.

- **Large (minimum 5 quart) slow cooker**

1	package (½ oz/14 g) dried porcini mushrooms	1
1 cup	boiling water	250 mL
¼ cup	all-purpose flour	50 mL
1 tsp	salt	5 mL
½ tsp	freshly ground black pepper	2 mL
6 to 8	sliced veal shanks	6 to 8
1 tbsp	olive oil	15 mL
1 tbsp	butter	15 mL
3	leeks, white part only, cleaned and thinly sliced (see Tips, page 66)	3
2	carrots, peeled and finely chopped	2
2	stalks celery, finely chopped	2
2	cloves garlic, finely chopped	2
1 tsp	dried thyme or 2 sprigs fresh thyme	5 mL
½ cup	dry white wine	125 mL

Lemon Gremolata

2	cloves garlic, minced	2
1 cup	finely chopped parsley	250 mL
	Grated zest of 1 lemon	
1 tbsp	extra virgin olive oil	15 mL

1. In a heatproof bowl, combine porcini mushrooms and boiling water. Let stand for 30 minutes. Drain through a fine sieve, reserving liquid. Pat mushrooms dry with paper towel and chop finely. Set aside.

2. In a bowl, mix together flour, salt and black pepper. Lightly coat veal shanks with mixture, shaking off the excess. Set any flour mixture remaining aside.

3. In a large skillet, heat olive oil and butter over medium heat. Add veal and cook until lightly browned on both sides. Transfer to slow cooker stoneware.

4. Add leeks, carrots and celery to pan and stir well. Reduce heat to low, cover and cook until vegetables are softened, about 10 minutes. Increase heat to medium. Add garlic, thyme and reserved mushrooms and cook, stirring, for 1 minute. Add reserved flour mixture, and cook, stirring, for 1 minute. Add wine and reserved mushroom liquid and bring to a boil.

5. Pour mixture over veal, cover and cook on Low for 12 hours, until veal is very tender.

6. *Lemon Gremolata*: Just before serving, combine garlic, parsley, lemon zest and olive oil in a small serving bowl and pass around the table, allowing guests to individually garnish.

Ribs in Tablecloth Stainer Sauce (page 126)

Pork and Lamb

Pork with Brandied Prunes

SERVES 8

A delightful blend of French and North African techniques, this rich stew combines prunes that have been plumped in brandy with a savory pork stew sweetened with honey. I like to serve this over whole wheat couscous, accompanied by a salad of shredded carrots.

Make ahead

This dish can be partially prepared before it is cooked. Complete Step 1. Heat oil and complete Step 3. Cover and refrigerate separately for up to 2 days. When you're ready to cook, either brown the pork as outlined in Step 2 or add it to the stoneware without browning. Stir well and continue with Step 4.

- **Works best in a large (minimum 5 quart) slow cooker**

½ cup	brandy or calvados	125 mL
2 cups	pitted prunes	500 mL
1 tbsp	olive oil	15 mL
2½ lbs	trimmed boneless pork shoulder, cut into 1-inch (2.5 cm) cubes, patted dry	1.25 kg
2	onions, thinly sliced on the vertical	2
4	cloves garlic, minced	4
2 tsp	grated lemon zest	10 mL
1 tsp	dried thyme leaves, crumbled	5 mL
½ tsp	cracked black peppercorns	2 mL
1 cup	chicken stock	250 mL
½ cup	dry white wine	125 mL
1 tbsp	tomato paste	15 mL
	Salt, optional	
2 tbsp	liquid honey	25 mL
¼ cup	snipped chives	50 mL

1. In a saucepan over medium heat, bring brandy to a boil. Add prunes, stir well and remove from heat. Cover and set aside.

2. In a skillet, heat oil over medium-high heat for 30 seconds. Add pork, in batches, and cook, stirring, adding a bit more oil if necessary, until browned, about 5 minutes per batch. Using a slotted spoon, transfer to slow cooker stoneware.

3. Reduce heat to medium. Add onions to pan and cook, stirring, until softened, about 3 minutes. Add garlic, lemon zest, thyme and peppercorns and cook, stirring, for 1 minute. Add stock, white wine and tomato paste and bring to a boil. Season to taste with salt, if using.

4. Transfer to slow cooker stoneware. Stir well. Cover and cook on Low for 6 hours or on High for 3 hours. Stir in honey and plumped prunes. Cover and cook on Low for 2 hours or on High for 1 hour, until pork is tender. Garnish with chives.

> **TIP**
> - If you're not afraid of pepper, increase the quantity of cracked black peppercorns to 1 tsp (5 mL). The extra nip provides a nice balance to the honey.

Pork Roast with Chili-Orange Sauce

SERVES 8

There's a lot more to Mexican cuisine than tacos and burritos — as demonstrated by the delicious sweet and spicy flavors of this pork roast. The combination of fruit and chile peppers derives from a simple country dish, but the results should inspire you to learn more about the cuisine of our neighbors to the south.

Make ahead

This dish can be partially prepared before it is cooked. Complete Steps 1 and 3. Cover and refrigerate mixture for up to 2 days. When you're ready to cook, heat 1 tbsp (15 mL) oil in skillet and brown roast (Step 2), or if you're pressed for time, omit this step and place roast directly in stoneware. Continue cooking as directed. Alternatively, cook roast overnight. Cover and refrigerate for up to 1 day. When ready to serve, spoon off congealed fat, remove meat from sauce and slice. Place sliced meat in a Dutch oven, cover with sauce and bring to a boil. Simmer, covered, for 10 minutes and serve.

- **Works best in a large (minimum 5 quart) slow cooker**

4	slices bacon, finely chopped	4
1	boneless pork shoulder blade (butt) roast, trimmed of excess fat, about 3 lbs (1.5 kg)	1
2	large onions, thinly sliced	2
3	cloves garlic, minced	3
1½ tbsp	chili powder	22 mL
1 tsp	salt	5 mL
1 tsp	cracked black peppercorns	5 mL
¼ cup	all-purpose flour	50 mL
1 tbsp	grated orange zest	15 mL
1½ cups	orange juice	375 mL
2	bananas, mashed	2
2	jalapeño peppers, finely chopped	2
	Hot cooked rice	

1. In a skillet, cook bacon over medium-high heat, until crisp. Remove with a slotted spoon and drain thoroughly on paper towel. Set aside.

2. In same pan, brown roast on all sides. Transfer to slow cooker stoneware.

3. Remove all but 1 tbsp (15 mL) fat from pan. Reduce heat to medium. Add onions and cook, stirring, until softened, about 3 minutes. Add garlic, chili powder, salt and peppercorns and cook, stirring, for 1 minute. Sprinkle flour over mixture and cook, stirring, for 1 minute. Add orange zest and orange juice and cook, stirring to scrape up any brown bits. Stir in bacon.

4. Pour mixture over pork. Cover and cook on Low for 8 to 10 hours or on High for 4 to 5 hours, until meat is very tender. Add bananas and jalapeño peppers and stir well. Cover and cook on High for about 15 minutes, until flavors meld. Serve over fluffy rice.

Ribs in Tablecloth Stainer Sauce

The colorful name of this sauce, which comes from the city of Oaxaca, in Mexico, is a literal translation from the Spanish. It is distinguished by the addition of fruit, such as pineapple and bananas, and you can vary the quantity of chiles to suit your taste. Three produce a pleasantly spicy sauce. Serve this with warm tortillas to soak up the ambrosial liquid.

Make ahead

This dish can be partially prepared the night before it is cooked. Complete Steps 2 and 4. Cover and refrigerate for up to 2 days, being aware that the chile mixture will lose some of its vibrancy if held for this long. (For best results, rehydrate chiles while the ribs are cooking or no sooner than the night before you plan to cook.) When you're ready to cook, broil the ribs (Step 1) and continue with the recipe.

- **Works best in a large (minimum 5 quart) slow cooker**
- **Preheat broiler**

4 lbs	country-style pork ribs (see Tip, page 132)	2 kg
1 tbsp	vegetable oil	15 mL
2	onions, thinly sliced on the vertical	2
4	cloves garlic, minced	4
1 tbsp	dried oregano leaves	15 mL
1	cinnamon stick piece (2 inches/5 cm)	1
1 tsp	salt	5 mL
½ tsp	cracked black peppercorns	2 mL
6	whole allspice	6
2	apples, peeled, cored and sliced	2
1	can (14 oz/398 mL) diced tomatoes, including juice	1
1 cup	chicken stock, divided	250 mL
3	dried ancho chiles	3
1	jalapeño pepper, coarsely chopped	1
2	bananas, peeled and sliced	2
1 tbsp	cider vinegar	15 mL
1 cup	pineapple chunks, drained if canned	250 mL

1. Position broiler rack 6 inches (15 cm) from heat source. Broil ribs on both sides, until lightly browned, about 7 minutes per side. Drain on paper towels and transfer to stoneware.

2. In a skillet, heat oil over medium heat for 30 seconds. Add onions and cook, stirring, until softened, about 3 minutes. Add garlic, oregano, cinnamon stick, salt, peppercorns and allspice and cook, stirring, for 1 minute. Add apples, tomatoes with juice and ½ cup (125 mL) of the chicken stock and bring to a boil.

3. Pour sauce over ribs. Cover and cook on Low for 6 hours or on High for 3 hours, until ribs are tender and falling off the bone.

4. Half an hour before recipe has finished cooking, in a heatproof bowl, soak ancho chiles in boiling water for 30 minutes, weighing down with a cup to ensure they remain submerged. Drain, discarding soaking liquid and stems and chop coarsely. Transfer to a blender. Add jalapeño, bananas, vinegar and remaining ½ cup (125 mL) of the chicken stock. Purée.

5. Add puréed chiles to stoneware, along with pineapple and stir well. Cover and Cook for 30 minutes, until hot and bubbly and flavors meld. Discard allspice and cinnamon stick.

Santa Fe-Style Ribs

If you like Southwestern flavors, you'll love these ribs, which are seasoned with mild New Mexico chiles, toasted cumin seeds and roasted garlic. I like to serve this with polenta, cooked with a jalapeño pepper and Monterey Jack cheese.

Make ahead

This dish can be partially prepared before it is cooked. Complete Step 2. Cover and refrigerate for up to 2 days. When you're ready to cook, continue with the recipe.

- **Works best in a large (minimum 5 quart) slow cooker**
- **Preheat broiler**

3½ to 4 lbs	country-style pork ribs (see Tip, page 132)	1.75 to 2 kg
2 tbsp	vegetable oil	25 mL
8	cloves garlic, slivered	8
1 tbsp	cumin seeds, toasted and ground (see Tip, page 178)	15 mL
1 tsp	dried oregano leaves	5 mL
1 tsp	salt	5 mL
½ tsp	cracked black peppercorns	2 mL
1	can (28 oz/796 mL) tomatoes, drained and coarsely chopped	1
2 tbsp	white vinegar	25 mL
3	dried New Mexico chile peppers	3
2 cups	boiling water	500 mL
	Polenta, optional	

1. Position broiler rack 6 inches (15 cm) from heat source. Broil ribs on both sides, until lightly browned, about 7 minutes per side. Drain on paper towels and transfer to slow cooker stoneware.

2. In a skillet, heat oil over medium heat for 30 seconds. Add garlic and cook, stirring often, until golden and softened, being careful that the garlic doesn't burn. Add toasted cumin, oregano, salt and peppercorns and cook, stirring, for 1 minute. Stir in tomatoes and vinegar and bring to a boil.

3. Pour sauce over ribs. Cover and cook on Low for 6 hours or on High for 3 hours, until ribs are tender and falling off the bone.

4. Half an hour before recipe has finished cooking, in a heatproof bowl, soak dried chiles in boiling water for 30 minutes, weighing down with a cup to ensure they remain submerged. Drain, discarding soaking liquid and stems and chop coarsely. Transfer to a blender. Scoop out ½ cup (125 mL) of the cooking broth from the ribs. Add to blender and purée. Stir puréed mixture into stoneware. Cover and cook for 30 minutes, until flavors meld. Cut pork into individual ribs if a whole piece of meat was used and place on a deep platter. (If desired, spread a layer of polenta on platter first.) Cover with sauce and serve.

Yucatecan-Style Ribs

This recipe is my version of a traditional dish served in Mexico's Yucatan peninsula, conchinita pibil (roughly translated as "small pig cooked in a pit"). While on a culinary tour of the Yucatan organized by Marilyn Tausend, I enjoyed an authentic version of this dish, prepared by Silvio Campos, a master of pibil cooking. Silvio cooks a whole pig in a brick-lined pit in the ground heated with a wood fire, unlike many of his contemporaries who utilize the more convenient oven. My recipe owes much to Rick Bayless and Diana Kennedy as well as to Silvio.

- **Work best in a large (minimum 5 quart) slow cooker**

Achiote Paste

3 tbsp	achiote seeds (see Tips, right)	45 mL
2 tsp	dried oregano leaves	10 mL
2 tsp	cumin seeds	10 mL
4	whole cloves	4
2	whole allspice	2
½ tsp	whole black peppercorns	2 mL
1	cinnamon stick piece (1 inch/2.5 cm)	1
1 tsp	fine sea salt	5 mL
6	puréed cloves garlic (see Tips, right)	6
2 tbsp	bitter orange juice (see Tips, right)	25 mL
¼ cup	water (approx.)	50 mL

Ribs

5 lbs	baby back or country-style pork ribs (see Tips, right)	2.5 kg
2	large pieces of banana leaf, thawed if frozen	2
¼ cup	bitter orange juice	50 mL

Sauce, optional

1	red onion, finely chopped	1
2	habanero chile peppers, seeds and veins removed, minced	2
1 tsp	salt	5 mL
¾ cup	bitter orange juice	175 mL
	Hot corn tortillas	

1. *Achiote Paste*: In a spice grinder, grind achiote seeds to a fine powder. Add oregano, cumin seeds, cloves, allspice, peppercorns and cinnamon stick and grind to a fine powder. Transfer to a small bowl. Add sea salt and garlic and mix well. Add orange juice and mix well. Add enough water to make a smooth paste. Cover and set aside for 6 hours or overnight.

2. *Ribs*: Set aside 2 tbsp (25 mL) of the achiote paste and rub the remainder all over the ribs, working it in with your fingers. Wrap the ribs in banana leaves. (If necessary, tie loosely, to avoid splitting the leaf, with string or strips of banana leaf.) Place wrapped ribs in a large bowl and refrigerate overnight.

3. When you're ready to cook, in a small bowl, combine reserved achiote paste and $1/4$ cup (50 mL) bitter orange juice. Place banana leafed-wrapped ribs in stoneware and cover with juice mixture. Cover and cook on High for 1 hour. Reduce heat to Low and cook for 8 hours, until ribs are tender and falling off the bone. Alternately, cook ribs on High for a total of $4^{1}/_2$ hours. To serve, lift out banana leaf package and place on a cutting board. Remove leaves and discard. Cut meat into individual ribs and place on a deep platter. Ladle sauce from slow cooker over meat.

4. *Sauce (optional)*: In a serving bowl, combine red onion, chile peppers, salt and orange juice. Set aside for several hours to allow the flavors to meld. Pass at the table with hot corn tortillas and allow guests to spoon over their ribs, to taste.

TIPS

- Achiote seeds are available in Latin American markets or the spice sections of well-stocked supermarkets.
- To purée garlic, use a fine, sharp-toothed grater, such as those made by Microplane.
- Bitter oranges are a staple in the Yucatan. If you don't have access to Latin American markets that carry them, you can substitute an equal quantity of juice made from Seville oranges, or a combination of grapefruit, orange and lime juice, or an equal quantity of mild (2%) cider vinegar. To make enough bitter orange substitute for this recipe, including the optional Sauce, combine 1 tsp (5 mL) grated lime zest, $1/2$ cup (125 mL) freshly squeezed lime juice, $1/3$ cup (75 mL) freshly squeezed orange juice and $1/3$ cup (75 mL) freshly squeezed grapefruit juice.
- Leave the ribs basically in full racks (you may need to cut a section of three or four ribs off each rack so they will fit in the slow cooker) or, if using country-style, in one piece. Layer any extra pieces on top, like an extra rack.

Hearty Ribs with Rigatoni

This is another dish that I like to serve on Friday night, when the busy week is over and we enjoy being able to relax with friends. With a basket of hot garlic bread, a big salad, plenty of robust red wine and lively conversation, it's a great way to wind down. While the cream is not essential, it's a nice enrichment for the sauce.

Make ahead

This dish can be partially prepared before it is cooked. Complete Step 2, heating 1 tbsp (15 mL) oil in pan before softening onions. Cover and refrigerate mixture for up to 2 days. When you're ready to cook, brown ribs (Step 1), and continue with the recipe. Alternatively, cook overnight, cover and refrigerate. When you're ready to serve, cook pasta, bring ribs and sauce to a boil in a Dutch oven and simmer for 10 minutes, until sauce is bubbly and meat is heated through. Then complete Step 4.

- **Works best in a large (minimum 5 quart) slow cooker**

1 tbsp	vegetable oil	15 mL
3 lbs	country-style pork ribs, cut into individual ribs	1.5 kg
2	onions, finely chopped	2
1	head garlic, peeled and finely chopped	1
1 tbsp	cracked black peppercorns	15 mL
1 tsp	salt	5 mL
4	sprigs fresh thyme or 1 tsp (5 mL) dried thyme leaves	4
½ tsp	ground nutmeg	2 mL
10	whole cloves	10
1	can (28 oz/796 mL) tomatoes, including juice, coarsely chopped (see Tips, page 34)	1
1 tbsp	tomato paste	15 mL
1 cup	dry red wine	250 mL
¼ cup	whipping (35%) cream, optional	50 mL
1 lb	rigatoni, cooked and drained	500 g
⅓ cup	finely chopped parsley	75 mL
	Freshly grated Parmesan cheese	

1. In a skillet, heat oil over medium-high heat for 30 seconds. Add ribs, in batches, and brown lightly on both sides. Using a slotted spoon, transfer to slow cooker stoneware. Drain off all but 1 tbsp (15 mL) fat from pan.

2. Reduce heat to medium. Add onions to pan and cook, stirring, until softened, about 3 minutes. Add garlic, peppercorns, salt, thyme, nutmeg and cloves and cook, stirring, for 1 minute. Add tomatoes with juice, tomato paste and wine. Bring to a boil and cook, stirring, until liquid is reduced by one-third, about 5 minutes, depending on the size of your pan.

3. Pour mixture into slow cooker stoneware and stir well. Cover and cook on Low for 6 hours or on High for 3 hours, until pork is tender and falling off the bone.

4. Discard whole cloves. Add cream, if using, and stir to combine. Place cooked pasta in a large, deep platter and spoon ribs and sauce over all. Garnish liberally with parsley and pass the Parmesan in a small bowl.

Italian-Style Ribs with Polenta

SERVES 6

Don't let the simplicity of this recipe fool you. Tender pork ribs are braised in a vegetable-based sauce, enhanced with wine and aromatic spices. The resulting sauce is rich-tasting but light, and the succulent ribs fall off the bone. I like to spoon the hot polenta over the bottom of a deep platter, lay the meat on top and cover with sauce. Garnish with additional sprigs of parsley for a presentation that looks as good as it tastes.

Make ahead

This dish can be partially prepared before it is cooked. Complete Step 2. Cover and refrigerate for up to 2 days. When you're ready to cook, broil ribs (Step 1) and complete Step 3.

- **Works best in a large (minimum 5 quart) slow cooker**
- **Preheat broiler**

3½ to 4 lbs	country-style pork ribs (see Tip, below)	1.75 to 2 kg
1 tbsp	vegetable oil	15 mL
2	onions, minced	2
2	carrots, peeled and chopped	2
4	stalks celery, chopped	4
4	cloves garlic, minced	4
2 tsp	dried Italian seasoning	10 mL
1 tsp	salt	5 mL
½ tsp	cracked black peppercorns	2 mL
6	whole cloves	6
6	whole allspice	6
1	cinnamon stick piece (2 inches/5 cm)	1
1	can (28 oz/796 mL) tomatoes, drained and coarsely chopped	1
½ cup	dry red wine	125 mL
¼ cup	flat-leaf parsley, finely chopped	50 mL
	Slow-Cooked Polenta (see recipe, page 264)	

1. Position broiler rack 6 inches (15 cm) from heat source. Broil ribs on both sides, until lightly browned, about 7 minutes per side. Drain on paper towels and transfer to slow cooker stoneware.

2. In a skillet, heat oil over medium heat for 30 seconds. Add onions, carrots and celery and cook, stirring, until softened, about 7 minutes. Add garlic, Italian seasoning, salt, peppercorns, cloves, allspice and cinnamon stick and cook, stirring, for 1 minute. Stir in tomatoes and red wine and bring to a boil.

3. Pour sauce over ribs. Cover and cook on Low for 6 hours or on High for 3 hours, until ribs are tender and falling off the bone. Discard cloves, allspice berries and cinnamon stick. Cut pork into individual ribs if a whole piece of meat was used. Garnish with parsley. Serve over hot polenta.

TIP

- This recipe works best if the ribs are in one big piece when cooked. (In my experience, this cut is usually only available from a butcher or in the pork roast section of the grocery store.) The single piece is easy to turn while broiling and will basically fall apart into individual servings after the meat is cooked.

Saucy Pinto Beans with Chorizo

SERVES 6 TO 8

Chorizo, a spicy sausage available in many supermarkets or specialty stores in either a soft or hard, cured version, gives this rustic dish an elegant touch. Serve this to guests with a basket of hot garlic bread, a big tossed salad and good Spanish wine, such as Rioja. Hot Italian sausage can be substituted for soft chorizo and cranberry or red kidney beans for pinto beans.

Make ahead

This dish can be partially assembled before it is cooked. Complete Steps 1 and 2 and refrigerate for up to 2 days. When you're ready to cook, continue with the recipe. Alternatively, the bean mixture may be cooked overnight in slow cooker. Cover and refrigerate until you're ready to serve, for up to 2 days. In a Dutch oven, bring to a boil, add reserved bacon, chili powder and cooked sausages (Step 4) and simmer for 15 minutes, until flavors meld.

- *Works best in a large (minimum 5 quart) slow cooker*

4 oz	bacon, cut into small cubes	125 g
2	onions, finely chopped	2
6	cloves garlic, minced	6
1 tbsp	cumin seeds, toasted and ground (see Tip, page 178)	15 mL
1 tsp	dried thyme leaves	5 mL
2 tbsp	balsamic vinegar	25 mL
1	can (5½ oz/156 mL) tomato paste	1
1 cup	beef stock	250 mL
4 cups	cooked dried or canned pinto beans, drained and rinsed	1 L
2 lbs	soft chorizo sausage	1 kg
2 tbsp	chili powder	25 mL

1. In a skillet, cook bacon over medium-high heat until crisp. Remove with a slotted spoon and drain on paper towel. Cover and refrigerate. Drain all but 1 tbsp (15 mL) fat from pan.

2. Reduce heat to medium. Add onions to pan and cook, stirring, until softened, about 3 minutes. Add garlic, toasted cumin and thyme and cook, stirring, for 1 minute. Add balsamic vinegar, tomato paste and stock.

3. Add to stoneware and stir well. Add beans and water, barely to cover. Stir well. Cover and cook on Low for 6 to 8 hours or on High for 3 to 4 hours, until hot and bubbly.

4. Forty-five minutes prior to serving, prick sausages all over with a fork and place in a large skillet. Cover with water, bring to boil and simmer for 10 minutes. Drain. Return sausage to pan and brown on all sides over medium-high heat. Cut into 2-inch (5 cm) lengths and add to beans, along with reserved bacon and chili powder. Cover and cook on High for 30 minutes, until mixture is hot and bubbly and flavors meld.

Not Your Granny's Pork and Beans

SERVES 8

This dish requires a bit of advance planning because the pork is marinated overnight in a salt and garlic rub, which imbues it with deep flavor. Otherwise it is simple, straightforward and loaded with flavor. To complement the Mediterranean ingredients, I like to accompany this with a platter of marinated roasted peppers. Add warm crusty bread, such as ciabatta and, if you're feeling festive, a robust Rioja, for a perfect meal. It makes a large quantity but reheats well.

Make ahead

This dish can be partially prepared before it is cooked. Complete Step 1. Heat 1 tbsp (15 mL) of the oil and complete Step 3. Cover and refrigerate meat and onion mixtures separately for up to 2 days. When you're ready to cook, either brown the pork as outlined in Step 2 or add it to the stoneware without browning. Stir well and continue with Step 4.

- **Works best in a large (minimum 5 quart) slow cooker**

1 tbsp	puréed garlic (see Tips, page 129)	15 mL
1 tsp	salt	5 mL
½ tsp	cracked black peppercorns	2 mL
2 lbs	trimmed boneless pork shoulder, cut into bite-size pieces	1 kg
2 tbsp	olive oil, divided	25 mL
3	onions, thinly sliced on the vertical	3
6	anchovy fillets, finely chopped	6
2 tsp	dried thyme leaves, crumbled	10 mL
1 cup	dry white wine	250 mL
1 tsp	white wine vinegar	5 mL
1	can (14 oz/398 mL) diced tomatoes, including juice (see Tips, page 202)	1
4 cups	cooked dried or canned white kidney or navy beans, drained and rinsed	1 L
1 tsp	paprika, preferably smoked, dissolved in 1 tbsp (15 mL) white wine or water	5 mL
1 cup	finely chopped parsley	250 mL
1 cup	chopped, pitted kalamata olives (about 48 olives)	250 mL

1. In a bowl large enough to accommodate the pork, combine garlic, salt and peppercorns. Add pork and toss until well coated with mixture. Cover and refrigerate overnight.

2. In a skillet, heat 1 tbsp (15 mL) of the oil over medium-high heat for 30 seconds. Pat pork dry with paper towel and cook, stirring, in batches, adding a bit more oil if necessary, until browned, about 5 minutes per batch. Using a slotted spoon, transfer to slow cooker stoneware.

3. Reduce heat to medium. Add onions and anchovies to pan and cook, stirring, adding more oil if necessary, until onions are softened, about 3 minutes. Add thyme and cook, stirring, for 1 minute. Add wine and vinegar and cook for 2 minutes, stirring and scraping up any brown bits on the bottom of the pan. Add tomatoes with juice and bring to a boil. Transfer to slow cooker stoneware. Add beans and stir well.

4. Cover and cook on Low for 8 to 10 hours or on High for 4 to 5 hours, until pork is very tender (it should be falling apart). Stir in paprika solution, parsley and olives. Cover and cook on High for 15 minutes, until heated through.

Sausage and Barley Jambalaya

SERVES 6

As this recipe demonstrates, barley is more than an ingredient to be added to the soup pot. A dense and chewy grain, barley is both nutritious and satisfying. It's a great comfort food, and I'm always looking for ways to include it in family meals. This flavorful mixture makes a great weeknight dinner or a terrific dish for a Friday night potluck with friends. Add a tossed salad, crusty country-style bread, some robust wine and enjoy.

Make ahead

This dish can be partially prepared before it is cooked. Complete Steps 1 and 2, chilling the cooked sausage and tomato mixtures separately. Refrigerate for up to 2 days. When you're ready to cook, continue with the recipe.

- **Works best in a large (minimum 5 quart) slow cooker**

1 lb	mild Italian sausage, removed from casings	500 g
2	onions, finely chopped	2
2	cloves garlic, minced	2
2 tsp	Cajun seasoning (see Tips, below)	10 mL
1 tsp	dried oregano leaves	5 mL
1 tsp	salt	5 mL
½ tsp	cracked black peppercorns	2 mL
1	can (28 oz/796 mL) tomatoes, including juice, coarsely chopped	1
3 cups	chicken stock	750 mL
1 cup	barley, thoroughly rinsed under cold running water (see Tips, below)	250 mL
8 oz	medium shrimp, cooked, peeled and deveined (see Tip, page 195)	250 g
1	roasted red pepper, finely chopped (see Tips, page 24)	1
1	long red chile or jalapeño pepper, finely chopped (see Tips, below)	1

1. In a skillet, cook sausage over medium-high heat, breaking up with a spoon, until no longer pink. Using a slotted spoon, transfer to slow cooker stoneware. Drain all but 1 tbsp (15 mL) fat from pan.

2. Reduce heat to medium. Add onions to pan and cook, stirring, until softened, about 3 minutes. Add garlic, Cajun seasoning, oregano, salt and peppercorns and cook, stirring, for 1 minute. Add tomatoes with juice and chicken stock and bring to a boil.

3. Pour mixture over sausage. Add barley and stir well. Cover and cook on Low for 6 to 8 hours or on High for 3 to 4 hours, until barley is tender. Add shrimp, roasted pepper and chile pepper. Cover and cook on High for 20 minutes, until shrimp is heated through.

TIPS

- Cajun seasoning is available in many supermarkets and specialty food stores. If you can't find it, substitute 1 tsp (5 mL) each dried thyme leaves and paprika to this recipe.
- Use whole, pot or pearl barley when making this recipe.
- If you don't have a fresh chile pepper, stir in hot pepper sauce to taste, after the jambalaya is cooked.

Pork and Black Bean Chili

Here's a festive and stick-to-your-ribs chili that is a perfect finish to a day in the chilly outdoors. I like to serve this with hot corn bread, a crisp green salad and a robust red wine or ice cold beer. Olé!

Make ahead

This dish can be partially prepared before it is cooked. Complete Steps 2 and 4, heating 1 tbsp (15 mL) oil in pan before softening the onions. Cover and refrigerate onion and chile mixtures separately for up to 2 days, being aware the chile mixture will lose some of its vibrancy if held for this long. (For best results, rehydrate chiles while the chili is cooking or no sooner than the night before you plan to cook.) When you're ready to cook, brown the pork, or if you're pressed for time, omit this step and continue with the recipe.

• **Works best in a large (minimum 5 quart) slow cooker**

1 tbsp	vegetable oil (approx.)	15 mL
2 lbs	trimmed boneless pork shoulder, cut into 1-inch (2.5 cm) cubes, patted dry	1 kg
2	onions, finely chopped	2
4	cloves garlic, minced	4
1 tbsp	cumin seeds, toasted and ground	15 mL
1 tbsp	dried oregano leaves	15 mL
1 tsp	salt	5 mL
½ tsp	cracked black peppercorns	2 mL
2 tbsp	tomato paste	25 mL
1½ cups	flat beer	375 mL
4 cups	cooked dried or canned black beans, drained and rinsed (see Basic Beans, page 219)	1 L
2	dried ancho chile peppers	2
2 cups	boiling water	500 mL
1 cup	coarsely chopped cilantro, stems and leaves	250 mL
½ cup	chicken stock	125 mL
1	chipotle pepper in adobo sauce	1
	Sour cream, optional	
	Crushed tortilla chips, optional	
	Finely chopped red or green onion, optional	

1. In a skillet, heat oil over medium-high heat for 30 seconds. Add pork, in batches, and cook, stirring, adding more oil if necessary, until browned, about 4 minutes per batch. Using a slotted spoon, transfer to stoneware. Reduce heat to medium.

2. Add onions to pan and cook, stirring, until softened, about 3 minutes. Add garlic, toasted cumin, oregano, salt and peppercorns and cook, stirring, for 1 minute. Stir in tomato paste and beer.

3. Pour mixture over meat. Add beans and stir to combine. Cover and cook on Low for 8 hours or on High for 4 hours, until pork is tender.

4. Half an hour before the recipe has finished cooking, in a heatproof bowl, soak ancho chiles in boiling water for 30 minutes, weighing down with a cup to ensure they remain submerged. Drain, discarding soaking liquid and stems and chop coarsely. Transfer to a blender. Add cilantro, stock and chipotle pepper. Purée.

5. Add chile mixture to pork and stir well. Cover and cook on High for 30 minutes, until flavors meld. Ladle into bowls and garnish with sour cream, crushed tortilla chips and chopped onion, if using.

Pasta with Sausage and Lentils

Here's a rich and nutritious pasta sauce that will serve a crowd and have people coming back for seconds. It freezes well, so if you're cooking for fewer people, divide it up and freeze the unused portions.

Make ahead

This dish can be partially prepared before it is cooked. Complete Steps 1 and 2, chilling cooked sausage and tomato mixtures separately. Refrigerate for up to 2 days. When you're ready to cook, continue with the recipe.

• *Works in slow cookers from 3½ to 6 quarts*

1 lb	mild Italian sausage, removed from casings	500 g
2	onions, finely chopped	2
2	large carrots, peeled, halved lengthwise and thinly sliced	2
2	stalks celery, thinly sliced	2
4	cloves garlic, minced	4
1 tsp	dried rosemary leaves	5 mL
4	whole cloves	4
1 tsp	salt	5 mL
½ tsp	cracked black peppercorns	2 mL
1	can (28 oz/796 mL) tomatoes, including juice, coarsely chopped	1
2 cups	chicken stock	500 mL
1 cup	dry red wine, water or additional stock	250 mL
2 cups	dried green or brown lentils, rinsed	500 mL
	Hot cooked pasta	
	Finely chopped parsley, optional	
	Freshly grated Parmesan cheese	

1. In a skillet, cook sausage over medium-high heat, breaking up with a spoon, until no longer pink. Using a slotted spoon, transfer to slow cooker stoneware. Drain all but 1 tbsp (15 mL) fat from pan.

2. Reduce heat to medium. Add onions, carrots and celery to pan and cook, stirring, until carrots are softened, about 7 minutes. Add garlic, rosemary, cloves, salt and peppercorns and cook, stirring, for 1 minute. Add tomatoes with juice, stock and wine and bring to a boil. Pour mixture over sausage.

3. Add lentils and stir to combine. Cover and cook on Low for 8 to 10 hours or on High for 4 to 5 hours, until mixture is hot and bubbly and lentils are tender.

4. Discard whole cloves. Place pasta in a large serving bowl. Spoon sauce over top and toss until well combined. Garnish with parsley, if using, and pass the Parmesan in a small bowl.

Curried Lamb with Apples and Bananas

SERVES 6 TO 8

Here's another lamb braise that is packed with flavor. The fruit adds nutrients as well as punch. This spicing produces a mildly flavored dish. If you like a bit of heat, add the second chile pepper or up to ¼ tsp (1 mL) cayenne (along with the chile), which nicely balances the sweetness of the fruit. Serve this over brown basmati rice and add steamed spinach to round out the meal.

Make ahead

This dish can be partially prepared before it is cooked. Complete Step 1. Heat oil and complete Step 3. Cover and refrigerate for up to 2 days. When you're ready to cook, either brown the lamb (Step 2) or add it to the stoneware without browning. Stir well and continue with Step 4.

- **Works in slow cookers from 3½ to 6 quarts**

1 tbsp	cumin seeds	15 mL
1 tsp	coriander seeds	5 mL
1 tbsp	olive oil (approx.)	15 mL
2 lbs	trimmed stewing lamb, cut into 1-inch (2.5 cm) cubes	1 kg
2	onions, finely chopped	2
4	cloves garlic, minced	4
1 tbsp	minced gingerroot	15 mL
2 tsp	turmeric	10 mL
1	cinnamon stick piece (2 inches/5 cm)	1
2	black cardamom pods, crushed	2
½ tsp	cracked black peppercorns	2 mL
1 cup	beef or chicken stock	250 mL
1 to 2	long red or green chile peppers, minced, or ¼ tsp (1 mL) cayenne dissolved in 1 tbsp (15 mL) boiling water	1 to 2
3	apples, peeled, cored and thinly sliced	3
2	bananas, thinly sliced	2
¼ cup	finely chopped cilantro or parsley leaves	50 mL

1. In a large dry skillet over medium heat, toast cumin and coriander seeds, stirring, until fragrant and cumin seeds just begin to brown, about 3 minutes. Immediately transfer to a mortar or a spice grinder and grind. Set aside.

2. In same skillet, heat oil over medium-high heat for 30 seconds. Add lamb, in batches, and cook, stirring, adding more oil if necessary, until browned, about 4 minutes per batch. Using a slotted spoon, transfer to slow cooker stoneware.

3. Reduce heat to medium. Add onions to pan and cook, stirring, until softened, about 3 minutes. Add garlic, gingerroot, turmeric, cinnamon stick, cardamom, peppercorns and reserved cumin and coriander and cook, stirring, until spices release their aroma, about 1 minute. Add stock and bring to a boil.

4. Pour sauce over lamb and stir well. Cover and cook on Low for 7 to 8 hours or on High for 3 to 4 hours, until lamb is very tender. Discard cinnamon stick and cardamom pods. Add chile peppers, apples and bananas, in batches, stirring to incorporate each batch before adding the next. Cover and cook on High for 30 minutes, until fruit is tender and hot. Garnish with cilantro.

Lamb with Artichokes

SERVES 6 TO 8

This is my version of a classic Greek dish, lamb cooked with artichokes, then finished with a lemony avgolemono sauce. It's absolutely luscious and makes a great dish for company or as part of a buffet. I like to serve this with couscous or hot orzo, a rice-shaped pasta, and a platter of steamed bitter greens, such as rapini, tossed in extra virgin olive oil and drizzled with lemon juice.

Make ahead

This dish can be partially prepared before it is cooked. Heat 1 tbsp (15 mL) of the oil and complete Step 2. Cover and refrigerate for up to 2 days. When you're ready to cook, either brown the lamb (Step 1) or add it to the stoneware without browning. Stir well and continue with the recipe.

• **Works best in a large (minimum 5 quart) slow cooker**

1 tbsp	olive oil (approx.)	15 mL
2 lbs	trimmed stewing lamb, cut into 1-inch (2.5 cm) cubes	1 kg
3	onions, finely chopped	3
4	cloves garlic, minced	4
2 tsp	grated lemon zest	10 mL
1 tsp	dried thyme leaves, crumbled	5 mL
½ tsp	salt	2 mL
½ tsp	cracked black peppercorns	2 mL
1 cup	vegetable or chicken stock	250 mL
2	cans (each 14 oz/398 mL) artichoke hearts, drained and halved (about 3 cups/750 mL)	2
2	eggs	2
½ cup	freshly squeezed lemon juice (approx.) (1 lemon)	125 mL
½ cup	finely chopped fresh dill	125 mL
	Salt, optional	
	Freshly ground black pepper, optional	

1. In a skillet, heat oil over medium-high heat for 30 seconds. Add lamb, in batches, and cook, stirring, adding more oil if necessary, until browned, about 4 minutes per batch. Using a slotted spoon, transfer to slow cooker stoneware.

2. Reduce heat to medium. Add onions to pan and cook, stirring, until softened, about 3 minutes. Add garlic, lemon zest, thyme, salt and peppercorns and cook, stirring, for 1 minute. Add stock and bring to a boil.

3. Transfer to slow cooker stoneware. Stir in artichokes. Cover and cook on Low for 7 to 8 hours or on High for 3 to 4 hours, until mixture is bubbly and lamb is tender. Spoon off 1 cup (250 mL) of the cooking liquid.

4. In a bowl, whisk eggs and lemon juice until frothy. Gradually add warm cooking liquid from the lamb, whisking constantly. Pour mixture into slow cooker and stir well. Stir in dill. Season to taste with salt and pepper, if using, and/or additional lemon juice. Serve immediately.

Irish Stew

This hearty and delicious stew is an old favorite that really can't be improved upon. All it needs is a green vegetable such as string beans or broccoli, crusty rolls or a loaf of country-style bread, and a big glass of Guinness or a robust red wine.

Make ahead

This recipe can be partially prepared before it is cooked. Complete Step 3, heating 1 tbsp (15 mL) of the oil in pan before softening vegetables. Cover and refrigerate for up to 2 days. When you're ready to cook, brown lamb (Steps 1 and 2) and complete Step 4.

• *Works best in a large (minimum 5 quart) slow cooker*

¼ cup	all-purpose flour	50 mL
1 tsp	salt	5 mL
½ tsp	cracked black peppercorns	2 mL
2 tbsp	vegetable oil (approx.)	25 mL
2 lbs	trimmed stewing lamb, cut into 1-inch (2.5 cm) cubes	1 kg
3	onions, finely chopped	3
2	large carrots, peeled and diced	2
1 tsp	dried thyme leaves	5 mL
2 tbsp	tomato paste	25 mL
1 tbsp	Worcestershire sauce	15 mL
1 cup	beef stock	250 mL
4	medium potatoes, peeled and cut into ½-inch (1 cm) cubes	4
1½ cups	green peas	375 mL

1. On a plate, combine flour, salt and peppercorns. Lightly coat lamb with mixture, shaking off the excess. Set any remaining flour mixture aside.

2. In a skillet, heat 1 tbsp (15 mL) of the oil over medium-high heat for 30 seconds. Add lamb, in batches, and cook, stirring, adding more oil if necessary, until browned, about 4 minutes per batch. Using a slotted spoon, transfer to slow cooker stoneware. Drain all but 1 tbsp (15 mL) fat from pan.

3. Reduce heat to medium. Add onions and carrots to pan and cook, stirring, until carrots are softened, about 7 minutes. Add thyme and reserved flour mixture and cook, stirring, for 1 minute. Stir in tomato paste, Worcestershire sauce and stock and bring to a boil.

4. Place potatoes in slow cooker stoneware. Add onion mixture and stir to combine. Cover and cook on Low for 8 to 10 hours or on High for 4 to 5 hours, until mixture is bubbly and potatoes are tender. Stir in peas. Cover and cook on High for 15 to 20 minutes, until peas are heated through.

Lamb Shanks Braised in Guinness

SERVES 4 TO 6

This Irish-inspired combination is a classic. Add a green vegetable and mounds of mashed potatoes, sprinkled with finely chopped green onion, to soak up the delicious sauce.

Make ahead

This dish can be partially prepared before it is cooked. Complete Step 3, heating 1 tbsp (15 mL) of the oil in pan before softening vegetables and sprinkling 1 tbsp (15 mL) of the flour over the vegetables. Cover and refrigerate for up to 2 days. When you're ready to cook, continue with the recipe.

- **Works best in a large (minimum 5 quart) slow cooker**

¼ cup	all-purpose flour	50 mL
1 tsp	salt	5 mL
½ tsp	cracked black peppercorns	2 mL
4 lbs	lamb shanks, whole or sliced (see Tip, below)	2 kg
2 tbsp	vegetable oil (approx.)	25 mL
4	onions, finely chopped	4
4	cloves garlic, minced	4
1 tsp	dried thyme leaves	5 mL
2 tbsp	tomato paste	25 mL
1½ cups	Guinness or other dark beer	375 mL
½ cup	beef stock	125 mL

1. On a plate, combine flour, salt and peppercorns. Lightly coat lamb shanks with mixture, shaking off the excess. Set any remaining flour mixture aside.

2. In a skillet, heat 1 tbsp (15 mL) of the oil over medium-high heat. Add lamb, in batches, and cook, turning, adding more oil if necessary, until lightly browned. Using tongs, transfer to slow cooker stoneware. Drain off all but 1 tbsp (15 mL) fat from pan.

3. Reduce heat to medium. Add onions to pan and cook, stirring, until softened, about 3 minutes. Add garlic and thyme and reserved flour mixture and cook, stirring, for 1 minute. Stir in tomato paste, beer and stock and bring to a boil. Cook, stirring, until mixture thickens.

4. Pour sauce over meat. Cover and cook on Low for 10 to 12 hours or on High for 5 to 6 hours, until meat is falling off the bone.

TIP
- Whether you cook the lamb shanks whole or have them cut into pieces is a matter of preference. However, if the shanks are left whole, you will be able to serve only four people — each will receive one large shank.

Lamb Shanks with Luscious Legumes

SERVES 6 TO 8

Lamb cooked with legumes in a flavorful wine-based sauce is a French tradition. No wonder — it is a mouth-watering combination. If you prefer more assertive flavors, bury a whole branch of fresh rosemary, stem and all, in the lamb before adding the sauce. Serve this with crusty bread, a green salad or garden-fresh tomatoes in vinaigrette, and a robust red wine for a memorable meal.

Make ahead

This dish can be partially prepared before it is cooked. Soak beans. Complete Step 4, heating 1 tbsp (15 mL) of the oil in pan before softening vegetables and sprinkling 1 tbsp (15 mL) of the flour over the vegetables. Cover and refrigerate for up to 2 days. When you're ready to cook, continue with the recipe.

• **Works best in a large (minimum 5 quart) slow cooker**

2 cups	dried white navy beans or flageolets, soaked, rinsed and drained	500 mL
1/4 cup	all-purpose flour	50 mL
1 tsp	salt	5 mL
1/2 tsp	cracked black peppercorns	2 mL
6	lamb shanks, whole or sliced	6
2 tbsp	vegetable oil (approx.)	25 mL
2	onions, finely chopped	2
2	carrots, peeled and diced	2
4	stalks celery, diced	4
6	cloves garlic, minced	6
1 tbsp	finely chopped rosemary	15 mL
	Grated zest and juice of 1 orange	
1 cup	beef stock	250 mL
1/2 cup	dry red wine	125 mL
	Finely chopped fresh parsley	

1. Place beans in slow cooker stoneware.

2. On a plate, combine flour, salt and peppercorns. Lightly coat lamb shanks with mixture, shaking off the excess. Set any remaining flour mixture aside.

3. In a skillet, heat 1 tbsp (15 mL) oil over medium-high heat. Add lamb, in batches, and cook, turning, adding more oil if necessary, until lightly browned on all sides. Using tongs, transfer to slow cooker stoneware. Drain all but 1 tbsp (15 mL) oil from pan.

4. Reduce heat to medium. Add onions, carrots and celery to pan and cook, stirring, until carrots are softened, about 7 minutes. Add garlic, rosemary and orange zest and cook, stirring, for 1 minute. Sprinkle reserved flour mixture over vegetables and cook, stirring, for 1 minute. Add orange juice, stock and wine and bring to a boil.

5. Pour mixture over lamb. Cover and cook on Low for 10 to 12 hours or on High for 5 to 6 hours, until lamb is falling off the bone and beans are tender. Transfer lamb and beans to a deep platter or serving dish and keep warm. In a saucepan over medium-high heat, reduce cooking liquid by one-third. Pour over lamb and garnish liberally with parsley.

Not-Too-Corny Turkey Chili with Sausage (page 175)

Poultry

Sage and Onion Chicken with Cranberry Rice

SERVES 6 TO 8

Simple but tasty, this dish has all the flavors of the Christmas turkey without the work. Add a tossed green salad or some marinated roasted red peppers to complete the meal.

Make ahead

This dish can be partially prepared before it is cooked. Complete Step 1. Cover and refrigerate overnight. The next morning, continue with the recipe.

- **Works best in a large (minimum 5 quart) slow cooker**
- **Lightly greased slow cooker stoneware**

1 tbsp	olive oil	15 mL
2	onions, finely chopped	2
4	cloves garlic, minced	4
1½ tsp	dried sage leaves	7 mL
½ tsp	cracked black peppercorns	2 mL
½ tsp	salt	2 mL
1 lb	mushrooms, sliced	500 g
1½ cups	brown and wild rice mixture, rinsed	375 mL
1 cup	dried cranberries	250 mL
3 cups	chicken stock (approx.)	750 mL
	Grated zest and juice of 1 orange	
3 lbs	skinless, bone-in chicken thighs (about 12 thighs)	1.5 kg

Topping

1 tbsp	butter	15 mL
1 tbsp	olive oil	15 mL
1 cup	fresh whole wheat bread crumbs	250 mL
2 tbsp	toasted sliced almonds	25 mL

1. In a skillet, heat oil over medium heat for 30 seconds. Add onions and cook, stirring, until softened, about 3 minutes. Add garlic, sage, peppercorns and salt and cook, stirring, for 1 minute. Add mushrooms and stir to coat. Add rice and stir to coat. Stir in cranberries. Add stock, orange zest and juice and bring to a boil. (You should have 4 cups/1 L of liquid in total. Squeeze the orange juice into a 1 cup/250 mL measure and add chicken stock to make up the 1 cup/250 mL, if necessary.)

2. Spoon half the rice mixture evenly over bottom of prepared slow cooker stoneware. Arrange chicken pieces evenly over top. Cover with remaining rice mixture.

3. Place two clean tea towels, each folded in half (so you will have four layers), over top of stoneware to absorb moisture. Cover and cook on Low for 6 hours or on High for 3 hours, until juices run clear when chicken is pierced with a fork.

4. *Topping:* In a skillet, heat butter and oil over medium heat. Add bread crumbs and toss until evenly coated. Cook, stirring, until golden, about 5 minutes. Stir in almonds. Spoon evenly over cooked rice and serve immediately.

The Captain's Curry

SERVES 6

This style of curry, made with a creamed curry sauce, was popular in the great American seaports during the 19th century. It gets its name from sea captains involved in the spice trade, who brought their wares to cities such as Charleston. Today, we associate coconut milk with our current interest in Asian foods. But citizens of the old South were quite familiar with this ingredient, which they made themselves using fresh coconuts from the West Indies.

Make ahead

This recipe can be partially prepared before it is cooked. Complete Step 1. Cover and refrigerate for up to 2 days. When you're ready to cook, continue with the recipe.

● *Works best in a large (minimum 5 quart) slow cooker*

1 tbsp	vegetable oil	15 mL
2	onions, finely chopped	2
2	stalks celery, thinly sliced	2
2	cloves garlic, minced	2
½ tsp	ground allspice	2 mL
½ tsp	freshly grated nutmeg	2 mL
1	cinnamon stick piece (3 inches/7.5 cm)	1
1	bay leaf	1
2 tbsp	all-purpose flour	25 mL
1 cup	chicken stock	250 mL
3 lbs	skinless, bone-in chicken thighs (about 12 thighs)	1.5 kg
1 cup	coconut milk, divided	250 mL
1 tbsp	curry powder	15 mL
½ tsp	cayenne pepper	2 mL
	Toasted sliced almonds, optional	
	Hot white rice	
	Mango chutney, optional	

1. In a skillet, heat oil over medium heat for 30 seconds. Add onions and celery and cook, stirring, until celery is softened, about 5 minutes. Add garlic, allspice, nutmeg, cinnamon stick and bay leaf and cook, stirring, for 1 minute. Sprinkle flour over mixture and cook, stirring, for 1 minute. Add stock. Bring to a boil and cook, stirring, until thickened.

2. Arrange chicken over bottom of slow cooker stoneware and cover with vegetable mixture. Cover and cook on Low for 6 hours or on High for 3 hours, until juices run clear when chicken is pierced with a fork.

3. In a small bowl, combine ¼ cup (50 mL) of the coconut milk with curry powder and cayenne. Mix well. Add to stoneware. Stir in remaining coconut milk and cook on High for 30 minutes, until flavors meld. Discard cinnamon stick and bay leaf. Garnish with almonds, if using, and serve over hot white rice, accompanied by chutney, if desired.

Chicken in Onion Buttermilk Gravy

SERVES 6

Here's a dish that is reminiscent of the old South — a rich onion-flavored gravy, punctuated with peas and finished with buttermilk to add a hint of tartness. I like to serve this with mounds of steamy mashed potatoes, sprinkled with finely chopped parsley, to soak up the sauce. Serve leftovers over hot buttermilk biscuits for a truly delicious lunch.

Make ahead

This dish can be partially prepared before it is cooked. Complete Step 2, heating 1 tbsp (15 mL) oil in pan before softening onions. Cover and refrigerate for up to 2 days. When you're ready to cook, brown chicken breasts (Step 1), or if you're pressed for time, omit this step and place chicken directly in slow cooker stoneware. Continue with the recipe.

- **Works best in a large (minimum 5 quart) slow cooker**

1 tbsp	vegetable oil	15 mL
3 lbs	skin-on, bone-in chicken breasts (see Tips, below)	1.5 kg
6	onions, sliced paper-thin	6
1 tsp	salt	5 mL
1/2 tsp	cracked black peppercorns	2 mL
1/2 tsp	dried thyme leaves	2 mL
1/4 cup	all-purpose flour	50 mL
1 1/2 cups	chicken stock	375 mL
1	bay leaf	1
1 1/2 cups	green peas, thawed if frozen	375 mL
3/4 cup	buttermilk (see Tips, below)	175 mL

1. In a nonstick skillet, heat oil over medium-high heat for 30 seconds. Add chicken, in batches, and brown lightly on all sides. Transfer to slow cooker stoneware.

2. Reduce heat to medium. Add onions to pan and cook, stirring, until softened and just beginning to turn brown, about 5 minutes. Add salt, peppercorns and thyme and cook, stirring, for 1 minute. Sprinkle flour over mixture and cook, stirring, for 1 minute. Add stock and bay leaf and cook, stirring, until mixture is thickened.

3. Pour mixture over chicken. Cover and cook on Low for 5 hours or on High for 2 1/2 hours, until juices run clear when chicken is pierced with a fork. Stir in peas and buttermilk. Cover and cook on High for 20 minutes, until peas are tender and mixture is hot and bubbly. Discard bay leaf.

TIPS

- If you prefer, use only skinless, bone-in chicken thighs when making this recipe. Do not brown and follow the method and Make-ahead instructions for The Captain's Curry (page 152). Increase the cooking time to 6 hours on Low or 3 hours on High.
- If you don't have buttermilk, use 1/2 cup (125 mL) milk mixed with 3 tbsp (45 mL) sour cream.

Indian-Style Cashew Chicken

I call this rich, comforting mélange Indian-Style to distinguish it from Thai Cashew Chicken, which is a very different dish, although equally delicious. I like to serve this over brown basmati rice with zesty mango chutney, but other robust fruit chutneys work well, too. Add a green vegetable, such as steamed broccoli, to round out the color palette.

Make ahead

This dish can be partially prepared before it is cooked. Complete Step 1. Cover and refrigerate for up to 2 days. When you're ready to cook, continue with the recipe.

• **Works best in a large (minimum 5 quart) slow cooker**

1 tbsp	olive oil	15 mL
2	onions, finely chopped	2
4	cloves garlic, minced	4
1 tbsp	minced gingerroot	15 mL
1 tbsp	cumin seeds, toasted and ground (see Tip, page 178)	15 mL
1 tsp	turmeric	5 mL
1 tsp	salt	5 mL
1/2 tsp	cracked black peppercorns	2 mL
1	can (14 to 19 oz/398 to 540 mL) diced tomatoes, including juice	1
3 lbs	skinless, bone-in chicken thighs (about 12 thighs)	1.5 kg
1/2 cup	dry roasted cashews or cashew pieces (see Tips, below)	125 mL
1/2 cup	coconut milk	125 mL
1	long red chile pepper, optional (see Tips, below)	1

1. In a skillet, heat oil over medium heat for 30 seconds. Add onions and cook, stirring, until softened, about 3 minutes. Add garlic, gingerroot, cumin, turmeric, salt and peppercorns and cook, stirring, for 1 minute. Add tomatoes with juice and bring to a boil.

2. Arrange chicken over bottom of slow cooker stoneware and cover with sauce. Cover and cook on Low for 6 hours or on High for 3 hours, until juices run clear when chicken is pierced with a fork.

3. In a blender, combine cashews, coconut milk and chile pepper, if using, and blend until smooth. Add to slow cooker stoneware and stir to combine. Cover and cook on High for 30 minutes, until mixture is hot and bubbly.

TIPS
- If you're buying cashews in bulk and planning to purée them, buy cashew pieces because they are much less costly. Reduce the quantity by about 1 tbsp (15 mL).
- If you don't have a long red chile and would still like a bit of heat in this recipe, blend 1/4 tsp (1 mL) cayenne pepper, or to taste, with the cashew mixture.
- If you prefer, use 1 tsp (5 mL) ground cumin instead of toasting and grinding the seeds yourself.

African-Style Braised Chicken in Peanut Sauce

SERVES 6

The combination of chicken with a spicy peanut sauce is usually associated with Thailand, where grilled chicken satay is served as an appetizer with peanut sauce on the side. Here's an unusual and delicious recipe that moves the delectable combination of hot peppers and peanuts into the main course. Serve with plenty of hot white rice.

Make ahead

This dish can be partially prepared before it is cooked. Complete Step 1. Cover and refrigerate for up to 2 days. When you're ready to cook, continue with the recipe.

• **Works best in a large (minimum 5 quart) slow cooker**

1 tbsp	vegetable oil	15 mL
2	onions, finely chopped	2
4	cloves garlic, minced	4
1 tsp	dried oregano leaves	5 mL
1 tsp	salt	5 mL
½ tsp	cracked black peppercorns	2 mL
½ cup	chicken stock	125 mL
½ cup	tomato sauce	125 mL
1	bay leaf	1
3 lbs	skinless, bone-in chicken thighs (about 12 thighs)	1.5 kg
½ cup	peanut butter	125 mL
2 tbsp	sherry or freshly squeezed lemon juice	25 mL
2 tsp	curry powder	10 mL
½ to 1	long red or green chile pepper, minced	½ to 1
1	red bell pepper, finely chopped	1
	Hot white rice	

1. In a skillet, heat oil over medium heat for 30 seconds. Add onions and cook, stirring, until softened, about 3 minutes. Add garlic, oregano, salt and peppercorns and cook, stirring, for I minute. Stir in stock, tomato sauce and bay leaf and bring to a boil.

2. Arrange chicken over bottom of slow cooker stoneware and cover with vegetable mixture. Cover and cook on Low for 6 hours or on High for 3 hours, until juices run clear when chicken is pierced with a fork.

3. In a bowl, combine peanut butter, sherry, curry powder and chile pepper. Add a little cooking liquid and stir to blend. Add to slow cooker along with red pepper. Cover and cook on High for 20 minutes, until pepper is tender and flavors meld. Discard bay leaf. Serve over hot white rice.

TIP

• If you prefer, substitute bone-in chicken breasts for the thighs. Leave the skin on and brown them in the oil before softening the vegetables. For more detailed instructions on cooking chicken breasts in the slow cooker and making part of the recipe ahead, follow the instructions for Chicken in Onion Buttermilk Gravy (page 153).

Chicken and Barley

I love the simple but appetizing combination of flavors in this delicious dish. Although we usually eat this as a family dinner, all it takes is a dressed-up salad — try a combination of Boston lettuce, mesclun greens, red onion and avocado in a balsamic vinaigrette — crusty rolls and some crisp white wine to make it perfect for guests.

Make ahead

This dish can be partially prepared before it is cooked. Complete Step 2, heating 1 tbsp (15 mL) oil in pan before softening vegetables. Cover and refrigerate overnight. The next morning, brown chicken (Step 1), or if you're pressed for time, omit this step and place chicken directly in slow cooker stoneware and continue with the recipe.

● *Works best in a large (minimum 5 quart) slow cooker*

1 tbsp	vegetable oil	15 mL
3 lbs	skin-on, bone-in chicken breasts (see Tips, below)	1.5 kg
2	onions, chopped	2
4	stalks celery, diced	4
4	cloves garlic, minced	4
1 tsp	salt	5 mL
½ tsp	cracked black peppercorns	2 mL
½ tsp	dried thyme leaves	2 mL
1 cup	barley, rinsed (see Tips, below)	250 mL
1	can (28 oz/796 mL) tomatoes, including juice, coarsely chopped	1
1 cup	dry white wine or chicken stock	250 mL
2	red bell peppers, chopped	2
	Finely chopped dill	

1. In a skillet, heat oil over medium-high heat for 30 seconds. Add chicken, in batches, and brown on all sides. Transfer to slow cooker stoneware.

2. Reduce heat to medium. Add onions and celery to pan and cook, stirring, until softened, about 5 minutes. Add garlic, salt, peppercorns and thyme and cook, stirring, for 1 minute. Add barley and stir until coated. Add tomatoes with juice and wine and bring to a boil.

3. Pour mixture over chicken. Cover and cook on Low for 5 hours or on High for 2½ hours, until juices run clear when chicken is pierced with a fork. Add peppers and cook on High for 15 minutes, until softened. Transfer mixture to a deep platter and garnish liberally with dill. Serve piping hot.

TIPS
● If you prefer, use only skinless, bone-in chicken thighs when making this recipe. Do not brown and follow the method and Make ahead instructions for The Captain's Curry (page 152). Increase the cooking time to 6 hours on Low or 3 hours on High.
● Use whole, pot or pearl barley in this recipe.

Mexican-Style Chicken with Cilantro and Lemon

SERVES 4 TO 6

With a sauce of pumpkin seeds, cumin seeds, oregano and cilantro, this dish reminds me of warm evening dinners in the courtyard of a charming Mexican hacienda. Mexicans have been thickening sauces with pumpkin seeds long before the Spanish arrived and, today, every cook has their own recipes for mole, one of the world's great culinary concoctions. Serve this with rice and fresh corn on the cob.

Make ahead

This dish can be partially prepared before it is cooked. Complete Steps 1 and 2. Cover and refrigerate puréed sauce overnight. The next morning, continue with the recipe.

● *Works in slow cookers from 3 1/2 to 6 quarts*

¼ cup	raw pumpkin seeds	50 mL
2 tsp	cumin seeds	10 mL
1 tbsp	vegetable oil	15 mL
2	onions, sliced	2
4	cloves garlic, minced	4
2 tbsp	tomato paste	25 mL
1 tsp	salt	5 mL
1 tsp	cracked black peppercorns	5 mL
1 tsp	dried oregano leaves	5 mL
¼ tsp	ground cinnamon	1 mL
1 cup	coarsely chopped cilantro, stems and leaves	250 mL
1 tbsp	grated lemon zest	15 mL
2 tbsp	freshly squeezed lemon juice	25 mL
½ cup	chicken stock	125 mL
3 lbs	skinless, bone-in chicken thighs (about 12 thighs)	1.5 kg
1 to 2	jalapeño peppers, chopped	1 to 2
	Finely chopped cilantro and green onion	
	Grated lemon zest	

1. In a skillet, over medium-high heat, toast pumpkin and cumin seeds, stirring constantly, until pumpkin seeds are popping and cumin is fragrant, about 3 minutes. Transfer to a small bowl and set aside.

2. In the same skillet, heat oil over medium heat for 30 seconds. Add onions to pan and cook, stirring, until softened, about 3 minutes. Add garlic, tomato paste, salt, peppercorns, oregano and cinnamon and cook, stirring, for 1 minute. Transfer contents of pan to a blender or food processor. Add cilantro, lemon zest and juice, stock, reserved pumpkin and cumin seeds and process until smooth.

3. Arrange chicken over bottom of slow cooker stoneware and cover with vegetable mixture. Cover and cook on Low for 6 hours or on High for 3 hours, until juices run clear when chicken is pierced with a fork. Stir in jalapeño peppers. When you're ready to serve, garnish with cilantro, green onion and lemon zest.

TIP
● Buy seeds and nuts at a health or bulk food store with high turnover, as they are likely to be much fresher than those in packages.

White Chicken Chili

Chili is one of my favorite weekday meals. I love its robust Tex-Mex flavors and the way the beans blend seamlessly with meat to create a sumptuous stew. This version, made from chicken and white beans, is lighter than traditional meat chilies. If you prefer a more colorful chili, use one red and one green bell pepper. Add a shredded carrot or sliced tomato salad, in season, and some whole grain bread to complete the meal.

Make ahead

This dish can be partially prepared before it is cooked. Complete Step 1. Cover and refrigerate for up to 2 days. When you're ready to cook, continue with the recipe.

- **Works best in a large (minimum 5 quart) slow cooker**

1 tbsp	olive oil	15 mL
2	onions, finely chopped	2
4	cloves garlic, minced	4
1 tbsp	cumin seeds, toasted and ground (see Tip, page 178)	15 mL
2 tsp	dried oregano leaves, crumbled	10 mL
1	cinnamon stick piece (2 inches/5 cm)	1
1 tsp	cracked black peppercorns	5 mL
2 cups	chicken stock	500 mL
2 lbs	skinless, boneless chicken thighs, quartered (about 12 thighs)	1 kg
2 cups	cooked dried or canned white kidney beans, drained and rinsed (see Basic Beans, page 219)	500 mL
2 tsp	dried ancho or New Mexico chile powder, dissolved in 1 tbsp (15 mL) freshly squeezed lime juice	10 mL
2	green bell peppers, finely chopped	2
1	jalapeño pepper, finely chopped	1
1	can (4½ oz/127 mL) diced mild green chiles, drained	1
1 cup	shredded Monterey Jack cheese	250 mL
	Finely chopped cilantro	
	Lime wedges, optional	

1. In a skillet, heat oil over medium heat for 30 seconds. Add onions and cook, stirring, until softened, about 3 minutes. Add garlic, toasted cumin, oregano, cinnamon stick and peppercorns and cook, stirring, for 1 minute. Add stock and bring to a boil.

2. Transfer to slow cooker stoneware. Add chicken and beans and stir well. Cover and cook on Low for 6 hours or on High for 3 hours, until juices run clear when chicken is pierced with a fork.

3. Stir in chili powder solution. Add bell peppers, jalapeño pepper and green chiles and stir well. Cover and cook on High for 20 to 30 minutes, until peppers are tender. Add cheese and cook, stirring, until melted, about 1 minute. Ladle into bowls and garnish with cilantro. Pass lime wedges at the table, if using.

Spanish-Style Chicken with Rice

SERVES 6

Here's a slow cooker version of the great Spanish dish Arroz con Pollo. Saffron is a pungent bittersweet spice garnered from a particular kind of crocus. It is expensive because it is difficult to harvest, but a little goes a long way and it has a unique and haunting flavor. This tasty one-dish meal is popular with everyone, especially my husband, who always has seconds. Serve with a green salad and hot crusty bread, and pass the hot pepper sauce for those who like heat.

Make ahead

This dish can be partially prepared before it is cooked. Complete Step 1. Cover and refrigerate overnight. The next morning, continue with the recipe.

● **Works best in a large (minimum 5 quart) slow cooker**

¼ tsp	saffron threads, soaked in 2 tbsp (25 mL) boiling water, or 1 tsp (5 mL) turmeric (see Tips, below)	1 mL
1 tbsp	vegetable oil	15 mL
2	onions, finely chopped	2
4	cloves garlic, minced	4
1 tsp	salt	5 mL
¼ tsp	freshly ground black pepper	1 mL
1½ cups	long-grain parboiled rice	375 mL
1	can (28 oz/796 mL) tomatoes, including juice, chopped	1
1½ cups	chicken stock (see Tips, below)	375 mL
3 lbs	skinless, bone-in chicken thighs (about 12 thighs)	1.5 kg
1	green bell pepper, finely chopped	1
1 cup	green peas, thawed if frozen	250 mL
	Sliced pimento-stuffed green olives, optional	
	Hot pepper sauce, optional	

1. In a skillet, heat oil over medium heat for 30 seconds. Add onions and cook, stirring, until softened, about 3 minutes. Add garlic, salt and pepper and cook, stirring, for 1 minute. Add rice and stir until grains are well coated with mixture. Stir in saffron, tomatoes with juice and stock.

2. Arrange chicken over bottom of slow cooker stoneware and cover with onion mixture. Place a clean tea towel, folded in half (so you will have two layers), over top of stoneware to absorb moisture. Cover and cook on Low for 6 hours or on High for 3 hours, until juices run clear when chicken is pierced with a fork. Stir in green pepper and peas, cover and cook on High for 20 minutes, until vegetables are tender. Garnish with olives, if using, and pass hot pepper sauce, if using.

> **TIPS**
> ● Buy saffron in threads, not powder. Although turmeric can be used to convey the saffron color in a dish, it will not replicate the flavor of the original.
> ● If you prefer, use 1 cup (250 mL) chicken stock and ½ cup (125 mL) dry white wine.

French-Country Chicken with Olives

I love the bold flavors of this hearty country-style dish. Served with a big bowl of fluffy mashed potatoes, there's nothing more satisfying on a chilly day. Accompany with crusty bread, a green salad and a robust red wine.

Make ahead

This dish can be partially prepared before it is cooked. Complete Steps 1 and 2. Cover and refrigerate for up to 2 days. When you're ready to cook, continue with the recipe.

• **Works best in a large (minimum 5 quart) slow cooker**

4	slices bacon or 2 oz (60 g) salt pork belly, cut in ¼-inch (0.5 cm) cubes	4
2	onions, finely chopped	2
4	cloves garlic, minced	4
1 tsp	dried Italian herb seasoning	5 mL
1 tsp	salt	5 mL
1 tsp	cracked black peppercorns	5 mL
¼ cup	all-purpose flour	50 mL
½ cup	dry white wine	125 mL
1 cup	tomato sauce	250 mL
½ cup	chicken stock	125 mL
1	bay leaf	1
3 to 4 lbs	skinless, bone-in chicken thighs	1.5 to 2 kg
½ cup	black olives, pitted and thinly sliced (see Tip, below)	125 mL
½ cup	green olives, pitted and thinly sliced	125 mL
	Finely chopped Italian parsley	

1. In a skillet, cook bacon or salt pork over medium-high heat until crisp. Drain on paper towels. If using bacon, when cool enough to handle, crumble, and set aside. Drain all but 2 tbsp (25 mL) fat from the pan.

2. Reduce heat to medium. Add onions and cook, stirring, until softened, about 3 minutes. Add garlic, Italian seasoning, salt and peppercorns and cook, stirring, for 1 minute. Sprinkle flour over mixture and cook, stirring, for 1 minute. Add wine and stir well. Add tomato sauce and stock and bring to a boil, stirring until mixture thickens. Add bay leaf and reserved bacon and stir to combine.

3. Arrange chicken over bottom of slow cooker stoneware and cover with mixture. Cover and cook on Low for 6 hours or on High for 3 hours, until juices run clear when chicken is pierced with a fork. Add olives, cover and cook on High for 15 minutes, until heated through. Discard bay leaf. Garnish with parsley.

TIP

• As a rule of thumb, the best olives do not come in cans or jars. Most of the canned black olives are processed in an alkaline solution, rendering them particularly tasteless. I always buy olives in bulk, from a trusted purveyor, and I make a point of tasting first.

Tuscan Chicken with Sage

This simple yet delicious chicken gets its distinctive, slightly peppery flavor from the addition of fresh sage, which has a pleasantly pungent flavor. In many ways, it's an Italian variation of coq au vin. Serve with a basic risotto, a robust green vegetable, such as broccoli or rapini, and hot crusty bread to soak up the sauce.

Make ahead

This dish can be partially prepared before it is cooked. Complete Step 3, heating 1 tbsp (15 mL) of the oil in pan before softening onions. Cover and refrigerate overnight. The next morning, continue with the recipe.

● *Works best in a large (minimum 5 quart) slow cooker*

3 lbs	skin-on, bone-in chicken breasts	1.5 kg
½ cup	all-purpose flour	125 mL
2 tbsp	olive oil (approx.)	25 mL
2	onions, finely chopped	2
2	cloves garlic, minced	2
½ cup	fresh sage leaves or 1 tsp (5 mL) dried sage (see Tip, below)	125 mL
1 tsp	salt	5 mL
½ tsp	cracked black peppercorns	2 mL
2 cups	dry robust red wine, such as Chianti	500 mL

1. On a plate, coat chicken on all sides with flour, shaking off the excess. Discard excess flour.

2. In a skillet, heat oil over medium-high heat for 30 seconds. Add chicken, in batches, and brown on all sides. Transfer to slow cooker stoneware.

3. Reduce heat to medium. Add onions to pan, adding additional oil, if needed. Cook, stirring, until softened, about 3 minutes. Add garlic, sage, salt and peppercorns and cook, stirring, for 1 minute. Pour in wine, bring to boil and cook, stirring, for 5 minutes, until sauce is reduced by one-third.

4. Pour mixture over chicken. Cover and cook on Low for 5 hours or on High for 2½ hours, until juices run clear when chicken is pierced with a fork. Serve immediately.

TIP

● For optimum results, make an effort to find fresh sage, which is often available in the produce section of well-stocked supermarkets or specialty stores. If you can't locate it, dried sage produces an acceptable substitute in this recipe.

Texas-Style Chicken Stew

SERVES 6

This tasty stew, which I adapted from a recipe that appeared in Saveur magazine, is an east Texas tradition. It makes a delicious weekday meal and is perfect for country weekends or tailgate parties. Add crusty rolls and a tossed green salad or coleslaw, for a great "down home" meal.

Make ahead

This dish can be partially prepared before it is cooked. Complete Steps 1 and 2. Cover and refrigerate for up to 2 days. When you're ready to cook, continue with the recipe.

• **Works best in a large (minimum 5 quart) slow cooker**

4	slices bacon	4
2	onions, chopped	2
4	cloves garlic, minced	4
1 tsp	dried oregano leaves, crumbled	5 mL
½ tsp	cracked black peppercorns	2 mL
	Salt	
1	can (14 oz/398 mL) diced tomatoes, including juice	1
1 cup	chicken stock	250 mL
3 lbs	skinless, bone-in chicken thighs (about 12 thighs)	1.5 kg
2	cans (each 14 oz/398 mL) cream-style corn	2
1 tbsp	chili powder, dissolved in 2 tbsp (25 mL) freshly squeezed lemon juice	15 mL
1 tsp	paprika (see Tip, below)	5 mL
Pinch	cayenne pepper, optional	Pinch

1. In a skillet, cook bacon over medium-high heat until crisp. Remove and drain thoroughly on paper towel and crumble. Cover and refrigerate until ready to use. Drain all but 1 tbsp (15 mL) of fat from pan.

2. Reduce heat to medium. Add onions to pan and cook, stirring, until softened, about 3 minutes. Add garlic, oregano, peppercorns and salt, to taste, and cook, stirring, for 1 minute. Add tomatoes with juice and stock and bring to a boil.

3. Arrange chicken over bottom of slow cooker stoneware and cover with vegetable mixture. Cover and cook on Low for 6 hours or on High for 3 hours, until juices run clear when chicken is pierced with a fork. Add corn, chili powder solution, paprika, cayenne, if using, and reserved bacon and stir well. Cover and cook on High for 30 minutes, until corn is heated through.

TIP

• Although any type of paprika, including hot paprika, works well in this recipe, I like to use smoked paprika, which lends a pleasant smoky undertone to the stew.

Classic Chicken Stew

I have a real soft spot for this creamy stew, which reminds me of chicken pot pie without the crust. I obtain a similar effect by serving it over crostini placed in the bottom of a soup plate. Add a tossed green salad for a complete and delicious meal.

Make ahead

This dish can be partially prepared before it is cooked. Complete Steps 1 and 2. Cover and refrigerate overnight. The next morning, continue with the recipe.

• **Works best in a large (minimum 5 quart) slow cooker**

1	potato, peeled and diced (see Tips, below)	1
1 tbsp	vegetable oil	15 mL
2	onions, finely chopped	2
4	stalks celery, diced	4
2	carrots, peeled and diced	2
½ tsp	dried thyme leaves or 3 whole sprigs of fresh thyme	2 mL
1	bay leaf	1
¼ cup	all-purpose flour	50 mL
1½ cups	chicken stock	375 mL
½ cup	dry white wine or chicken stock	125 mL
	Salt and freshly ground black pepper	
3 lbs	skinless, bone-in chicken thighs (about 12 thighs)	1.5 kg
1 cup	green peas, thawed if frozen	250 mL
½ cup	cream, optional (see Tips, below)	125 mL

1. In a saucepan, combine potato and cold water to cover. Bring to a boil and cook for 2 minutes. Remove from heat. Cover and set aside.

2. In a skillet, heat oil over medium heat for 30 seconds. Add onions, celery and carrots and cook, stirring, until carrots are softened, about 7 minutes. Add thyme, bay leaf and flour and cook, stirring, for 1 minute. Add stock and white wine and cook, stirring, until mixture comes to a boil and thickens, about 4 minutes. Drain reserved potato and add to mixture. Season to taste with salt and pepper.

3. Arrange chicken over bottom of slow cooker stoneware and cover with vegetable mixture. Cover and cook on Low for 6 hours or on High for 3 hours, until juices run clear when chicken is pierced with a fork. Add peas and cream, if using, and stir well. Cover and cook on High for 20 minutes, until peas are tender and mixture is hot and bubbly.

TIPS

• Because the chicken only cooks for 6 hours on Low the potatoes will be a bit firm unless they are blanched prior to adding to the stew.
• Any kind of cream from half-and-half (10%) to the richest whipping (35%) cream works well in this recipe.

Spanish Chicken Stew

SERVES 6 TO 8

Both the Spanish and the Portuguese claim the spicy chorizo sausage for their own and this dish owes something to both cultures. I like to serve this with hot cornbread and a big green salad.

Make ahead

This dish can be partially prepared before it is cooked. Complete Step 1. Cover and refrigerate mixture for up to 2 days. When you're ready to cook, continue with the recipe.

● **Works best in a large (minimum 5 quart) slow cooker**

1 tbsp	vegetable oil	15 mL
2	onions, finely chopped	2
4	cloves garlic, finely chopped	4
1 tsp	dried thyme leaves	5 mL
1 tsp	salt	5 mL
1 tsp	cracked black peppercorns	5 mL
½ cup	dry sherry	125 mL
1	can (28 oz/796 mL) tomatoes, including juice, coarsely chopped (see Tips, page 34)	1
2 cups	cooked dried or canned white beans, rinsed and drained (see Basic Beans, page 219)	500 mL
3 lbs	skinless, bone-in chicken thighs (about 12 thighs) (see Tips, below)	1.5 kg
1 tbsp	paprika	15 mL
8 oz	hard chorizo sausage, cut into ¼-inch (0.5 cm) slices or removed from casing and chopped (see Tips, below)	250 g
1 cup	large green pimento-stuffed olives, thinly sliced	250 mL

1. In a skillet, heat oil over medium heat for 30 seconds. Add onions and cook, stirring, until softened, about 3 minutes. Add garlic, thyme, salt and peppercorns and cook, stirring, for 1 minute. Add sherry and tomatoes with juice and bring to a boil. Cook, stirring, until liquid is reduced by one-third, about 5 minutes.

2. Add beans to tomato mixture. Arrange chicken over bottom of slow cooker stoneware and cover with tomato mixture. Cover and cook on Low for 6 hours or on High for 3 hours, until juices run clear when chicken is pierced with a fork. Stir in paprika, chorizo and olives. Cover and cook on High for 15 minutes, until heated through and flavors meld.

TIPS

- If you prefer, substitute bone-in chicken breasts for the thighs. Leave the skin on and brown them in the oil before softening the vegetables. Be sure not to overcook as breasts tend to dry out in the slow cooker. For more detailed instructions on cooking chicken breasts in the slow cooker and making part of the recipe ahead, follow the instructions for Chicken in Onion Buttermilk Gravy (page 153).
- If you can't find hard chorizo sausage, substitute an equal quantity of pepperoni or kielbasa.

Indonesian Chicken

SERVES 6

Although this chicken dish is remarkably easy, its slightly sweet yet spicy coconut-milk sauce gives it an exotic flavor. For a more fiery version, increase the quantity of chili sauce. Serve over fluffy white rice.

Make ahead

This dish can be partially prepared before it is cooked. Complete Step 2, heating 1 tbsp (15 mL) oil in pan before softening onions. Cover and refrigerate puréed mixture for up to 2 days. When you're ready to cook, brown chicken (Step 1), or if you're pressed for time, omit browning and place chicken directly in stoneware. (If you're not browning the chicken, this recipe works best with skinless chicken thighs, which need to be cooked for about 6 hours on Low or 3 hours on High.) Continue with the recipe.

- **Works best in a large (minimum 5 quart) slow cooker**

1 tbsp	vegetable oil	15 mL
3 lbs	skin-on, bone-in chicken breasts (see Tips, below)	1.5 kg
2	onions, sliced	2
4	cloves garlic, minced	4
1 tbsp	minced gingerroot	15 mL
1 tsp	ground coriander	5 mL
1 tsp	turmeric	5 mL
8	almonds, blanched and peeled	8
1 cup	chicken stock	250 mL
1	stalk lemongrass, bruised and cut into 2-inch (5 cm) pieces, or 1 tbsp (15 mL) grated lemon zest (see Tips, below)	1
1 cup	coconut milk	250 mL
1½ tsp	soy sauce, preferably dark	7 mL
1 tsp	brown sugar	5 mL
1 tbsp	Asian chili sauce, such as sambal oelek	15 mL

1. In a skillet, heat oil over medium-high heat for 30 seconds. Add chicken and cook, turning, until brown on all sides. Transfer to slow cooker. Drain all but 1 tbsp (15 mL) fat from the pan.

2. Reduce heat to medium. Add onions to pan and cook, stirring, until softened, about 3 minutes. Add garlic, gingerroot, coriander, turmeric and almonds and cook, stirring, for 1 minute. Add stock and stir. Transfer contents of pan to food processor or blender and process until smooth.

3. Pour mixture over chicken and add lemongrass. Cover and cook on Low for 5 hours or on High for 2½ hours, until juices run clear when chicken is pierced with a fork.

4. Discard lemongrass. Stir in coconut milk, soy sauce, brown sugar and chili sauce. Cover and cook on High for 20 minutes.

TIPS

- If you prefer, use only skinless, bone-in chicken thighs when making this recipe. Do not brown and follow the method and Make-ahead instructions for The Captain's Curry (page 152).
- Lemongrass is available in Asian markets and many supermarkets. Before adding lemongrass to a recipe, "smash" it with the flat side of a chef's knife, so it can release its flavor when it cooks.

Balsamic Braised Chicken with Olives

SERVES 6

Here's a tasty Mediterranean-inspired dish that is simple yet elegant. Serve this over creamy Slow-Cooked Polenta (see recipe, page 264) or hot couscous for a delectable meal.

Make ahead

This dish can be partially prepared before it is cooked. Complete Step 2, heating 1 tbsp (15 mL) oil in pan before softening onions. Cover and refrigerate for up to 2 days. When you're ready to cook, brown chicken (Step 1), or if you're pressed for time, omit this step and add chicken directly to slow cooker stoneware. (If you're not browning the chicken, I recommend making this recipe using skinless, bone-in chicken thighs, which do not need to be browned but do need to be cooked for about 6 hours on Low or 3 hours on High.) Continue with the recipe.

- **Works best in a large (minimum 5 quart) slow cooker**

1 tbsp	vegetable oil	15 mL
3½ lbs	skin-on, bone-in chicken breasts (see Tip, below)	1.75 kg
2	onions, finely chopped	2
4	cloves garlic, minced	4
1 tsp	salt	5 mL
½ tsp	cracked black peppercorns	2 mL
½ tsp	dried thyme leaves	2 mL
2 cups	chopped peeled tomatoes, including juice, if canned	500 mL
½ cup	chicken stock	125 mL
2 tbsp	balsamic vinegar	25 mL
2 tbsp	chopped pitted black olives	25 mL
2 tbsp	drained capers, optional	25 mL

1. In a skillet, heat oil over medium-high heat for 30 seconds. Add chicken, in batches, and brown on all sides. Transfer to slow cooker stoneware.

2. Reduce heat to medium. Add onions to pan and cook, stirring, until softened, about 3 minutes. Add garlic, salt, peppercorns and thyme and cook, stirring, for 1 minute. Add tomatoes, stock and balsamic vinegar and bring to a boil.

3. Pour mixture over chicken. Cover and cook on Low for 5 hours or on High for 2½ hours, until juices run clear when chicken is pierced with a fork. Add olives and capers, if using, and stir well. Serve immediately.

TIP
- If you prefer, use only skinless, bone-in chicken thighs when making this recipe. Do not brown and follow the method and Make ahead instructions for The Captain's Curry (page 152).

Spicy Chinese Chicken

I've been making variations of this basic recipe for more than twenty years and I still love it. This one is particularly good, as the vinegar, brown sugar and chile pepper add a nice complexity to the basic sauce.

Make ahead

This dish can be assembled the night before it is cooked and, in fact, improves in flavor for marinating in the sauce overnight. Complete Step 1. Add chicken to sauce and refrigerate overnight. The next day, transfer mixture to stoneware in slow cooker and continue with the recipe.

● **Works best in a large (minimum 5 quart) slow cooker**

¾ cup	chicken stock	175 mL
¼ cup	soy sauce, preferably dark (see Tips, below)	50 mL
3 tbsp	rice vinegar	45 mL
2 tsp	packed brown sugar	10 mL
4	green onions, white and green parts, cut into 2-inch (5 cm) pieces	4
4	cloves garlic, minced	4
1 tbsp	minced gingerroot	15 mL
1 tsp	cracked black peppercorns	5 mL
3 lbs	skinless, bone-in chicken pieces (see Tips, below)	1.5 kg
1	long red or green chile or 2 Thai chiles, finely chopped (see Tip, page 86)	1
3 tbsp	cornstarch, dissolved in 2 tbsp (25 mL) cold water	45 mL
	Hot cooked rice	

1. In a bowl, combine chicken stock, soy sauce, rice vinegar and brown sugar, stirring well to ensure sugar is dissolved. Add green onions, garlic, gingerroot and peppercorns.

2. Arrange chicken over bottom of slow cooker stoneware and cover with sauce. Cover and cook on Low for 5 to 6 hours or on High for 2½ to 3 hours, until juices run clear when chicken is pierced with a fork.

3. With a slotted spoon, transfer chicken to a platter and cover with foil to keep warm. Strain liquid into a saucepan and add chile peppers. Whisk in cornstarch mixture. Bring to a boil. Reduce heat to simmer and stir for about 3 minutes or until thickened and glossy. Pour over chicken. Serve with hot fluffy rice.

TIPS

● Dark soy sauce, which is aged for a longer period of time than the lighter version, is thicker and more flavorful and works better in braising-type recipes such as this one. It is available in Asian grocery stores and many supermarkets with an Asian section. If you can't find it, use the same quantity of light soy sauce mixed with 1 tbsp (15 mL) molasses.

● Since chicken breasts tend to dry out when cooked in the slow cooker, I recommend making this dish with skinless legs and/or thighs. If you are using chicken breasts, cook them for the shortest time.

Not-Too-Corny Turkey Chili with Sausage

SERVES 6 TO 8

This delicious chili, which is loaded with vegetables and the complex flavors of a variety of hot peppers, is mild enough to be enjoyed by all family members, even with the addition of a chipotle pepper in adobo sauce. It's perfect for those evenings when everyone is running off to differently timed events or for winter weekends in the country. Just keep the slow cooker on Warm, have some crusty rolls on hand and tell people to help themselves.

Make ahead

This dish can be partially prepared before it is cooked. Complete Steps 1 and 3, chilling sausage and chile mixtures separately. Cover and refrigerate for up to 2 days, being aware that the chile mixture will lose some of its vibrancy if held for this long. (For best results, complete Step 3 while the chili is cooking or no sooner than the night before you plan to cook.) When you're ready to cook, continue with the recipe.

- **Works best in a large (minimum 5 quart) slow cooker**

1 tbsp	vegetable oil	15 mL
1 lb	mild Italian sausage, removed from casings	500 g
2	onions, finely chopped	2
4	stalks celery, diced	4
6	cloves garlic, minced	6
1 tbsp	cumin seeds, toasted and ground (see Tip, page 178)	15 mL
1 tbsp	dried oregano leaves	15 mL
1 tsp	salt	5 mL
1	can (28 oz/796 mL) diced tomatoes, including juice	1
1 lb	skinless, boneless turkey, cut into ½-inch (1 cm) cubes	500 g
2 cups	cooked dried or canned pinto beans, drained and rinsed	500 mL
2	dried ancho, guajillo or New Mexico chiles	2
2 cups	boiling water	500 mL
1 cup	coarsely chopped cilantro, stems and leaves	250 mL
½ cup	chicken stock	125 mL
2 tsp	chili powder	10 mL
1	chipotle chile in adobo sauce, optional	1
1	red or green bell pepper, diced	1
2 cups	corn kernels, thawed, if frozen	500 mL

1. In a skillet, heat oil over medium heat. Add sausage, onions and celery and cook, stirring, until sausage is no longer pink, about 10 minutes. Add garlic, toasted cumin, oregano and salt and cook, stirring, for 1 minute. Add tomatoes with juice and bring to a boil.

2. Transfer to slow cooker stoneware. Add turkey and pinto beans to stoneware. Cover and cook on Low for 6 hours or on High for 3 hours, until turkey is no longer pink inside.

3. Half an hour before recipe has finished cooking, in a heatproof bowl, soak dried chiles in boiling water for 30 minutes, weighing down with a cup to ensure they remain submerged. Drain, discarding soaking liquid and stems and chop coarsely. Transfer to a blender. Add cilantro, stock, chili powder and chipotle pepper, if using, and purée.

4. Add chile mixture to stoneware along with bell pepper and corn kernels and stir well. Cover and cook on High for 30 minutes, until pepper is tender and flavors meld.

Turkey Mole

In many parts of Mexico, no special occasion is complete without turkey cooked in mole poblano. Since the authentic version is quite a production, I've simplified this slow cooker version, which is delicious nonetheless. Serve with hot tortillas, fluffy white rice and creamed corn.

Make ahead

This dish can be partially prepared before it is cooked. Complete Steps 2 and 4, heating 1 tbsp (15 mL) oil in pan before softening onions. Cover and refrigerate puréed sauces separately for up to 2 days, being aware that the chile mixture will lose some of its vibrancy if held for this long. (For best results, complete Step 4 while the turkey is cooking or no sooner than the night before you plan to cook.) When you're ready to cook, brown turkey (Step 1), or remove skin from turkey, omit browning and place directly in stoneware. Continue with the recipe.

- **Works best in a large (minimum 5 quart) slow cooker**

1 tbsp	vegetable oil	15 mL
1	skin-on turkey breast, about 2 to 3 lbs (1 to 1.5 kg)	1
2	onions, sliced	2
4	cloves garlic, sliced	4
4	whole cloves	4
1	cinnamon stick piece (2 inches/5 cm)	1
1 tsp	salt	5 mL
1 tsp	cracked black peppercorns	5 mL
1	can (28 oz/796 mL) tomatillos, drained	1
½ oz	unsweetened chocolate, broken in pieces	15 g
1 cup	chicken stock, divided	250 mL
2	dried ancho, New Mexico or guajillo chiles	2
2 cups	boiling water	500 mL
½ cup	coarsely chopped cilantro stems and leaves	125 mL
1 tbsp	chili powder	15 mL
1 to 2	jalapeño peppers, chopped	1 to 2
3 tbsp	diced mild green chiles, optional	45 mL

1. In a skillet, heat oil over medium-high heat for 30 seconds. Add turkey, in batches, and brown on all sides. Transfer to slow cooker stoneware.

2. Reduce heat to medium. Add onions to pan and cook, stirring, until softened, about 3 minutes. Add garlic, cloves, cinnamon stick, salt and peppercorns and cook, stirring, for 1 minute. Transfer mixture to blender. Add tomatillos, chocolate and ½ cup (125 mL) of the stock and process until smooth.

3. Pour sauce over turkey, cover and cook on Low for 8 hours or on High for 4 hours, until juices run clear when turkey is pierced with a fork or meat thermometer reads 170°F (77°C).

4. Half an hour before recipe has finished cooking, in a heatproof bowl, soak dried chiles in boiling water for 30 minutes, weighing down with a cup to ensure they remain submerged. Drain, discarding soaking liquid and stems and chop coarsely. Transfer to a blender. Add cilantro, remaining ½ cup (125 mL) of the chicken stock, chili powder and jalapeño pepper and purée. Add to stoneware along with mild green chiles, if using, and stir gently to combine. Cover and cook on High for 30 minutes, until flavors meld.

Turkey Sloppy Joes

Kids love this savory mixture, which is perfect for those busy evenings when you have to rush out after eating dinner. Serve this over hot split onion buns and accompany with a tossed salad for a tasty and nutritious meal.

Make ahead

This dish can be partially prepared before it is cooked. Complete Steps 1 and 2, chilling cooked meat and onion mixtures separately. Cover and refrigerate for up to 2 days. When you're ready to cook, combine and continue with the recipe.

• **Works in slow cookers from 3½ to 6 quarts**

2 tbsp	vegetable oil, divided	25 mL
1½ lbs	ground turkey	750 g
2	onions, finely chopped	2
4	cloves garlic, minced	4
2 tsp	cumin seeds, toasted and ground (see Tip, below)	10 mL
2 tsp	dried oregano leaves	10 mL
1 tsp	salt	5 mL
½ tsp	cracked black peppercorns	2 mL
1 cup	tomato-based chili sauce	250 mL
2 cups	shredded Monterey Jack cheese	500 mL
1	green bell pepper, finely chopped, optional	1
1	jalapeño pepper, minced, optional	1
1 tbsp	Worcestershire sauce	15 mL
1 tsp	paprika, preferably smoked	5 mL
	Hot onion buns	

1. In a skillet, heat 1 tbsp (15 mL) of the oil over medium heat for 30 seconds. Add turkey and cook, breaking up meat with a wooden spoon, until no longer pink. Using a slotted spoon, transfer to slow cooker stoneware. Drain and discard liquid from pan.

2. Add remaining oil to pan. Add onions and cook, stirring, until softened, about 3 minutes. Add garlic, toasted cumin, oregano, salt and peppercorns and cook, stirring, for 1 minute. Add chili sauce and bring to a boil.

3. Transfer mixture to slow cooker stoneware. Cover and cook on Low for 8 hours or on High for 4 hours, until mixture is hot and bubbly. Add cheese and green pepper and jalapeño pepper, if using, Worcestershire sauce and paprika. Cover and cook on High for 20 minutes, until cheese is melted and pepper is softened. Spoon over hot split onion buns and serve.

TIP

• To toast cumin seeds: Place seeds in a dry skillet over medium heat, stirring, until fragrant, about 3 minutes. Immediately transfer to a mortar or a spice grinder and grind. You can substitute 1 tsp (5 mL) ground cumin for the cumin seeds if you prefer.

Turkey in Puff Pastry

SERVES 6 TO 8

I've always enjoyed the many variations of this comfort food classic. Here, succulent chunks of turkey are served in a creamy sauce embellished with mushrooms and sweet red pepper. The velvety sauce contrasts with the crunchy crust of a vol-au-vent. For a celebratory dinner, add a salad of mushrooms, bacon bits and baby spinach in a mustard vinaigrette, and a glass of cold white wine.

Make ahead

This dish can be partially prepared before it is cooked. Complete Step 1. Cover and refrigerate for up to 2 days. When you're ready to cook, continue with the recipe.

• **Works best in a large (minimum 5 quart) slow cooker**

2 tbsp	vegetable oil	25 mL
2	onions, finely chopped	2
4	stalks celery, cut into 1/4-inch (0.5 cm) dice	4
1 tbsp	dried tarragon leaves	15 mL
1 tsp	salt	5 mL
1/2 tsp	freshly ground black pepper	2 mL
1 lb	cremini mushrooms, halved or quartered (see Tips, below)	500 g
1/4 cup	all-purpose flour	50 mL
1/2 cup	chicken stock	125 mL
1/2 cup	dry white wine	125 mL
2 lbs	skinless, boneless turkey, cut into 1/2-inch (1 cm) cubes	1 kg
1	red bell pepper, diced	1
1/2 cup	whipping (35%) cream	125 mL
8	frozen puff pastry shells (see Tips, below)	8

1. In a large skillet, heat oil over medium heat for 30 seconds. Add onions and celery and cook, stirring, until celery is softened, about 5 minutes. Add tarragon, salt and pepper and cook, stirring, for 1 minute. Add mushrooms and toss to coat. Sprinkle flour over mixture and cook, stirring, for 1 minute. Add stock and wine and stir until thickened (mixture will be very thick).

2. Arrange turkey over bottom of stoneware and cover with mushroom mixture. Cover and cook on Low for 6 to 7 hours or on High for 3 to 4 hours, until turkey is no longer pink inside. Add red pepper and cream. Cover and cook on High for 20 to 25 minutes, until heated through.

3. Bake pastry shells according to package directions. Fill with turkey mixture and serve piping hot.

> ### TIPS
> • I prefer the stronger flavor of cremini mushrooms in this recipe, but white mushrooms work well, too.
> • Make your own puff pastry if you are so inclined, but using frozen puff pastry shells, which are readily available at the supermarket, makes this an easy weeknight meal.

Best-Ever Turkey Breast

SERVES 4 TO 6

If you want to celebrate a holiday with turkey but don't feel like cooking an entire bird, try this tasty alternative. Accompany with roast or mashed potatoes, Brussels sprouts and cranberry ketchup for a great festive meal.

Make ahead

This dish can be partially prepared before it is cooked. Complete Steps 1 and 3. Cover and refrigerate for up to 2 days. When you're ready to cook, heat 1 tbsp (15 mL) oil in pan and brown turkey breast (Step 2), or if you're pressed for time, remove skin from turkey breast, omit browning and place directly in slow cooker stoneware. If you are not browning the turkey, omit the optional brandy flambé. Continue with the recipe.

- *Works best in a large (minimum 5 quart) slow cooker*

2	slices bacon	2
1	skin-on turkey breast, about 2 to 3 lbs (1 to 1.5 kg)	1
2 tbsp	brandy or cognac, optional	25 mL
2	onions, finely chopped	2
4	carrots, peeled and diced	4
4	stalks celery, diced	4
2	cloves garlic, minced	2
1 tsp	ground sage	5 mL
6	whole cloves or allspice	6
1 tsp	salt	5 mL
½ tsp	cracked black peppercorns	2 mL
¼ cup	all-purpose flour	50 mL
¾ cup	dry white wine or chicken stock	175 mL

1. In a skillet, cook bacon over medium-high heat until crisp. Remove from pan and drain on paper towel. Crumble and set aside. Drain all but 2 tbsp (25 mL) fat from pan.

2. Add turkey breast to pan and brown on all sides. Turn turkey skin side up and sprinkle with brandy, if using. Ignite, stand back and wait for flames to subside. Transfer to slow cooker stoneware.

3. Reduce heat to medium. Add onions, carrots and celery to pan and cook, stirring, until vegetables are softened, about 7 minutes. Add garlic, sage, cloves, salt and peppercorns and cook, stirring, for 1 minute. Sprinkle flour over mixture and cook, stirring, for 1 minute. Stir in reserved bacon and wine and cook, stirring, until mixture is thickened.

4. Spoon sauce over turkey breast. Cover and cook on Low for 6 hours or on High for 3 hours, until turkey is tender and no longer pink inside or an instant-read meat thermometer reads 170°F (77°C). Transfer turkey to a warm platter, spoon sauce over and serve piping hot.

New World Bouillabaisse (page 184)

Fish and Seafood

New World Bouillabaisse

SERVES 6

Traditional bouillabaisse contains a wide variety of Mediterranean fish, which leads many to conclude that it can only be made in proximity to the Mediterranean Sea. But in my opinion, this elevates the dish to a status that defies its origins. Bouillabaisse was originally a one-pot meal fishermen made from their daily catch. This simple stew is distinguished by the inclusion of saffron, and a rapid reduction of the broth, which intensifies the flavor and emulsifies the olive oil. Serve this delicious meal-in-a bowl in soup plates followed by a simple salad and fresh fruit for dessert.

- **Works best in a large (minimum 5 quart) slow cooker**
- **Large square of cheesecloth**

3 tbsp	olive oil, divided	45 mL
1 tsp	fennel seeds, toasted and ground (see Tips, right)	5 mL
1 lb	medium shrimp, peeled and deveined	500 g
1 lb	halibut, cut into 1-inch (2.5 cm) cubes	500 g
2	onions, chopped	2
2	carrots, peeled and diced	2
1	large bulb fennel, cored and thinly sliced on the vertical	1
6	cloves garlic, minced	6
1 tsp	salt	5 mL
½ tsp	cracked black peppercorns	2 mL
1	can (28 oz/ 796 mL) diced tomatoes, including juice	1
2	potatoes, peeled and diced	2
4 cups	water	1 L
2 cups	dry white wine	500 mL
2 lbs	fish trimmings	1 kg
4	sprigs parsley	4
2	sprigs fresh thyme (see Tips, right)	2
2	bay leaves	2
1 tsp	saffron threads dissolved in 1 tbsp (15 mL) boiling water	5 mL
24	mussels, cleaned	24
	Crostini (see Tips, right)	

Rouille

¼ cup	mayonnaise	50 mL
1	roasted red pepper, peeled and chopped	1
2	cloves garlic minced	2
Pinch	cayenne pepper	Pinch

1. In a bowl, combine 2 tbsp (25 mL) of the olive oil and toasted fennel. Add shrimp and halibut and toss until coated. Cover and refrigerate for 2 hours or overnight, stirring occasionally.

Make ahead

This dish can be partially prepared before it is cooked. Complete Steps 1 and 2. Cover and refrigerate fish and tomato mixtures separately overnight. The next morning, continue with the recipe. You can also make the rouille the night before you plan to cook.

2. In a skillet, heat remaining oil over medium heat for 30 seconds. Add onions, carrots and fennel and cook, stirring, until carrots are softened, about 7 minutes. Add garlic, salt and peppercorns and cook, stirring, for 1 minute. Add tomatoes with juice and bring to a boil. Transfer to slow cooker stoneware.

3. Add potatoes, water and wine to slow cooker and stir well. In a large square of cheesecloth, tie fish trimmings, parsley, thyme and bay leaves. Place in stoneware, ensuring all or most is submerged in the sauce. Cover and cook on Low for 8 to 10 hours or on High for 4 to 5 hours, until vegetables are very tender. Remove package of fish trimmings and discard.

4. Place a colander over a large saucepan and add the soup. Transfer solids to a food processor and purée. Bring liquids in saucepan to a boil over medium-high heat and cook until reduced by about one-third, about 10 minutes. Add dissolved saffron and mussels and cook for 5 minutes, until mussels open. Discard any mussels that do not open. Add marinated shrimp and halibut and cook until fish is tender. Add reserved puréed solids and heat until heated through.

5. *Rouille:* In a mini-chopper, combine mayonnaise, red pepper, garlic and cayenne. Process until smooth. To serve, spread crostini with rouille, place in the bottom of a soup plate and ladle the soup over them.

TIPS

- To toast fennel seeds: Place seeds in a dry skillet over medium heat, stirring, until fragrant, about 3 minutes. Immediately transfer to a mortar or a spice grinder and grind.
- If you don't have fresh thyme, you can use $1/2$ tsp (2 mL) dried thyme. Add it to the recipe in Step 2, along with the garlic.
- To make crostini: Preheat broiler. Brush baguette slices on both sides with olive oil and toast under broiler, turning once.

Manhattan Clam Chowder

Manhattan clam chowder is appealing because it is a lighter alternative to traditional New England-style chowder. However, I find that its tomato-based broth often seems harsh. The solution is to add a touch of cream. This creates a chowder with the zest of Manhattan and the creamy smoothness of New England — the best of both worlds.

Make ahead

This dish can be partially prepared before it is cooked. Complete Steps 1 and 2. Cover and refrigerate broth for up to 2 days. When you're ready to cook, continue with the recipe.

● **Works in slow cookers from 3 1/2 to 6 quarts**

4	slices bacon	4
2	onions, finely chopped	2
2	stalks celery, thinly sliced	2
1	can (28 oz/796 mL) tomatoes, including juice, chopped	1
1 cup	bottled clam juice	250 mL
1 cup	water or dry white wine	250 mL
2	potatoes, diced	2
2 1/2 lbs	clams, cleaned (see Tips, below)	1.25 kg
1/2 cup	whipping (35%) cream	125 mL
	Finely chopped fresh parsley	

1. In a skillet, cook bacon over medium-high heat until crisp. Drain well on paper towel and crumble. Cover and refrigerate until ready to use. Drain all but 1 tbsp (15 mL) fat from pan.

2. Reduce heat to medium. Add onions and celery to pan and cook, stirring, until softened, about 5 minutes. Add tomatoes with juice, clam juice and water and bring to boil. Transfer to slow cooker stoneware.

3. Add potatoes and stir well. Cover and cook on Low for 8 hours or on High for 4 hours, until potatoes are tender.

4. Discard any clams that are open. In a large saucepan over medium-high heat, bring 1/2 cup (125 mL) water to a rapid boil. Add clams, cover and cook, shaking the pot until all the clams open. Discard any that do not open. Strain cooking liquid through a fine sieve into a bowl. Using a fork, remove clam meat from shells. Add clam cooking liquid and meat to slow cooker along with cream and reserved bacon. Cover and cook on High for 15 minutes, until heated through. Ladle soup into bowls and garnish liberally with parsley.

TIPS
● To clean clams, scrub thoroughly with a wire brush and soak in several changes of cold salted water.
● Substitute 2 cans (each 5 oz/142 g) baby clams, drained and rinsed, for the fresh clams, if desired.

Seafood Jambalaya

Like its Spanish relative, paella, Jambalaya is an ever-changing mixture depending upon the cook's whim and the available ingredients. This recipe uses Italian sausage, instead of the more traditional ham or andouille and produces a medium-spicy result. For more heat, add a hot pepper along with the shrimp. For a more authentic Jambalaya, substitute thinly sliced andouille, a Louisiana smoked sausage, for the hot Italian sausage. Since andouille is quite strongly flavored, I suggest using only 8 oz (250 g). Add, along with the shrimp, without browning.

Make ahead

This dish can be partially prepared before it is cooked. Complete Steps 1 and 2. Cover and refrigerate sausage and vegetable mixtures separately for up to 2 days. Cook, peel and devein shrimp and refrigerate overnight. The next day, combine sausage and vegetables in slow cooker stoneware and continue with the recipe.

• **Works best in a large (minimum 5 quart) slow cooker**

1 tbsp	vegetable oil	15 mL
1 lb	mild Italian sausage, casings removed	500 g
2	onions, finely chopped	2
2	stalks celery, cut into ¼ -inch (0.5 cm) dice	2
4	cloves garlic, finely chopped	4
1 tsp	salt	5 mL
1 tsp	dried thyme leaves	5 mL
1 tsp	dried oregano leaves	5 mL
½ tsp	cracked black peppercorns	2 mL
1	bay leaf	1
2 cups	chicken stock	500 mL
1	can (28 oz/796 mL) tomatoes, including juice, chopped (see Tips, page 34)	1
8 oz	skinless, boneless chicken breasts or thighs, cut into 1-inch (2.5 cm) cubes	250 g
2 cups	long-grain rice, preferably parboiled	500 mL
1 lb	medium shrimp, cooked, peeled and deveined (see Tip, page 195)	500 g
2 tbsp	Worcestershire sauce	25 mL
1	hot banana pepper or long red or green chile, finely chopped, optional	1

1. In a skillet, heat oil over medium-high heat for 30 seconds. Add sausage and cook, breaking up with a spoon, until no longer pink, about 10 minutes. Using a slotted spoon, transfer to slow cooker stoneware. Drain all but 1 tbsp (15 mL) fat from pan.

2. Reduce heat to medium. Add onions and celery and cook, stirring, until softened, about 5 minutes. Add garlic, salt, thyme, oregano and peppercorns and cook, stirring, for 1 minute. Add bay leaf, chicken stock and tomatoes with juice and bring to a boil. Transfer to slow cooker.

3. Add chicken and rice and stir well. Place two clean tea towels, each folded in half (so you will have four layers), across the top of the stoneware to absorb moisture. Cover and cook on Low for 6 to 8 hours or on High for 3 to 4 hours. Stir in shrimp, Worcestershire sauce and hot pepper, if using. Cover and cook on High for 20 to 30 minutes, or until shrimp are heated through. Discard bay leaf and serve.

Savory Vegetable Stew with Chili-Crusted Halibut

SERVES 4 TO 6

This tasty stew is a meal in itself. All it needs is crusty bread to soak up the sauce.

Make ahead

This dish can be partially prepared before it is cooked. Complete Step 1. Cover and refrigerate for up to 2 days. When you're ready to cook, continue with the recipe.

- **Works in slow cookers from 3½ to 6 quarts**

1 tbsp	vegetable oil	15 mL
2	onions, finely chopped	2
2	carrots, peeled and finely chopped	2
1 tsp	dried oregano leaves	5 mL
1 tsp	salt	5 mL
½ tsp	cracked black peppercorns	2 mL
2 cups	bottled clam juice	500 mL
2 cups	dry white wine	500 mL
2 cups	water	500 mL
1 tbsp	freshly squeezed lime juice	15 mL
2	potatoes, cut into ¼-inch (0.5 cm) dice	2
1	green bell pepper, chopped	1
1 cup	buttermilk (see Tip, below)	250 mL
½ cup	cornmeal	125 mL
1 tsp	chili powder	5 mL
1½ lbs	halibut fillets, cut into ½-inch (1 cm) squares	750 g
2 tbsp	vegetable oil	25 mL

1. In a skillet, heat 1 tbsp (15 mL) oil over medium heat for 30 seconds. Add onions and carrots and cook, stirring, until carrots are softened, about 7 minutes. Add oregano, salt and peppercorns and cook, stirring, for 1 minute. Transfer to slow cooker stoneware. Add clam juice, white wine, water and lime juice.

2. Add potatoes to stoneware and stir well. Cover and cook on Low for 8 to 10 hours or on High for 4 to 5 hours, until vegetables are tender. Stir in green pepper and buttermilk. Cover and cook on High for 20 minutes or until pepper is soft.

3. In a plastic bag, combine cornmeal and chili powder. Add halibut and toss until evenly coated. In a skillet, heat 2 tbsp (25 mL) oil over medium-high heat for 30 seconds. Add fish, in batches as necessary, and sauté, turning once, until nicely browned and fish flakes easily when pierced with a knife. Discard any excess cornmeal mixture. Place fish in bowl. Ladle stew over top.

TIP
- If you don't have buttermilk, mix ¾ cup (175 mL) milk with 3 tbsp (45 mL) sour cream.

Portuguese Sausage and Shellfish Stew

SERVES 6

This robust Portuguese-inspired dish is easy to make yet produces impressive results. I like to serve this with a big green salad, hot Portuguese cornbread and a crisp white wine.

Make ahead

This dish can be partially prepared before it is cooked. Complete Step 1. Cover and refrigerate mixture for up to 2 days. When you're ready to cook, continue with the recipe.

- **Works best in a large (minimum 5 quart) slow cooker**

1 lb	soft chorizo sausage, removed from casings	500 g
1	onion, finely chopped	1
4	stalks celery, thinly sliced	4
4	cloves garlic, minced	4
¼ tsp	salt	1 mL
¼ tsp	cracked black peppercorns	1 mL
1 tsp	saffron threads, soaked in 1 tbsp (15 mL) boiling water, optional	5 mL
2 cups	dry white wine	500 mL
1	can (14 oz/398 mL) diced tomatoes, including juice	1
½ cup	bottled clam juice	125 mL
½ cup	water	125 mL
1 tsp	paprika, preferably smoked	5 mL
1	green bell pepper, finely chopped	1
1 lb	medium shrimp, cooked, shelled and deveined (see Tip, page 195)	500 g
12	clams (see Tips, below)	12
	Finely chopped fresh parsley	

1. In a skillet, cook chorizo, onion and celery over medium heat, until sausage is no longer pink, about 10 minutes. Add garlic, salt, peppercorns and saffron, if using, and cook, stirring, for 1 minute. Using a slotted spoon, transfer to slow cooker stoneware. Add wine, tomatoes with juice, clam juice and water and stir well.

2. Cover and cook on Low for 6 hours or on High for 3 hours.

3. Add paprika, green pepper and shrimp and stir to combine. Cover and cook on High for 20 minutes. Meanwhile, discard any clams that are open. In a large saucepan over medium-high heat, bring ½ cup (125 mL) cooking liquid from stew to a rapid boil. Add clams, cover and cook, shaking the pot until all the clams open. Discard any that do not open. Return clams with liquid to stew. Garnish liberally with parsley and serve in big bowls.

TIPS
- If using fresh clams, clean them first by scrubbing thoroughly with a wire brush and soaking in several changes of cold salted water.
- If desired, substitute 2 cans (each 5 oz/142 g) baby clams, drained and rinsed, for the fresh clams. Stir into stew along with the shrimp.

Poached Salmon

*Although I love
salmon cooked almost
any way, poaching
produces the moistest
result. The problem is,
successfully poaching
a large piece of salmon
used to require a fish
poacher, a piece of
kitchen equipment
that was rarely used
yet relatively costly
and cumbersome to
store. A large oval slow
cooker is the ideal
solution. It produces
great results with
little fuss. Serve
poached salmon, warm
or cold, as the focus
of an elegant buffet
or dinner, attractively
garnished with sliced
lemon and sprigs of
parsley or dill and
accompany with your
favorite sauce.*

Make ahead

You can make the
poaching liquid before
you intend to cook.
Cover and refrigerate
for up to 2 days.

- **Works best in a large (minimum 5 quart) oval slow cooker**

Poaching Liquid

6 cups	water	1.5 L
1	onion, chopped	1
2	stalks celery, chopped, or 1/2 tsp (2 mL) celery seeds	2
4	sprigs parsley	4
1/2 cup	white wine or freshly squeezed lemon juice	125 mL
8	whole black peppercorns	8
1	bay leaf	1

Salmon

1	fillet of salmon (about 3 lbs/1.5 kg)	1
	Lemon slices	
	Sprigs fresh parsley or dill	

1. *Poaching Liquid:* In a saucepan, combine water, onion, celery, parsley, white wine, peppercorns and bay leaf over medium heat. Bring to a boil and simmer for 30 minutes. Strain and discard solids.

2. *Salmon:* Preheat slow cooker on High for 15 minutes. Fold a 2-foot (60 cm) piece of foil in half lengthwise. Place on bottom and up sides of stoneware, allowing it to overhang the casing a bit. Lay salmon over foil strip. Return poaching liquid to a boil and pour over salmon (see Tips, below). Cover and cook on High for 1 hour. Remove stoneware from slow cooker. Allow salmon to cool in stoneware for 20 minutes. If serving cold, place stoneware in refrigerator and allow salmon to chill in liquid. When cold, lift out and transfer to a platter. If serving hot, lift out and transfer to a platter. Garnish with lemon slices and sprigs of parsley and serve.

TIPS

- Make sure that the salmon is completely covered with the poaching liquid. If you do not have sufficient liquid, add water to cover.
- When the salmon is cooked, it should feel firm to the touch and the skin should peel off easily.

Halibut in Indian-Spiced Tomato Sauce

SERVES 4 TO 6

This robust fish recipe is almost a meal in itself. I like to serve it with fresh green beans and naan, an Indian bread, to soak up the sauce.

Make ahead

This dish can be partially prepared before it is cooked. Complete Step 1. Cover and refrigerate for up to 2 days. When you're ready to cook, continue with the recipe.

• **Works in slow cookers from 3½ to 6 quarts**

2 tbsp	vegetable oil, divided	25 mL
2	onions, finely chopped	2
2	cloves garlic, minced	2
½ tsp	minced gingerroot	2 mL
2	whole cloves	2
2	white or green cardamom pods	2
1	cinnamon stick piece (2 inches/5 cm)	1
½ tsp	caraway seeds	2 mL
1 tsp	salt	5 mL
½ tsp	cracked black peppercorns	2 mL
1	can (28 oz/796 mL) tomatoes, including juice, coarsely chopped	1
2	potatoes, peeled and diced	2
1	long green chile pepper, seeded and finely chopped	1
¼ cup	all-purpose flour	50 mL
1 tsp	turmeric	5 mL
½ tsp	ground coriander	2 mL
¼ tsp	cayenne pepper	1 mL
1½ lbs	halibut fillets, cut into 1-inch (2.5 cm) squares	750 g

1. In a skillet, heat 1 tbsp (15 mL) of the oil over medium heat for 30 seconds. Add onions and cook, stirring, until softened, about 3 minutes. Add garlic, gingerroot, cloves, cardamom, cinnamon stick, caraway seeds, salt and peppercorns and cook, stirring, for 1 minute. Add tomatoes with juice and bring to a boil. Transfer to slow cooker stoneware.

2. Add potatoes and stir well. Cover and cook on Low for 8 to 10 hours or on High for 4 to 5 hours, until potatoes are tender. Stir in chile pepper.

3. On a plate, mix together flour, turmeric, coriander and cayenne. Roll halibut in mixture until lightly coated. Discard excess flour. In a skillet, heat remaining oil over medium-high heat for 30 seconds. Add dredged halibut and sauté, in batches if necessary, stirring, until fish is nicely browned and cooked to desired doneness. Spoon tomato mixture into a serving dish and layer halibut on top.

Shrimp Creole

This classic Louisiana dish needs only fluffy white rice, a green salad and hot crusty bread to make a delicious meal. For a special treat, add crisp white wine.

Make ahead

This dish can be partially prepared, in stages, before it is cooked. Complete Step 1. Cover and refrigerate mixture for up to 2 days. Chop parsley, zest lemon and slice green pepper. Cover and refrigerate overnight. Cook shrimp. Peel and devein and refrigerate overnight. The next day, continue with the recipe.

● **Works in slow cookers from 3½ to 6 quarts**

1 tbsp	vegetable oil	15 mL
1	onion, finely chopped	1
4	stalks celery, cut into ¼-inch (0.5 cm) dice	4
2	cloves garlic, minced	2
1 tsp	dried oregano leaves	5 mL
½ tsp	dried thyme leaves	2 mL
½ tsp	salt	2 mL
½ tsp	cracked black peppercorns	2 mL
1	can (28 oz/796 mL) tomatoes, drained and chopped (see Tips, page 34)	1
½ cup	fish stock, bottled clam juice or white wine	125 mL
¼ cup	finely chopped parsley	50 mL
	Grated zest of 1 lemon	
1 tbsp	Worcestershire sauce	15 mL
1 lb	medium shrimp, cooked, peeled and deveined (see Tip, below)	500 g
1	green bell pepper, thinly sliced	1
½ to 1	long red or green chile pepper, finely chopped (see Tip, page 86)	½ to 1
	Hot cooked rice	

1. In a skillet, heat oil over medium heat for 30 seconds. Add onion and celery and cook, stirring, until softened, about 5 minutes. Add garlic, oregano, thyme, salt and peppercorns and cook, stirring, for 1 minute. Add tomatoes and stock and bring to a boil. Transfer to slow cooker stoneware.

2. Cover and cook on Low for 6 to 8 hours or on High for 3 to 4 hours, until hot and bubbly. Add parsley, lemon zest and Worcestershire sauce and stir. Add shrimp, green pepper and chile pepper and stir thoroughly. Cover and cook on High for 20 minutes, or until peppers are soft and shrimp are heated through. Serve over hot rice.

TIP

● To prepare shrimp for this recipe, immerse shrimp, in shells, in a large pot of boiling salted water. Cook over High heat, until the shells turn pink, about 2 to 3 minutes. Drain and let cool, then peel and devein.

Mussels in Lemongrass Tomato Broth

SERVES 4 AS A MAIN COURSE OR 6 AS A STARTER

This is a variation of a recipe that appeared in New World Noodles by Bill Jones and Stephen Wong. I particularly enjoy the unusual and slightly Indonesian flavors of the delicious broth. This works equally well as the centerpiece of a light meal or as a dramatic first course.

Make ahead

This dish can be partially prepared before it is cooked. Complete Step 1. Cover and refrigerate broth for up to 2 days. When you're ready to cook, continue with the recipe.

- **Works in slow cookers from 3½ to 6 quarts**

1 tbsp	vegetable oil	15 mL
1	onion, finely chopped	1
2	cloves garlic, minced	2
1 tsp	gingerroot, minced	5 mL
1 tsp	whole coriander seeds	5 mL
1	cinnamon stick piece (2 inches/5 cm)	1
1	stalk lemongrass, coarsely chopped	1
½ tsp	salt	2 mL
½ tsp	whole black peppercorns	2 mL
1	can (28 oz/796 mL) tomatoes, including juice, chopped	1
2 cups	vegetable stock, or 1 cup (250 mL) bottled clam juice mixed with 1 cup (250 mL) water	500 mL
3 lbs	mussels, cleaned (see Tip, below)	1.5 kg
	Finely chopped cilantro	
	Hot pepper sauce, optional	

1. In a skillet, heat oil over medium heat for 30 seconds. Add onion and cook, stirring, until softened, about 3 minutes. Add garlic, gingerroot, coriander seeds, cinnamon stick, lemongrass, salt and peppercorns and cook, stirring, for 1 minute. Add tomatoes with juice and vegetable stock and bring to a boil. Transfer to slow cooker stoneware.

2. Cover and cook on Low for 8 to 10 hours or on High for 4 to 5 hours, until broth is flavorful. Strain broth through a fine-mesh strainer into a large saucepan, pressing out liquid with a wooden spoon. Discard solids.

3. Bring broth to a boil. Add mussels, cover and cook until mussels open. Discard any that do not open. Ladle mussels and broth into bowls, garnish with cilantro and serve. Pass hot pepper sauce, if desired.

TIP

- Farmed mussels are very clean and only need to be thoroughly rinsed under water before use in this recipe. If the mussels are not farmed, they will need to be carefully scrubbed with a wire brush under cold running water. Any fibrous beard should be trimmed with a sharp knife. The mussels should be tightly closed, or they should close when you tap them. If not, discard before cooking. Discard any that do not open after they are cooked.

Snapper Vera Cruz

SERVES 4

This traditional Mexican recipe has many variations. Most often, filleted fish is fried and covered with a sauce that is cooked separately. For this slow cooker version, I've sliced the fish very thinly and poached it in the sauce during the last 20 minutes of cooking. For an authentic Mexican touch, serve with hot tortillas to soak up the sauce. Feel free to use any firm white fish instead of snapper.

Make ahead

This dish can be partially prepared before it is cooked. Complete Step 1. Cover and refrigerate mixture for up to 2 days. When you're ready to cook, continue with the recipe.

● **Works in slow cookers from 3½ to 6 quarts**

1 tbsp	vegetable oil	15 mL
1	onion, finely chopped	1
2	cloves garlic, minced	2
½ tsp	dried oregano leaves	2 mL
¼ tsp	ground cinnamon	1 mL
⅛ tsp	ground cloves	0.5 mL
1	can (28 oz/796 mL) tomatoes, drained and chopped (see Tips, page 34)	1
½ cup	fish stock or bottled clam juice	125 mL
1½ lbs	skinless snapper fillets, cut in half lengthwise and sliced as thinly as possible on the horizontal	750 g
1 to 2	jalapeño peppers, finely chopped	1 to 2
2 tbsp	freshly squeezed lemon juice	25 mL
1 tbsp	drained capers	15 mL
10	olives, pitted and thinly sliced	10
	Hot tortillas, optional	

1. In a skillet, heat oil over medium heat for 30 seconds. Add onion and cook, stirring, until softened, about 3 minutes. Add garlic, oregano, cinnamon and cloves and cook, stirring, for 1 minute. Add tomatoes and stock and bring to a boil. Transfer to slow cooker stoneware.

2. Cover and cook on Low for 6 hours or on High for 3 hours, until hot and bubbly. Stir in fish, jalapeño peppers and lemon juice. Cover and cook on High for 20 minutes, or until fish is cooked through. Stir in capers and pour mixture onto a deep platter. Garnish with olives and serve with hot tortillas, if desired.

Luscious Fish Chowder

This recipe makes a nicely peppery chowder, but if you're heat averse, omit the cayenne. Although you can make an acceptable soup using water, clam juice or a good fish stock produce better results. I make mine with whipping cream because I prefer a richer chowder, but milk works well, too.

Make ahead

This chowder can be partially prepared before it is cooked. Complete Steps 1 and 2. Cover and refrigerate for up to 2 days. When you're ready to cook, continue with the recipe.

- **Works in slow cookers from 3½ to 6 quarts**

2	slices bacon, chopped	2
3	leeks, white part only, cleaned and thinly sliced (see Tips, page 202)	3
3	stalks celery, thinly sliced	3
½ tsp	dried thyme leaves	2 mL
2 tbsp	all-purpose flour	25 mL
5 cups	fish stock or water or 2 cups (500 mL) bottled clam juice diluted with 3 cups (750 mL) water	1.25 L
1	bay leaf	1
1	medium potato, cut into ½-inch (1 cm) cubes	1
¼ tsp	cayenne pepper, or to taste (see Tip, below)	1 mL
1 cup	milk or whipping (35%) cream	250 mL
2 lbs	skinless firm white fish fillets, such as halibut or snapper, cut into 1-inch (2.5 cm) cubes	1 kg
	Finely chopped parsley or chives	

1. In a skillet, cook bacon over medium-high heat, until crisp. Using a slotted spoon, remove and drain on paper towel. Cover and refrigerate until ready to use. Drain all but 1 tbsp (15 mL) fat from pan.

2. Reduce heat to medium. Add leeks and celery and cook, stirring, until softened, about 5 minutes. Stir in thyme and flour and cook, stirring, for 1 minute. Add stock and bay leaf. Bring to a boil and cook, stirring, until slightly thickened. Transfer mixture to slow cooker stoneware.

3. Add potato and stir. Cover and cook on Low for 8 to 10 hours or on High for 4 to 5 hours, until vegetables are tender.

4. Stir in cayenne. Add milk, fish and reserved bacon. Cover and cook on High for 30 minutes, or until fish is cooked through. Discard bay leaf. Ladle into individual bowls and garnish liberally with parsley.

TIP

- If you prefer, substitute 1 finely chopped fresh chile, such as jalapeño or cayenne, for the ground cayenne.

Sweet Potato Lasagna (page 218)

Meatless Mains

Cheesy Fennel and Leek Bake

SERVES 4

This Mediterranean-inspired dish is delightfully different and equally delicious over hot polenta, mashed potatoes or a white bean purée (see Tip, page 266).

Make ahead

This dish can be partially prepared before it is cooked. Complete Step 1. Cover and refrigerate for up to 2 days. When you're ready to cook, continue with the recipe.

• **Works in slow cookers from 3 1/2 to 6 quarts**

1 tbsp	vegetable oil (approx.)	15 mL
2	bulbs fennel, cored, leafy stems discarded, and sliced on the vertical	2
3	leeks, white part with a bit of green, cleaned and thinly sliced (see Tips, below)	3
4	cloves garlic, minced	4
2 tsp	dried Italian seasoning	10 mL
1 tsp	salt, or to taste	5 mL
1/2 tsp	cracked black peppercorns	2 mL
1	can (14 oz/398 mL) diced tomatoes, including juice (see Tips, below)	1
1 cup	shredded Italian cheese, such as mozzarella or Fontina, or a prepared mix of shredded Italian cheeses	250 mL

1. In a skillet, heat oil over medium-high heat for 30 seconds. Add fennel, in batches, and cook, stirring, until lightly browned, about 5 minutes per batch. Transfer to slow cooker stoneware. Reduce heat to medium and add more oil to pan, if necessary. Add leeks and cook, stirring, until softened, about 5 minutes. Add garlic, Italian seasoning, salt and peppercorns and cook, stirring, for 1 minute. Add tomatoes with juice and bring to a boil. Transfer to slow cooker stoneware.

2. Cover and cook on Low for 6 hours or High for 3 hours, until fennel is tender. Stir in cheese. Cover and cook on High for 15 minutes, until cheese is melted and mixture is bubbly.

TIPS
• To clean leeks: Fill sink full of lukewarm water. Split leeks in half lengthwise and submerge in water, swishing them around to remove all traces of dirt. Transfer to a colander and rinse under cold water.
• If you don't have a 14 oz (398 mL) can of diced tomatoes, use 2 cups (500 mL) canned tomatoes with juice, coarsely chopped.

Sweet Potatoes and Carrots with Chickpea Topping

SERVES 4

This tasty and nutritious combination of sweet potatoes, carrots and pineapple, finished with a chickpea topping makes a delightfully different main course. Refrigerate any leftovers and transform them into an interesting side dish. Simply purée in a food processor fitted with a metal blade, then reheat in the microwave or over low heat on the stovetop.

Make ahead

This dish can be partially prepared the night before it is cooked. Complete Steps 1 and 2. Cover and refrigerate overnight. The next morning, continue with the recipe.

- **Works best in a large (minimum 5 quart) slow cooker**
- **Greased slow cooker stoneware**

2	sweet potatoes (each about 8 oz/250 g), peeled and cut into ½-inch (1 cm) cubes	2
6	carrots, peeled and thinly sliced	6
1	can (14 oz/398 mL) crushed pineapple, drained, ¼ cup (50 mL) juice reserved	1
2 tbsp	packed brown sugar	25 mL
Topping		
2 cups	cooked dried or canned chickpeas, drained and rinsed (see Basic Beans, page 219)	500 mL
1 tbsp	minced garlic	15 mL
½ cup	vegetable stock	125 mL
	Salt and freshly ground pepper	

1. In prepared stoneware, combine sweet potato, carrots and pineapple. In a small bowl, combine brown sugar and reserved pineapple juice. Add to stoneware and stir to blend.

2. *Topping:* In a food processor fitted with a metal blade, process chickpeas, garlic and vegetable stock until mixture is well combined but chickpeas are still a little chunky. Season to taste with salt and pepper. Spread mixture evenly over sweet potato mixture.

3. Cover and cook on Low for 8 hours or on High for 4 hours until vegetables are tender.

Tofu in Indian-Spiced Tomato Sauce

SERVES 4 TO 6

This robust dish makes a lively and different meal. I like to serve it with fresh green beans and naan, an Indian bread, to soak up the sauce.

Make ahead

This dish can be partially prepared before it is cooked. Complete Step 1. Cover and refrigerate for up to 2 days. When you're ready to cook, continue with the recipe.

• *Works in slow cookers from 3 1/2 to 6 quarts*

1 tbsp	vegetable oil	15 mL
2	onions, finely chopped	2
2	cloves garlic, minced	2
1/2 tsp	minced gingerroot	2 mL
6	whole cloves	6
4	pods white or green cardamom	4
1	cinnamon stick piece (2 inches/5 cm)	1
1 tsp	caraway seeds	5 mL
1 tsp	salt	5 mL
1/2 tsp	cracked black peppercorns	2 mL
1	can (28 oz/796 mL) tomatoes, including juice, coarsely chopped	1
1	long green chile pepper, seeded and finely chopped	1

Tofu

1/4 cup	all-purpose flour	50 mL
1 tsp	curry powder	5 mL
1/4 tsp	cayenne pepper	1 mL
8 oz	firm tofu, cut into 1-inch (2.5 cm) squares	250 g
1 tbsp	vegetable oil	15 mL

1. In a skillet, heat oil over medium heat for 30 seconds. Add onions and cook, stirring, until softened, about 3 minutes. Add garlic, gingerroot, cloves, cardamom, cinnamon stick, caraway seeds, salt and peppercorns and cook, stirring, for I minute. Add tomatoes with juice and bring to a boil. Transfer to slow cooker stoneware.

2. Cover and cook on Low for 8 hours or on High for 4 hours, until hot and bubbly. Stir in chile pepper.

3. *Tofu:* On a plate, mix together flour, curry powder and cayenne. Roll tofu in mixture until lightly coated. Discard excess flour mixture. In a skillet, heat oil over medium-high heat for 30 seconds. Add dredged tofu and sauté, stirring, until nicely browned. Spoon tomato mixture into a serving dish. Discard cloves, cardamom and cinnamon stick. Layer tofu on top.

Vegetable Stroganoff

SERVES 6

This robust stew makes a delicious dinner with a salad and crusty bread. You can also serve it over hot noodles.

Make ahead

This dish can be partially prepared before it is cooked. Complete Step 1. Cover and refrigerate for up to 2 days. When you're ready to cook, continue with the recipe.

• **Works best in a large (minimum 5 quart) slow cooker**

1 tbsp	butter, divided	15 mL
2	large leeks, white part only, cleaned and thinly sliced (see Tips, page 202)	2
4	stalks celery, thinly sliced	4
2	cloves garlic, minced	2
1 tsp	dried thyme leaves	5 mL
1 tsp	cracked black peppercorns	5 mL
1 tsp	salt	5 mL
1	can (28 oz/796 mL) tomatoes, including juice, coarsely chopped	1
1 cup	vegetable stock	250 mL
1 lb	portobello or cremini mushrooms, stems removed and sliced (see Tips, below)	500 g
2 to 3	potatoes, peeled and cut into 1/2-inch (1 cm) cubes	2 to 3
1/4 cup	whipping (35%) cream	50 mL
3 oz	good-quality blue cheese, crumbled, and at room temperature (see Tips, below)	90 g

1. In a skillet, melt butter over medium heat. Add leeks and celery and cook, stirring, until softened, about 5 minutes. Add garlic, thyme, peppercorns and salt and cook, stirring, for I minute. Add tomatoes with juice and vegetable stock and bring to a boil. Transfer to slow cooker stoneware.

2. Stir in mushrooms and potatoes. Cover and cook on Low for 8 to 10 hours or on High for 4 to 5 hours, until potatoes are tender. Stir in cream and cheese. Cover and cook on High for 15 minutes, or until cheese is melted into sauce and mixture is hot and bubbly.

TIPS
- If you're using portobello mushrooms, discard the stem, cut them into quarters and thinly slice. If you're using cremini mushrooms, trim off the tough end of the stem and cut them into quarters. Save the stems for making vegetable stock.
- Use only good-quality blue cheese such as Maytag or Italian Gorgonzola for this recipe as blue cheese of lesser quality tends to be very harsh.
- If you are in a hurry, warm the cream and cheese, before adding to the stoneware. Stir in and serve as soon as the cheese melts.

Coconut-Braised Carrots with Cashews and Peas

SERVES 6 TO 8

Here's a recipe that takes a classic combination — peas and carrots — and gives it an exotic twist with the addition of cumin, ginger, cashews, a hint of chile and coconut milk, among other ingredients. The results are deliciously different. I like to serve this as a main course, over brown basmati rice, accompanied by a tossed green salad, but it also makes an excellent side dish.

Make ahead

This dish can be partially prepared before it is cooked. Complete Steps 1 and 2. Cover and refrigerate cashews and onion mixture separately for up to 2 days. When you're ready to cook, continue with the recipe.

- **Works in slow cookers from $3\frac{1}{2}$ to 6 quarts**

1 tbsp	olive oil	15 mL
½ cup	raw cashews	125 mL
1	onion, finely chopped	1
2	cloves garlic, minced	2
1 tsp	cumin seeds, toasted and ground	5 mL
½ tsp	fennel seeds, toasted and ground (see Tip, below)	2 mL
½ tsp	each salt and cracked black peppercorns	2 mL
6	large carrots, peeled and thinly sliced	6
⅔ cup	coconut milk	150 mL
2 tsp	minced gingerroot	10 mL
½ tsp	turmeric	2 mL
2 cups	frozen peas, thawed	500 mL
1	long green or red chile pepper, minced,	1
¼ cup	finely chopped cilantro leaves	50 mL

1. In a skillet, heat oil over medium heat for 30 seconds. Add cashews and cook, stirring, until they begin to brown, about 2 minutes. Remove from heat and, using a slotted spoon, transfer cashews to a blender or food processor. Set aside.

2. Add onion to pan and cook, stirring, until softened, about 3 minutes. Add garlic, toasted cumin and fennel, salt and peppercorns and cook, stirring, for 1 minute. Transfer to stoneware. Stir in carrots.

3. Add coconut milk, gingerroot and turmeric to cashews in food processor or blender and process until smooth, about 2 minutes. Spoon mixture into stoneware. Add ¼ cup (50 mL) water to food processor and blend until any remaining mixture falls to the bottom and is well incorporated. (If you are using a blender you may need more water.) Pour over carrots and stir well.

4. Cover and cook on Low for 6 hours or on High for 3 hours, until carrots are tender. Stir in peas and chile pepper. Cover and cook on High for 20 minutes, until peas are tender and mixture is hot. Sprinkle with cilantro and serve.

TIP

- In a dry skillet over medium heat, toast cumin and fennel seeds, stirring, until fragrant and cumin seeds just begin to brown, about 3 minutes. Immediately transfer to a mortar or a spice grinder and grind.

Onion-Braised Potatoes with Spinach

SERVES 8

Served with brown rice and a salad, this tasty braise makes a great weeknight dinner. It also works well as part of a multi-dish Indian meal.

Make ahead

This dish can be partially prepared before it is cooked. Complete Step 1. Cover and refrigerate for up to 2 days. When you're ready to cook, continue with the recipe.

• **Works best in a large (minimum 5 quart) slow cooker**

1 tbsp	olive oil	15 mL
4	onions, thinly sliced on the vertical	4
4	cloves garlic, minced	4
1 tbsp	minced gingerroot	15 mL
1 tbsp	cumin seeds, toasted and ground (see Tip, page 178)	15 mL
1 tsp	salt	5 mL
1 tsp	cracked black peppercorns	5 mL
2	black cardamom pods, crushed	2
1	can (14 oz/398 mL) diced tomatoes, including juice (see Tips, page 202)	1
1 cup	vegetable stock	250 mL
2 lbs	new potatoes, scrubbed and quartered (about 24 potatoes)	1 kg
1 lb	fresh spinach, stems removed, or 1 package (10 oz/300 g) spinach leaves, thawed if frozen (see Tips, page 22)	500 g
1/4 tsp	cayenne pepper	1 mL
2 tbsp	freshly squeezed lemon juice	25 mL

1. In a skillet, heat oil over medium heat for 30 seconds. Add onions and cook, stirring, until softened, about 3 minutes. Add garlic, gingerroot, toasted cumin, salt, peppercorns and cardamom and cook, stirring, for 1 minute. Add tomatoes with juice and vegetable stock and bring to a boil. Transfer to slow cooker stoneware.

2. Add potatoes and stir well. Cover and cook on Low for 8 hours or on High for 4 hours, until potatoes are tender. Discard cardamom pods. Add spinach, in batches, stirring after each batch until all the leaves are submerged in the liquid. In a small bowl, dissolve cayenne in lime juice. Add to slow cooker and stir well. Cover and cook on High for 10 minutes, until spinach is wilted and flavors have melded.

TIP

• This dish cooks for longer than most vegetarian dishes because it contains potatoes, which, unless they are diced, take a long time to cook in the slow cooker. New potatoes cook more quickly than mature potatoes, but before adding the final ingredients in this recipe check to make sure the potatoes are tender. If not, continue cooking until the potatoes are cooked, increasing the temperature to High, if necessary.

Potatoes with Creamy Corn Topping

SERVES 6 TO 8

This dish reminds me of scalloped potatoes, a childhood favorite, dressed up to become a main course. It's much lighter and more nutritious than that old favorite and has an abundance of interesting flavors. Add a green salad or crisp green beans, sprinkled with toasted sesame seeds to complete the meal.

Make ahead

This dish can be partially prepared before it is cooked. Complete Steps 1 through 3. Cover and refrigerate corn and tomato mixtures separately overnight. The next morning, continue with the recipe.

- **Works best in a large (minimum 5 quart) slow cooker**
- **Greased slow cooker stoneware**

4 cups	corn kernels, thawed if frozen	1 L
½ cup	evaporated milk	125 mL
1 tbsp	butter	15 mL
½ tsp	freshly grated nutmeg	2 mL
	Freshly ground black pepper	
1 cup	shredded mozzarella	250 mL
1	can (28 oz/796 mL) tomatoes, including juice	1
½ cup	loosely packed parsley leaves	125 mL
1 tsp	salt	5 mL
4	medium potatoes, thinly sliced, preferably with a mandoline (see Tip, below)	4
1	red onion, halved and thinly sliced on the vertical	1

1. In a food processor, combine corn and evaporated milk. Process until combined, but corn is still a little chunky.

2. In a skillet, melt butter over medium-low heat. Add corn mixture and cook, stirring, until thickened, about 5 minutes. Add nutmeg, pepper, to taste, and mozzarella and stir until cheese is melted. Set aside.

3. Rinse out food processor work bowl. Add tomatoes with juice, parsley and salt and process until smooth.

4. Spread potatoes evenly over bottom of prepared slow cooker stoneware. Spread red onion over top and cover with tomato mixture.

5. Spread corn mixture evenly over top of tomato mixture. Cover and cook on Low for 8 hours or High for 4 hours, until potatoes are tender and mixture is hot and bubbly.

TIP
- Because potatoes turn brown on contact with air they shouldn't be sliced until you are ready to cook this dish.

Vegetable Goulash

SERVES 4

This hearty and delicious stew is the perfect pick-me-up after a day in the chilly outdoors. Serve over hot cooked noodles, topped with a dollop of sour cream, if desired. Accompany with dark rye bread and a salad of shredded carrots. For a special occasion, see Variation, below.

Make ahead

This dish can be partially prepared before it is cooked. Complete Steps 1, 2 and 3. Cover and refrigerate for up to 2 days. When you're ready to cook, continue with the recipe.

Variation
Vegetable Pot Pie
If desired, add $\frac{1}{2}$ cup (125 mL) whipping (35%) cream to the cooked goulash. Ladle into a casserole dish or 4 ovenproof ramekins. Top with thawed prepared puff pastry, cut to fit. Bake for 20 to 25 minutes in a 400°F (200°C) oven, until pastry is puffed and browned.

• **Works in slow cookers from $3\frac{1}{2}$ to 6 quarts**

4	dried shiitake mushrooms	4
1 cup	hot water	250 mL
2 tbsp	vegetable oil, divided	25 mL
8 oz	fresh shiitake mushrooms, stems removed and coarsely chopped	250 g
1	onion, finely chopped	1
4	stalks celery, diced	4
2	carrots, peeled and diced	2
2	parsnips, peeled and diced	2
1 tsp	caraway seeds, coarsely crushed	5 mL
$\frac{1}{2}$ tsp	salt	2 mL
$\frac{1}{2}$ tsp	cracked black peppercorns	2 mL
1 tbsp	all-purpose flour	15 mL
2 cups	vegetable stock	500 mL
2 tsp	paprika	10 mL
1	green bell pepper, seeded and diced	1

1. Soak dried mushrooms in hot water for 30 minutes. Drain and pat dry. Cut into quarters.

2. In a skillet, heat 1 tbsp (15 mL) of the oil over medium heat for 30 seconds. Add fresh mushrooms and cook, stirring, for 1 minute. Transfer to slow cooker stoneware.

3. Heat remaining oil in pan. Add onion, celery, carrots and parsnips and cook, stirring, until softened, about 7 minutes. Add caraway seeds, salt, peppercorns and reserved dried shiitake mushrooms and cook, stirring, for 1 minute. Add flour and cook, stirring, for 1 minute. Add stock and cook, stirring, until thickened, about 3 minutes. Transfer to slow cooker stoneware.

4. Cover and cook on Low for 6 hours or on High for 3 hours, until vegetables are tender. Stir in paprika and green pepper. Cover and cook on High, until pepper is soft, about 15 minutes.

Potato and Pea Coconut Curry

SERVES 6

Sweet and white potatoes, cooked in an aromatic sauce, is a simple but very tasty combination. If you have time, finish this curry with either of the Crispy Onion or Crispy Shallot toppings (see Variation, below), which adds delicious flavor and texture to the dish. Serve with warm naan or over hot rice.

Make ahead

This dish can be partially prepared before it is cooked. Complete Step 1. Cover and refrigerate for up to 2 days. When you're ready to cook, continue with the recipe.

Variation
Alternate Toppings
If you want to dress this dish up, substitute Crispy Onion Topping (see Variation, page 216) or Crispy Shallot Topping (see recipe, page 227) for the cilantro garnish.

• *Works in slow cookers from 3½ to 6 quarts*

1 tbsp	vegetable oil	15 mL
2	onions, finely chopped	2
4	cloves garlic, minced	4
1 tbsp	minced gingerroot	15 mL
½ tsp	cracked black peppercorns	2 mL
1 cup	vegetable stock	250 mL
2	large sweet potatoes (each about 8 oz/250 g) peeled and cut into 1-inch (2.5 cm) cubes	2
2	potatoes, peeled and diced	2
2 tsp	Thai red curry paste (see Tips, below)	10 mL
1 cup	coconut milk, divided	250 mL
2 cups	sweet green peas, thawed if frozen	500 mL
	Finely chopped cilantro (see Variations, left)	

1. In a skillet, heat oil over medium heat for 30 seconds. Add onions and cook, stirring, until softened, about 3 minutes. Add garlic, gingerroot and peppercorns and cook, stirring, for 1 minute. Add stock and bring to a boil. Transfer to slow cooker stoneware.

2. Add sweet potatoes and potatoes. Cover and cook on Low for 6 to 8 hours or on High for 3 to 4 hours, until potatoes are tender.

3. In a small bowl, combine curry paste and ¼ cup (50 mL) of the coconut milk. Stir until blended. Add to stoneware along with remaining coconut milk and stir well. Add peas and stir well. Cover and cook on High for 30 minutes, until peas are tender and flavors have melded. Garnish with cilantro.

TIPS
• Some curry pastes contain products such as shrimp paste or fish sauce, so if you're a vegetarian, check the label to ensure that yours is fish- and seafood-free.
• If you're a heat seeker, you can increase the quantity of curry paste, but this quantity is quite enough for me.

Peppery Peas with Sweet Potato

SERVES 4 TO 6

This Indian-inspired dish makes a nice weekday meal served over hot rice or an Indian bread, such as naan, and accompanied by a green salad. Finish it simply, with finely chopped cilantro or with Crispy Onion Topping (see Variation, below).

Make ahead

This dish can be partially prepared before it is cooked. Soak peas overnight according to the long soak method. Complete Step 1. Cover and refrigerate onion mixture overnight. The next morning, continue with the recipe.

Variation

Crispy Onion Topping
Substitute crispy onions for cilantro. Cut 3 onions in half vertically, then cut them vertically into paper-thin slices. In a large skillet, heat 1 tbsp (15 mL) vegetable oil or clarified butter over medium-high heat and cook the onion slices, stirring constantly, until they are crisp and brown, about 10 minutes.

- **Works in slow cookers from 3¹/₂ to 6 quarts**

1 cup	split yellow peas, soaked and drained (see page 219)	250 mL
1 tbsp	olive oil	15 mL
1	onion, finely chopped	1
2	carrots, peeled and chopped	2
4	cloves garlic, minced	4
1 tbsp	minced gingerroot	15 mL
1 tsp	cracked black peppercorns	5 mL
1 tsp	turmeric	5 mL
2 tsp	cumin seeds, toasted and ground	10 mL
1 tsp	coriander seeds, toasted and ground (see Tips, below)	5 mL
1	can (14 oz/398 mL) diced tomatoes, including juice (see Tips, page 202)	1
1 cup	vegetable or chicken stock	250 mL
1	large sweet potato (about 1 lb/500 g) peeled and cut into ¹/₂-inch (1 cm) cubes	1
¹/₂ tsp	cayenne pepper	2 mL
1 tbsp	freshly squeezed lime juice	15 mL
1	green bell pepper, seeded and diced	1
	Finely chopped cilantro	

1. In a skillet, heat oil over medium heat for 30 seconds. Add onion and carrots and cook, stirring, until carrot is softened, about 7 minutes. Add garlic, gingerroot, peppercorns, turmeric, cumin and coriander and cook, stirring, for 1 minute. Add tomatoes with juice and stock and bring to a boil. Transfer to slow cooker.

2. Stir in sweet potato and soaked peas. Cover and cook on High for 5 hours, until peas are tender. In a small bowl, dissolve cayenne in lime juice. Add to slow cooker and stir well. Stir in green pepper. Cover and cook on High for 20 minutes, until green pepper is tender. Garnish with cilantro just before serving.

TIPS

- For convenience substitute 1 tsp (5 mL) ground cumin and ¹/₂ tsp (2 mL) ground coriander for the whole seeds. Add along with the turmeric.
- In a dry skillet over medium heat, toast cumin and coriander seeds, stirring, until fragrant and they just begin to brown, about 3 minutes. Immediately transfer to a mortar or a spice grinder and grind.
- Cooking this recipe on High ensures the split yellow peas will be tender.

Sweet Potato Lasagna

SERVES 6 TO 8

This delicious lasagna is very easy to make. I like to serve it with steamed spinach sprinkled with toasted sesame seeds or a tossed green salad topped with sliced avocado.

Make ahead

This dish can be partially prepared before it is cooked. Complete Steps 1 and 2. Cover and refrigerate overnight. The next morning, continue with the recipe.

- **Works best in a large (minimum 5 quart) oval slow cooker**
- **Greased slow cooker stoneware**

12	brown rice lasagna noodles (see Tips, below)	12
1 tbsp	olive oil	15 mL
4 cups	tomato sauce	1 L
2 cups	ricotta cheese	500 mL
3	medium sweet potatoes, peeled and thinly sliced	3
1 tbsp	dried Italian seasoning	15 mL
2 cups	shredded lower-fat mozzarella cheese	500 mL
¼ cup	freshly grated Parmesan cheese	50 mL

1. Cook lasagna noodles in a pot of boiling salted water, until slightly undercooked, or according to package instructions, undercooking by 2 minutes. Drain, toss with oil and set aside.

2. Spread 1 cup (250 mL) of the tomato sauce over bottom of prepared slow cooker stoneware. Cover with 3 noodles. Spread with one-third each of the ricotta, sweet potatoes and dried Italian seasoning and one-quarter of the tomato sauce and mozzarella. Repeat twice. Cover with final layer of noodles. Pour remaining sauce over top. Sprinkle with remaining mozzarella and the Parmesan cheese.

3. Cover and cook on Low for 6 hours or on High for 3 hours, until sweet potatoes are tender and mixture is hot and bubbly.

TIP

- I've used brown rice noodles in this pasta because they are a gluten-free alternative. If you prefer, substitute whole wheat lasagna noodles, which are higher in fiber, or oven-ready noodles for convenience. If using oven-ready noodles, skip Step 1.

Basic Beans

MAKES APPROXIMATELY 2 CUPS (500 ML) COOKED BEANS (SEE TIPS, BELOW)

Loaded with nutrition and high in fiber, dried beans are one of our most healthful edibles. As a key ingredient in many of our best-loved dishes, they can also be absolutely delicious. The slow cooker excels at turning these unappetizing bullets into potentially sublime fare. It is also extraordinarily convenient — since discovering the slow cooker, I don't cook dried beans any other way. I put presoaked beans into the slow cooker before I go to bed and when I wake up, they are ready for whatever recipe I plan to make.

Variation
Basic Lentils
Cook as above (Step 3) but do not presoak lentils. Just rinse them well and pick out any bits of dirt.

- **Works in slow cookers from 3½ to 6 quarts**

1 cup	dried beans or chickpeas	250 mL
3 cups	water	750 mL

1. *Long soak:* In a bowl, combine beans and water. Soak for at least 6 hours or overnight. Drain and rinse thoroughly with cold water. Beans are now ready for cooking.

2. *Quick soak:* In a pot, combine beans and water. Cover and bring to a boil. Boil for 3 minutes. Turn off heat and soak for 1 hour. Drain and rinse thoroughly under cold water. Beans are now ready to cook.

3. *Cooking:* In slow cooker, combine 1 cup (250 mL) presoaked beans and 3 cups (750 mL) fresh cold water. Season with garlic, bay leaves or a bouquet garni made from your favorite herbs tied together in a cheesecloth, if desired. Season to taste with salt. Cover and cook on Low for 10 to 12 hours or overnight. Drain and rinse. If not using immediately, cover and refrigerate. The beans are now ready for use in your favorite recipe.

TIPS
- This recipe may be doubled or tripled to suit the quantity of beans required for a recipe.
- Once cooked, legumes should be covered and stored in the refrigerator, where they will keep for 4 to 5 days. Cooked legumes can also be frozen in an airtight container. They will keep frozen for up to 6 months.
- In most recipes, 1 can (14 to 19 oz/398 to 540 mL) of beans, drained and rinsed, can be substituted for 1 cup (250 mL) dried beans, soaked, cooked and drained.

Greek Bean Sauce with Feta

SERVES 4 TO 6

This lip-smacking sauce is particularly delicious as a topping for polenta, but it also works well with brown rice and pasta, particularly orzo. If serving it with pasta, use a whole wheat version or boost the nutritional content by adding bulgur (see Variation, below).

Make ahead

This dish can be partially prepared before it is cooked. Complete Step 1. Cover and refrigerate for up to 2 days. When you're ready to cook, continue with the recipe.

Variation

Greek Bean Sauce with Bulgur

If you're serving this sauce with pasta, you can boost the nutritional content by stirring in 2 cups (500 mL) of soaked bulgur before adding the feta and dill.

• **Works in slow cookers from 3½ to 6 quarts**

1 tbsp	olive oil	15 mL
2	onions, diced	2
2	cloves garlic, minced	2
1 tsp	dried oregano leaves, crumbled	5 mL
1 tsp	salt	5 mL
½ tsp	cracked black peppercorns	2 mL
1	cinnamon stick piece (1 inch/2.5 cm) (see Tips, below)	1
1	can (28 oz/796 mL) tomatoes, including juice, coarsely crushed	1
3 cups	frozen sliced green beans	750 mL
1	batch Slow-Cooked Polenta, (see recipe, page 264), optional	1
½ cup	crumbled feta cheese (see Tips, below)	125 mL
¼ cup	finely chopped dill	50 mL

1. In a large skillet, heat oil over medium heat for 30 seconds. Add onions and cook, stirring, until softened, about 3 minutes. Add garlic, oregano, salt, peppercorns and cinnamon stick and cook, stirring, for 1 minute. Add tomatoes with juice, stirring and breaking up with a spoon. Transfer to slow cooker stoneware.

2. Stir in beans. Cover and cook on Low for 6 hours or High for 3 hours, until hot and bubbly. Discard cinnamon stick. To serve, ladle over hot polenta, if using, and sprinkle with feta and dill.

TIPS

• The cinnamon in this recipe adds a lovely note to the sauce but be careful not to overdo it. This is the appropriate amount. More would overwhelm the other flavors.
• Use goat or sheep milk feta in this recipe to suit your preference.

Tagine of Squash and Chickpeas with Mushrooms

SERVES 6

I love the unusual combination of flavorings in this dish, which meld beautifully. The taste of the cinnamon and ginger really come through, and the bittersweet combination of lemon and honey, with a sprinkling of currants adds a perfect finish. Serve this over whole grain couscous to complete the Middle Eastern flavors and provide vegetarians with a complete protein. Add a leafy green vegetable, such as spinach or Swiss chard, to complete the meal.

Make ahead

This dish can be partially prepared before it is cooked. Complete Step 1. Cover and refrigerate for up to 2 days. When you're ready to cook, continue with the recipe.

- **Works in slow cookers from 3½ to 6 quarts**

1 tbsp	olive oil	15 mL
1	onion, finely chopped	1
2	carrots, peeled and diced (about 1 cup/250 mL)	2
4	cloves garlic, minced	4
2 tbsp	minced gingerroot (see Tip, below)	25 mL
1 tsp	turmeric	5 mL
½ tsp	salt	2 mL
½ tsp	cracked black peppercorns	2 mL
1	cinnamon stick piece (2 inches/5 cm)	1
8 oz	cremini mushrooms, stemmed and halved	250 g
1	can (28 oz/796 mL) tomatoes, including juice, coarsely chopped	1
3 cups	cubed (1 inch/2.5 cm), peeled butternut squash or pumpkin	750 mL
2 cups	cooked dried or canned chickpeas, drained and rinsed (see Basic Beans, page 219)	500 mL
1 tbsp	liquid honey	15 mL
1 tbsp	freshly squeezed lemon juice	15 mL
¼ cup	currants, optional	50 mL

1. In a large skillet, heat oil over medium heat for 30 seconds. Add onion and carrots and cook, stirring, until carrots are softened, about 7 minutes. Add garlic, gingerroot, turmeric, salt, peppercorns and cinnamon stick and cook, stirring, for 1 minute. Add mushrooms and toss until coated. Add tomatoes with juice and bring to a boil. Transfer to slow cooker stoneware.

2. Add squash and chickpeas and stir well. Cover and cook on Low for 8 hours or on High for 4 hours, until vegetables are tender.

3. In a small bowl, combine honey and lemon juice. Add to slow cooker and stir well. To serve, sprinkle with currants, if using.

TIP

- I prefer a strong gingery flavor in this dish. If you're ginger-averse, reduce the amount.

Cannelloni with Tomato Eggplant Sauce

SERVES 8

Here's a great recipe for cannelloni that is remarkably easy to make. Oven-ready pasta is filled with ricotta and baby spinach and bathed in a tomato eggplant sauce. Add some crusty bread and a salad of roasted peppers or crisp greens for a terrific meal.

Make ahead

This dish can be partially prepared before it is cooked. Complete Steps 1 and 2, letting tomato sauce cool before pouring over cannelloni. Refrigerate overnight in slow cooker stoneware. The next morning, continue with the recipe.

• **Works best in a large (minimum 5 quart) slow cooker**

Sauce

2 tbsp	olive oil	25 mL
1	medium eggplant, peeled, cut into 2-inch (5 cm) cubes, and drained of excess moisture (see Tips, page 20)	1
2	cloves garlic, minced	2
1/4 tsp	freshly ground black pepper	1 mL
3 cups	tomato sauce	750 mL

Filling

2 cups	ricotta cheese	500 mL
1/2 cup	freshly grated Parmesan cheese	125 mL
1 1/2 cups	chopped baby spinach	375 mL
1 tsp	freshly grated nutmeg	5 mL
1	egg, beaten	1
1/4 tsp	salt	1 mL
1/4 tsp	freshly ground black pepper	1 mL
24	oven-ready cannelloni shells	24

1. *Sauce:* In a skillet, heat oil over medium heat for 30 seconds. Add eggplant, in batches, and cook, stirring, until it begins to brown. Return all eggplant to pan. Add garlic and black pepper and cook, stirring, for 1 minute. Add tomato sauce, stir well and bring to a boil. Remove from heat and set aside.

2. *Filling:* In a bowl, combine ricotta, Parmesan, spinach, nutmeg, egg, salt and pepper. Using your fingers, fill pasta shells with mixture and place filled shells side by side in slow cooker stoneware, then on top of each other when bottom layer is complete. Pour sauce over shells.

3. Cover and cook on Low for 8 hours or on High for 4 hours, until hot and bubbly.

> **TIP**
> • Be sure to use oven-ready cannelloni in this recipe. It is a great time saver and it cooks to perfection in the slow cooker.

Cheese Torta with Artichokes and Sun-Dried Tomatoes

SERVES 6

This tasty Italian-inspired torta is like a luscious airy cheesecake. Served with salad, it makes a great light supper and is a perfect dish to serve for brunch.

Make ahead

This dish can be partially prepared before it is cooked. Complete Step 1. Cover and refrigerate for up to 2 days. When you're ready to cook, continue with the recipe.

- **Large (minimum 5 quart) slow cooker**
- **Greased 6-cup (1.5 L) baking dish**

1	can (14 oz/398 mL) artichoke hearts, drained (see Tips, below)	1
½ cup	coarsely chopped sun-dried tomatoes in olive oil, drained	125 mL
2 tbsp	snipped chives	25 mL
4	eggs	4
1	package (1 lb/500 g) ricotta cheese (see Tips, below)	1
1 cup	freshly grated Parmesan cheese	250 mL
	Salt	
	Freshly ground black pepper	

1. In a food processor fitted with a metal blade, combine artichoke hearts, sun-dried tomatoes and chives. Pulse until artichokes are finely chopped. Transfer to a bowl and set aside.

2. Add eggs to food processor work bowl and pulse until beaten. Add ricotta and Parmesan and process until mixture is well blended and the ricotta is smooth. Add reserved artichoke mixture and pulse to blend. Season to taste with salt and pepper. Spoon into prepared dish. Cover with foil and secure with string. Place dish in slow cooker stoneware and add enough boiling water to come 1 inch (2.5 cm) up the sides. Cover and cook on High for 2½ to 3 hours, until a knife inserted in the torta comes out clean. Serve immediately.

TIPS

- If you prefer, use frozen artichoke hearts, thawed, to make this recipe. You'll need 6 artichoke hearts.
- If you aren't using packaged ricotta, you'll need 2 cups (500 mL) loosely packed.

Parsnip and Coconut Curry with Crispy Shallots

SERVES 6

The combination of sweet parsnips, spicy curry, mellow coconut milk and crispy shallots is absolutely delicious. I like to serve this over hot rice or with a warm Indian bread such as naan, alongside a small platter of stir-fried bok choy, drizzled with toasted sesame oil and sprinkled with toasted sesame seeds.

Make ahead

This dish can be partially prepared before it is cooked. Complete Step 1. Cover and refrigerate overnight. The next morning, continue with the recipe.

* **Works in slow cookers from 3 1/2 to 6 quarts**

1 tbsp	vegetable oil	15 mL
1	large onion, finely chopped	1
4	stalks celery, thinly sliced	4
6	parsnips, peeled and diced	6
1 tbsp	minced gingerroot	15 mL
2 tsp	cumin seeds, toasted and ground (see Tip, below)	10 mL
1 cup	vegetable stock	250 mL
2 tsp	curry powder	10 mL
1 cup	coconut milk	250 mL
1 cup	green peas, thawed if frozen	250 mL

Crispy Shallot Topping

2 tbsp	vegetable oil	25 mL
1/2 cup	diced shallots	125 mL

1. In a skillet, heat oil over medium heat for 30 seconds. Add onion, celery and parsnips and cook, stirring, until vegetables are softened, about 7 minutes. Add gingerroot and toasted cumin and cook, stirring for 1 minute. Stir in vegetable stock. Transfer mixture to slow cooker stoneware.

2. Cover and cook on Low for 8 hours or High for 4 hours, until vegetables are tender.

3. In a small bowl, place curry powder. Gradually add coconut milk, stirring until blended. Add to slow cooker along with the green peas. Cover and cook on High for 20 to 30 minutes, until peas are cooked and mixture is bubbly.

4. *Crispy Shallot Topping:* Meanwhile, in a skillet, heat oil over medium-high heat for 30 seconds. Add shallots and cook, stirring until they are browned and crispy, about 5 minutes. Ladle curry into individual serving bowls and top with shallots.

TIP
* To toast cumin seeds: Place seeds in a dry skillet over medium heat, stirring, until fragrant, about 3 minutes. Immediately transfer to a mortar or a spice grinder and grind. If you prefer to use ground cumin, substitute half of the quantity called for.

Rigatoni and Cheese

VEGETARIAN FRIENDLY

SERVES 4

Here's a comfort food favorite that works well in the slow cooker when made with rigatoni rather than the traditional macaroni. Serve with a tossed salad and crusty bread for a tasty family meal.

Make ahead

This dish can be partially prepared before it is cooked. Complete Steps 1, 2 and 3. Cover and refrigerate for up to 2 days. When you're ready to cook, continue with the recipe.

- **Works best in a large (minimum 5 quart) slow cooker**
- **Lightly greased slow cooker stoneware**

3 cups	rigatoni	750 mL
1	can (28 oz/796 mL) tomatoes, drained, reserving 1 cup (250 mL) liquid (see Tips, page 34)	1
1	can (10 oz/284 mL) condensed cream of mushroom soup	1
1 tsp	dried oregano leaves	5 mL
1 tsp	salt	5 mL
½ tsp	cracked black peppercorns	2 mL
2½ cups	shredded Cheddar cheese	625 mL
½ cup	freshly grated Parmesan cheese	125 mL
½ cup	fine fresh bread crumbs	125 mL
2 tbsp	melted butter	25 mL

1. In a large pot of boiling salted water, cook rigatoni until barely tender, about 7 minutes once water returns to a boil. Drain and set aside.

2. In a food processor, combine tomatoes plus reserved liquid, soup, oregano, salt and peppercorns. Pulse three or four times, until tomatoes are coarsely chopped and mixture is combined.

3. In slow cooker stoneware, combine rigatoni, Cheddar cheese and tomato mixture.

4. In a bowl, mix together Parmesan cheese and bread crumbs. Sprinkle evenly over rigatoni. Drizzle with butter. Place two clean tea towels, each folded in half (so you will have four layers), over top of slow cooker stoneware to absorb moisture. Cover and cook on Low for 8 hours or on High for 4 hours, until hot and bubbly.

Easy Vegetable Chili

SERVES 4 TO 6

Not only is this chili easy to make, it is also delicious. The mild dried chiles add interesting flavor, along with a nice bit of heat. Only add the jalapeño if you're a heat seeker.

Make ahead

This dish can be partially prepared before it is cooked. Complete Steps 1 and 3. Cover and refrigerate tomato and chile mixtures separately for up to 2 days, being aware that the chile mixture will lose some of its vibrancy if held for this long. (For best results, rehydrate the chiles while the dish is cooking or no sooner than the night before you plan to cook.) When you're ready to cook, continue with the recipe.

• **Works in slow cookers from 3 1/2 to 6 quarts**

1 tbsp	vegetable oil	15 mL
2	onions, chopped	2
4	stalks celery, thinly sliced	4
4	cloves garlic, minced	4
2 tsp	cumin seeds, toasted and ground (see Tip, page 227)	10 mL
2 tsp	dried oregano leaves, crumbled	10 mL
1 tsp	salt	5 mL
1	can (14 oz/398 mL) diced tomatoes, including juice	1
2 cups	cooked dried or canned red kidney beans, drained and rinsed (see Basic Beans, page 219)	500 mL
2	dried New Mexico, ancho or guajillo chile peppers	2
2 cups	boiling water	500 mL
1 cup	coarsely chopped cilantro, leaves and stems	250 mL
1 cup	vegetable stock, tomato juice or water	250 mL
1	jalapeño pepper, coarsely chopped, optional	1
2 cups	corn kernels	500 mL
1	green bell pepper, chopped	1

1. In a skillet, heat oil over medium heat for 30 seconds. Add onions and celery and cook, stirring, until softened, about 5 minutes. Add garlic, toasted cumin, oregano and salt, and cook, stirring, for 1 minute. Add tomatoes with juice and bring to a boil. Transfer to slow cooker.

2. Add beans and stir well. Cover and cook on Low for 6 to 8 hours or on High for 3 to 4 hours, until hot and bubbly.

3. Half an hour before the recipe is finished cooking, in a heatproof bowl, soak dried chiles in boiling water for 30 minutes, weighing down with a cup to ensure they remain submerged. Drain, discarding soaking liquid and stems and chop coarsely. Transfer to a blender. Add cilantro, stock and jalapeño, if using. Purée.

4. Add chile mixture to stoneware and stir well. Add corn and green pepper and stir well. Cover and cook on High for 20 minutes, until pepper is tender and mixture is hot and bubbly.

Red Beans and Greens

SERVES 6 TO 8

Few meals could be more healthful than this delicious combination of hot leafy greens over flavorful beans. I like to make this with collard greens but other dark leafy greens such as kale work well, too. The smoked paprika makes the dish more robust but it isn't essential. If you're cooking for a smaller group, make the full quantity of beans, spoon off what is needed, and serve with the appropriate quantity of cooked greens. Refrigerate or freeze the leftover beans for another meal.

Make ahead

This dish can be partially prepared before it is cooked. Complete Steps 1 and 2. Cover and refrigerate for up to 2 days. When you're ready to cook, continue with the recipe.

- **Works in slow cookers from 3¹/₂ to 6 quarts**

2 cups	dried red kidney beans	500 mL
1 tbsp	vegetable oil	15 mL
2	large onions, finely chopped	2
2	stalks celery, finely chopped	2
4	cloves garlic, minced	4
1 tsp	dried oregano leaves	5 mL
1 tsp	salt	5 mL
¹/₂ tsp	cracked black peppercorns	2 mL
¹/₂ tsp	dried thyme leaves	2 mL
¹/₄ tsp	ground allspice or 6 whole allspice (tied in a piece of cheesecloth)	1 mL
2	bay leaves	2
4 cups	vegetable stock	1 L
1 tsp	paprika, preferably smoked, optional	5 mL
Greens		
2 lbs	greens, such as collards, thoroughly washed, stems removed and chopped	1 kg
	Butter or butter substitute	
1 tbsp	balsamic vinegar	15 mL
	Salt and freshly ground black pepper	

1. Soak beans according to either method in Basic Beans (see page 219). Drain and rinse and set aside.

2. In a skillet, heat oil over medium heat for 30 seconds. Add onions and celery and cook, stirring, until softened, about 5 minutes. Add garlic, oregano, salt, peppercorns, thyme, allspice and bay leaves and cook, stirring for 1 minute. Transfer to slow cooker stoneware. Add beans and vegetable stock.

3. Cover and cook on Low for 8 to 10 hours or on High for 4 to 5 hours, until beans are tender. Stir in smoked paprika, if using.

4. *Greens:* In a large pot or steamer, steam greens until tender, about 10 minutes for collards. Toss with butter or butter substitute and balsamic vinegar. Season to taste with salt and pepper. Add to beans and stir to combine. Serve immediately.

Light Chili

SERVES 4 TO 6

This is my favorite light chili. I love the rich, creamy sauce and the flavors of the spices. Serve this with a good dollop of sour cream, your favorite salsa and a sprinkling of chopped cilantro.

Make ahead

This dish can be partially prepared before it is cooked. Chop jalapeño and bell peppers and shred cheese. Cover and refrigerate. Complete Step 1. Cover and refrigerate for up to 2 days. When you're ready to cook, continue with the recipe.

- **Works in slow cookers from 3 1/2 to 6 quarts**

1 tbsp	vegetable oil	15 mL
2	onions, finely chopped	2
6	cloves garlic, minced	6
1 tbsp	cumin seeds, toasted and ground (see Tip, page 227)	15 mL
1 tbsp	dried oregano leaves	15 mL
1 tsp	salt	5 mL
1 tsp	cracked black peppercorns	5 mL
1	can (28 oz/796 mL) tomatoes, including juice, chopped (see Tips, page 34)	1
2 cups	vegetable stock	500 mL
8 oz	portobello mushrooms, stems removed, cut into 1-inch (2.5 cm) cubes	250 g
2 cups	cooked dried or canned white kidney beans, drained and rinsed (see Basic Beans, page 219)	500 mL
1 to 2	jalapeño peppers, finely chopped	1 to 2
2	green bell peppers, diced	2
1 1/2 cups	shredded Monterey Jack cheese	375 mL
1	can (4 1/2 oz/127 mL) diced mild green chiles, drained	1
	Sour cream	
	Salsa	
	Finely chopped cilantro	

1. In a skillet, heat oil over medium heat for 30 seconds. Add onions and cook, stirring, until softened, about 3 minutes. Add garlic, toasted cumin, oregano, salt and peppercorns and cook, stirring, for 1 minute. Add tomatoes with juice and stock and bring to a boil. Cook, stirring, until liquid is reduced by one-third, about 5 minutes. Transfer to slow cooker stoneware.

2. Add mushrooms and beans and stir to combine Cover and cook on Low for 6 to 8 hours or on High for 3 to 4 hours, until mixture is hot and bubbly. Stir in jalapeño peppers, green peppers, cheese and mild green chiles. Cover and cook on High for 20 to 30 minutes, until peppers are tender and cheese is melted. Ladle into bowls and top with sour cream, salsa and chopped cilantro.

Peas and Greens

SERVES 4

This delicious combination of black-eyed peas and greens, which is a Greek tradition, is a great dish for busy weeknights. It also makes a wonderful side dish for roasted meat, particularly lamb.

Make ahead

This dish can be partially prepared before it is cooked. Complete Step 1. Cover and refrigerate for up to 2 days. When you're ready to cook, continue with the recipe.

● *Works in slow cookers from 3½ to 6 quarts*

1 tbsp	vegetable oil	15 mL
2	onions, finely chopped	2
1	bulb fennel, cored, leafy stems discarded, and sliced on the vertical	1
4	cloves garlic, minced	4
½ tsp	salt, or to taste	2 mL
½ tsp	cracked black peppercorns	2 mL
¼ tsp	fennel seeds, toasted and ground (see Tips, below)	1 mL
1	can (14 oz/398 mL) diced tomatoes, including juice	1
2 cups	cooked dried or canned black-eyed peas, drained and rinsed (see Basic Beans, page 219)	500 mL
2 tbsp	freshly squeezed lemon juice	25 mL
1 tsp	paprika (see Tips, below)	5 mL
4 cups	chopped spinach or Swiss Chard (about 1 bunch), stems removed	1 L

1. In a skillet, heat oil over medium heat for 30 seconds. Add onions and fennel and cook, stirring, until fennel is softened, about 5 minutes. Add garlic, salt, peppercorns and toasted fennel and cook, stirring, for 1 minute. Add tomatoes with juice and bring to a boil. Transfer to slow cooker stoneware.

2. Add peas and stir well. Cover and cook on Low for 8 hours or on High for 4 hours, until peas are tender. In a small bowl, combine lemon juice and paprika, stirring, until paprika dissolves. Add to slow cooker stoneware and stir well. Add spinach, stirring, until submerged. Cover and cook on High for 20 minutes, until spinach is tender.

TIPS

● To toast fennel seeds: Place seeds in a dry skillet over medium heat and cook, stirring, until fragrant and they just begin to brown, about 3 minutes. Immediately transfer to a mortar or a spice grinder and grind. (Or place the seeds on a cutting board and use the bottom of a wine bottle or measuring cup.)

● Use any kind of paprika in this recipe. Hot paprika will add the zest heat seekers prefer. Smoked paprika will enhance the flavor with a pleasant smokiness.

Poached Eggs on Spicy Lentils

SERVES 4

This delicious combination is a great cold-weather dish. Add the chiles if you prefer a little spice and accompany with warm Indian bread, such as naan, and hot white rice. The Egg and Lentil Curry (see Variation, below) is a great dish for a buffet table or as part of an Indian-themed meal.

Make ahead

This dish can be partially prepared before it is cooked. Complete Step 1. Cover and refrigerate for up to 2 days. When you're ready to cook, continue with the recipe.

Variation

Egg and Lentil Curry
Substitute 4 to 6 hard-cooked eggs for the poached. Peel them and cut into halves. Ladle the curry into a serving dish, arrange the eggs on top and garnish with parsley.

• **Works in slow cookers from 3½ to 6 quarts**

1 tbsp	vegetable oil	15 mL
1½ cups	finely chopped onions	375 mL
1 tbsp	minced garlic	15 mL
1 tbsp	minced gingerroot	15 mL
1 tsp	ground coriander	5 mL
1 tsp	cumin seeds, toasted and ground (see Tip, page 178)	5 mL
1 tsp	cracked black peppercorns	5 mL
1 cup	dried red lentils, rinsed	250 mL
1	can (28 oz/796 mL) tomatoes, including juice, coarsely chopped	1
2 cups	vegetable stock	500 mL
1 cup	coconut milk	250 mL
	Salt	
1	long green chile pepper or 2 Thai birds-eye chiles, finely chopped, optional	1
4	poached eggs (see Tip, below)	4
	Finely chopped parsley, optional	

1. In a skillet, heat oil over medium heat for 30 seconds. Add onions and cook, stirring, until softened, about 3 minutes. Add garlic, gingerroot, coriander, toasted cumin and peppercorns and cook, stirring, for 1 minute. Add lentils, tomatoes with juice and vegetable stock and bring to a boil. Transfer to slow cooker stoneware.

2. Cover and cook on Low for 8 hours or on High for 4 hours, until lentils are tender and mixture is bubbly. Stir in coconut milk, salt, to taste, and chile pepper, if using. Cover and cook for 20 to 30 minutes, until heated through.

3. When ready to serve, ladle into soup bowls and top each serving with a poached egg. Garnish with parsley, if using.

TIP

• To poach eggs: In a deep skillet, bring about 2 inches (5 cm) lightly salted water to a boil over medium heat. Reduce heat to low. Break eggs into a measuring cup and, holding the cup close to the surface of the water, slip the eggs into the pan. Cook until whites are set and centers are still soft, 3 to 4 minutes. Remove with a slotted spoon.

Lentil Shepherd's Pie

SERVES 6 TO 8

This flavorful combination is the ultimate comfort food dish. Don't worry if you're serving fewer people — the leftovers taste great reheated.

Make ahead

This recipe can be partially prepared before it is cooked. Complete Step 1 and refrigerate overnight. The next morning, continue with the recipe.

- **Works best in a large (minimum 5 quart) slow cooker**

1 tbsp	vegetable oil	15 mL
2 cups	finely chopped onions	500 mL
4	stalks celery, thinly sliced	4
2	large carrots, peeled and thinly sliced	2
1 tbsp	finely chopped garlic	15 mL
1 tsp	salt	5 mL
½ tsp	dried thyme leaves	2 mL
½ tsp	cracked black peppercorns	2 mL
1½ cups	dried brown or green lentils, rinsed	375 mL
1	can (28 oz/796 mL) tomatoes, including juice, coarsely chopped	1
2 cups	vegetable stock	500 mL
Topping		
4 cups	mashed potatoes (see Tip, below)	1 L
1 cup	dry bread crumbs	250 mL
½ cup	shredded Cheddar cheese, optional	125 mL

1. In a large skillet, heat oil over medium heat for 30 seconds. Add onions, celery and carrots and cook, stirring, until vegetables are softened, about 7 minutes. Add garlic, salt, thyme and peppercorns and cook, stirring, for 1 minute. Add lentils and tomatoes with juice and bring to a boil. Transfer to slow cooker stoneware and stir in vegetable stock.

2. *Topping*: In a bowl, combine mashed potatoes and bread crumbs. Mix well. Spread mixture evenly over lentil mixture. Sprinkle cheese over top, if using. Cover and cook on Low for 7 to 8 hours or on High for 3 to 4 hours, until hot and bubbly.

TIP

- You can use leftover mashed potatoes in this recipe or even prepared mashed potatoes from the supermarket. However, if your potatoes contain milk, don't add the topping mixture to the slow cooker until the mixture has cooked. Spread topping over the hot lentil mixture. Cover and cook on High for 30 minutes, until the potatoes are hot and the cheese has melted.

Lentil Sloppy Joes

SERVES 4

Here's a kids' favorite that grown-ups enjoy, too. It makes a great dinner for those busy nights when everyone is coming and going at different times. Leave the slow cooker on Low or Warm, the buns on the counter, the fixin's of salad in the fridge and let everyone help themselves.

Make ahead

This dish can be partially prepared before it is cooked. Complete Step 1. Cover and refrigerate for up to 2 days. When you're ready to cook, continue with the recipe.

● *Works in slow cookers from 3½ to 6 quarts*

1 tbsp	vegetable oil	15 mL
1	onion, finely chopped	1
4	stalks celery, diced	4
4	cloves garlic, minced	4
½ tsp	dried oregano leaves	2 mL
½ tsp	salt	2 mL
	Freshly ground black pepper	
½ cup	tomato ketchup	125 mL
¼ cup	water	50 mL
1 tbsp	balsamic vinegar	15 mL
1 tbsp	brown sugar	15 mL
1 tbsp	Dijon mustard	15 mL
2 cups	cooked brown or green lentils, drained and rinsed (see Tip, below)	500 mL
	Hot pepper sauce, optional	
	Toasted hamburger buns	

1. In a skillet, heat oil over medium heat for 30 seconds. Add onion and celery and cook, stirring, until softened, about 5 minutes. Add garlic, oregano, salt and pepper, to taste, and cook, stirring for 1 minute. Stir in ketchup, water, balsamic vinegar, brown sugar and mustard. Transfer to slow cooker stoneware.

2. Add lentils and stir well. Cover and cook on Low for 6 hours or on High for 3 hours, until hot and bubbly. Add hot pepper sauce, to taste, if using. Ladle over hot toasted buns and serve immediately.

> **TIP**
> ● Use 1 can (14 to 19 oz/398 to 540 mL) green or brown lentils, drained and rinsed or cook dried lentils (see Basic Beans, page 219).

Rice and Bulgur Pilaf (page 256)

Grains and Sides

Carrot Bread

**MAKES 1 LOAF
OR 8 SERVINGS**

*Serve this tasty bread
as a snack or for a
healthy breakfast on
the run.*

- **Large (minimum 5 quart) oval slow cooker**
- **Greased 8-by 4-inch (20 by 10 cm) approx. loaf pan or 6-cup
  (1.5 L) soufflé or baking dish (see Tip, below)**

1½ cups	all-purpose flour	375 mL
½ cup	whole wheat flour (see Tips, page 244)	125 mL
2 tsp	baking powder	10 mL
1 tsp	ground cinnamon	5 mL
½ tsp	ground cloves	2 mL
½ tsp	salt	2 mL
½ cup	packed brown sugar	125 mL
¼ cup	granulated sugar	50 mL
3 tbsp	vegetable oil	45 mL
1	egg, beaten	1
¾ cup	plain yogurt	175 mL
1½ cups	shredded peeled carrots	375 mL
¾ cup	chopped pecans	175 mL

1. In a bowl, combine all-purpose and whole wheat flours, baking powder, cinnamon, cloves and salt.

2. In a separate bowl, beat together brown and granulated sugars, vegetable oil, egg and yogurt. Add to flour mixture, stirring just until combined. Fold in carrots and pecans.

3. Spoon batter into prepared pan. Cover tightly with foil and secure with a string. Place pan in slow cooker stoneware and pour in enough boiling water to come 1 inch (2.5 cm) up the sides of the dish. Cover and cook on High for 4 hours, until a tester inserted in the center of the loaf comes out clean. Unmold and serve warm or let cool.

> **TIP**
> - This bread, like the others in this book, can be made in almost any kind of baking dish that will fit into your slow cooker. I have a variety of baking pans that work well: A small loaf pan (about 8-by 4-inches/20 by 10 cm) makes a traditionally shaped bread; a round (6-cup/1.5 L) soufflé dish or a square 7-inch/17.5 cm) baking dish produces slices of different shapes. All taste equally good.

Whole Wheat Soda Bread

**MAKES 1 LOAF
OR 8 SERVINGS**

*This homey bread
is easy to make
and is a delicious
accompaniment to
many main course
dishes. It also makes
a very tasty snack
served warm with
sliced Cheddar cheese.
Add a crisp apple or
some freshly sliced
pear to complete
the treat.*

- **Large (minimum 5 quart) oval slow cooker**
- **Lightly greased 8-by 4-inch (20 by 10 cm) approx. loaf pan or 6 cup (1.5 L) soufflé or baking dish (see Tips, below)**

1 cup	whole wheat flour (see Tips, below)	250 mL
1 cup	all-purpose flour	250 mL
¾ tsp	baking soda	4 mL
¾ tsp	salt	4 mL
1¼ cups	buttermilk	300 mL

1. In a large bowl, mix together whole wheat and all-purpose flours, baking soda and salt. Make a well in the center, pour buttermilk into well and mix just until blended. Spread into prepared pan.

2. Cover pan tightly with foil and secure with string. Place pan in slow cooker stoneware and pour in enough boiling water to come 1 inch (2.5 cm) up the sides of the dish. Cover and cook on High for 2½ to 3 hours, until bread springs back when touched lightly in the center. Unmold and serve warm.

TIPS

- This bread, like the others in this book, can be made in almost any kind of baking dish that will fit into your slow cooker. I have a variety of baking pans that work well: a small loaf pan (about 8-by 4-inches/20 by 10 cm) makes a traditionally shaped bread; a round (6-cup/1.5 L) soufflé dish or a square (7-inch/17.5 cm) baking dish produces slices of different shapes. All taste equally good.
- Because whole wheat flour contains more oil than all-purpose flour, it quickly becomes rancid at room temperature and should be stored in the freezer. It will keep for up to a year and can be used in its frozen state. Buy it in small quantities from a source with high turnover. If possible, smell before you buy, and if the flour smells the slightest bit rancid, give it a pass.

Steamed Brown Bread

MAKES 1 LARGE LOAF OR 3 SMALL LOAVES, DEPENDING UPON THE CONTAINER USED

Served warm, this slightly sweet bread is a delicious accompaniment to baked beans. It also goes well with wedges of Cheddar cheese.

- *Large (minimum 5 quart) oval slow cooker*
- *Three 19-oz (540 mL) vegetable cans, washed, dried and sprayed with vegetable oil spray, or one 8-cup (2 L) lightly greased soufflé or baking dish*

1 cup	all-purpose flour	250 mL
1 cup	whole wheat flour (see Tips, page 244)	250 mL
½ cup	rye flour	125 mL
½ cup	cornmeal	125 mL
2 tbsp	granulated sugar	25 mL
1 tsp	salt	5 mL
1 tsp	baking soda	5 mL
1½ cups	buttermilk	375 mL
½ cup	mild-flavored or fancy molasses	125 mL
2 tbsp	olive oil	25 mL

1. In a bowl, mix together all-purpose, whole wheat and rye flours, cornmeal, sugar, salt and baking soda. Make a well in the center.

2. In a separate bowl, mix together buttermilk, molasses and olive oil. Pour into well and mix until blended.

3. Spoon batter into prepared cans (in equal amounts) or baking dish. Cover top(s) with foil and secure with a string. Place in slow cooker stoneware and pour in enough boiling water to come 1 inch (2.5 cm) up the sides of the cans or dish. Cover and cook on High for 2 hours, if using cans, or 3 hours, if using a baking dish, until bread springs back when touched lightly in the center. Unmold and serve warm.

Hot Breakfast Cereals

SERVES 4

Serve grits with milk or a dairy alternative and/or fruit as a breakfast cereal. If you're splurging and enjoying a traditional English-style breakfast, they also make a delicious side.

Although starting your day with a bowl of rice may seem unconventional to many North Americans, in large parts of the world it is the norm. Both brown rice and wheat berries are nutritious whole grains. Cooked with flavorful rice milk and enhanced with the addition of raisins, they provide a delicious breakfast that will keep you energized throughout the day.

- **These recipes work best in a small (maximum 3^1/$_2$ quart) slow cooker**
- **Greased slow cooker stoneware**

Breakfast Grits

4 cups	water	1 L
½ tsp	salt	2 mL
1 cup	grits (not instant, preferably stone-ground)	250 mL
	Toasted pecans, optional	
	Sliced bananas, optional	

1. In a saucepan over medium heat, bring water and salt to a boil. Gradually add grits, stirring until smooth and blended. Transfer to prepared stoneware. Cover and cook on High for 4 hours or on Low for 8 hours or overnight. Garnish with pecans and add bananas, if using.

Rice and Wheat Berries

½ cup	brown rice	125 mL
½ cup	wheat berries	125 mL
4 cups	vanilla-flavored rice milk	1 L
½ cup	water	125 mL
½ cup	raisins	125 mL

1. In prepared slow cooker stoneware, combine rice, wheat berries, rice milk and water. Place a clean tea towel, folded in half (so you will have two layers), over top of stoneware to absorb moisture. Cover and cook on High for 4 hours or on Low for up to 8 hours or overnight. Just before serving, place raisins in a microwave-safe bowl and cover with water. Microwave for 20 seconds to soften. Add to hot cereal. Stir well and serve.

TIP
- Remember to store whole grains, such as rice and wheat berries, in the refrigerator in airtight containers as their high content of healthful oils predisposes them to early spoilage.

Hot Breakfast Cereals

SERVES 4

Hot cereal is one of my favorite ways to begin the day, and happily, you can use your slow cooker to ensure that all family members get off to a nutritious start. Cook the cereal overnight and leave the slow cooker on Warm in the morning. Everyone can help themselves according to their schedules. Thanks to my editor, Carol Sherman, who, inspired by the idea of waking up to ready-to-eat hot cereal, came up with the idea of adding rolled oats to multigrain cereal. For a crunchier version, use Irish oatmeal or steel-cut oats, instead of traditional rolled oats in either recipe.

- *These recipes work best in a small (maximum 3½ quart) slow cooker*
- *Greased slow cooker stoneware*

Hot Multigrain Cereal (pictured right)

1 cup	multigrain cereal, or ½ cup (125 mL) multigrain cereal and ½ cup (125 mL) rolled oats	250 mL
¼ tsp	salt	1 mL
4 cups	water	1 L
2	all-purpose apples, peeled and thickly sliced	2
¼ to ⅓ cup	raisins, optional	50 to 75 mL

1. In prepared slow cooker stoneware, combine multigrain cereal, salt, water and apples. Cover and cook on Low for 8 hours or overnight. Just before serving, place raisins, if using, in a microwave-safe bowl and cover with water. Microwave for 20 seconds to soften. Add to hot cereal. Stir well and serve.

TIP
- Multigrain cereals are one way of ensuring that you maximize the nutritional benefits of cereal grains. You can buy them pre-packaged, usually in 3, 5 or 7-grain combinations or under a brand name, or you can make your own by combining your favorite grains. Store multigrain cereal in an airtight container in a cool, dry place.

Hot Oatmeal

1¼ cups	rolled oats	300 mL
½ tsp	salt	2 mL
4 cups	water	1 L

1. In prepared slow cooker stoneware, combine oats, salt and water. Cover and cook on Low for 8 hours or overnight. Stir well and serve.

TIP
- Rolled oats, often called porridge when cooked, are probably the most popular breakfast cereal. For variety, try steel-cut oats, Irish oatmeal or Scotch oats, which have an appealing chewy texture.

Basic Grits

SERVES 4

Add variety to your diet by serving grits, instead of pasta, topped with a tasty sauce for a light lunch or dinner. Grits are dried broken grains of corn with a pleasant nutty taste that adapts well to many flavors. In fact, they are one of my favorite grains.

- **Works best in a small (3½ quart) slow cooker**
- **Lightly greased slow cooker stoneware**

4 cups	water	1 L
1 tbsp	olive oil	15 mL
½ tsp	salt	2 mL
½ tsp	freshly ground black pepper	2 mL
1 cup	grits (not instant, preferably stone-ground)	250 mL

1. In a saucepan over medium heat, bring water, olive oil, salt and pepper to boil. Gradually add grits, stirring constantly until smooth and blended. Continue cooking and stirring, until grits are slightly thickened, about 4 minutes. Transfer to prepared stoneware. Cover and cook on Low for 8 hours or on High for 4 hours, until set. Serve immediately.

TIP

- Whole grain stone-ground grits (the tastiest and most nutritious kind) take a long time to cook. Preparing them on the stovetop requires about 2 hours of attention and frequent stirring. If, like me, you're a grits lover, having a slow cooker is very advantageous. Once you put them in the stoneware and turn the appliance on, you can forget about them until they are done.

Grits with Sautéed Mushrooms

SERVES 4

What could be simpler — or more delicious — than this medley of sautéed mushrooms? Prepare the mushrooms and the makings of a salad before you leave for work in the morning and in a matter of minutes, you'll have a delicious meal on the table after you arrive home.

1	Basic Grits (see recipe, page 250)	1
1 tbsp	olive oil	15 mL
1 tbsp	butter or olive oil	15 mL
1 lb	mixed mushrooms, stemmed and sliced	500 g
1	clove garlic, minced	1
	Salt and freshly ground black pepper	
1 tbsp	freshly squeezed lemon juice	15 mL
¼ cup	freshly grated Parmesan cheese, optional	50 mL
¼ cup	finely chopped parsley leaves or chives	50 mL

1. In a skillet, heat olive oil and butter over medium-high heat, until butter melts. Add mushrooms and cook, stirring, until they lose their liquid, about 7 minutes. Add garlic. Season to taste with salt and pepper and cook, stirring, for 1 minute. Remove from heat. Add lemon juice and toss well.

2. To serve, spoon grits onto a platter, top with mushrooms, sprinkle with Parmesan, if using, and garnish with parsley.

TIP
- If you happen to have truffle salt in your pantry, use it instead of regular salt to season the mushrooms for an added hit of mouth-watering flavor.

Grits with Spinach Sauce

SERVES 4

This delicious no-fuss dish, which is equally good over polenta, is a weekday favorite at our house. Put the grits on to cook before you leave the house in the morning and whip up the sauce when you come home. Add a sliced tomato salad in season to complete the colors.

1	Basic Grits (see recipe, page 250)	1
1 lb	fresh spinach, stems removed, or 1 package (10 oz/300 g) spinach leaves, thawed if frozen (see Tips, below)	500 g
1/3 cup	tahini (see Tips, below)	75 mL
2 tbsp	freshly squeezed lemon juice	25 mL
2	green onions, white part only, chopped	2
2	cloves garlic, minced	2
1/2 tsp	cumin seeds, toasted and ground (see Tips, below)	2 mL
	Salt and freshly ground black pepper	

1. In a large pot, cook spinach until wilted, about 5 minutes, or just until heated through if using frozen. Drain and transfer to a food processor. Add tahini, lemon juice, green onions, garlic and toasted cumin. Season to taste with salt and black pepper.

2. To serve, spoon grits onto a platter and top with spinach sauce.

TIPS

- If you are using fresh spinach leaves in this recipe, take care to wash them thoroughly, as they can be quite gritty. To wash spinach: Fill a clean sink with lukewarm water. Remove the tough stems and submerge the tender leaves in the water, swishing to remove the grit. Rinse thoroughly in a colander under cold running water, checking carefully to ensure that no sand remains. If you are using frozen spinach in this recipe, thaw and squeeze the excess moisture out before adding to the slow cooker.

- Look for tahini (sesame seed paste) in well-stocked supermarkets and natural or specialty food stores.

- To toast cumin seeds: Place seeds in a dry skillet over medium heat, stirring, until fragrant, about 3 minutes. Immediately transfer to a mortar or a spice grinder and grind. If you prefer to use ground cumin, substitute one-third of the quantity called for.

Mushroom Cholent

SERVES 8

Cholent made with brisket, which is prepared on Friday and left to cook overnight, is the traditional midday meal for the Jewish Sabbath. In this version, portobello mushrooms provide heartiness and a mirepoix containing parsnips, as well as the traditional vegetables, adds sweetness and flavor. The mushrooms contribute to a surprisingly rich gravy and the results are very good indeed.

Make ahead

This dish can be assembled the night before it is cooked. Using the Long Soak method, soak the beans overnight. Complete Step 2. Cover and refrigerate vegetable mixture overnight. The next morning, continue with the recipe.

- **Works best in a large (minimum 5 quart) slow cooker**

1 cup	dried white navy beans	250 mL
1 tbsp	vegetable oil	15 mL
2	onions, finely chopped	2
4	stalks celery, diced	4
2	carrots, peeled and diced	2
2	parsnips, peeled and diced	2
6	cloves garlic, minced	6
1 tbsp	minced gingerroot	15 mL
2 tsp	paprika	10 mL
1 tsp	salt	5 mL
1 tsp	cracked black peppercorns	5 mL
4 cups	vegetable stock	1 L
2	potatoes, peeled and cut into 1/2-inch (1 cm) cubes	2
12 oz	portobello mushroom caps (about 4 large)	375 g
1 cup	barley, rinsed (see Tips, below)	250 mL

1. Soak beans according to either method in Basic Beans (see page 219). Drain and rinse and set aside.

2. In a skillet, heat oil over medium heat for 30 seconds. Add onions, celery, carrots and parsnips and cook, stirring, until softened, about 7 minutes. Add garlic, gingerroot, paprika, salt and peppercorns and cook, stirring for 1 minute. Stir in stock and remove from heat.

3. Pour half the contents of pan into slow cooker stoneware. Set remainder aside. Spread potatoes evenly over mixture. Arrange mushrooms evenly over potatoes, cutting one to fit, if necessary. Spread barley and reserved beans evenly over mushrooms. Add remaining onion mixture to stoneware.

4. Cover and cook on Low for 10 to 12 hours, or on High for 5 to 6 hours until beans are tender.

TIPS
- Although traditional wisdom holds that adding salt to dried beans before they are cooked will make them tough, when food scientist Shirley Corriher actually tested this premise she found the opposite to be true. Adding salt to beans while they cooked produced a more tender result.
- Use whole, pot or pearl barley in this recipe.

Brown Rice Chili

SERVES 6

This tasty chili is an ideal dish for vegetarians as the combination of rice and beans produces a complete protein. I think the flavor is outstanding when it's made using reconstituted dried chiles. Just be aware that chiles described as New Mexico can range widely in heat. If you are using New Mexico chiles in this recipe, check to make certain that they are not described as "hot." The "mild" variety is called for.

Make ahead

This dish can be partially prepared before it is cooked. Complete Steps 1 and 3. Cover and refrigerate onion and chile mixtures separately, overnight. (For best results, rehydrate chiles while the chili is cooking.) When you're ready to cook, continue with the recipe.

• **Works best in a large (minimum 5 quart) slow cooker**

1 tbsp	vegetable oil	15 mL
2	onions, chopped	2
4	stalks celery, chopped	4
1 cup	brown rice, rinsed	250 mL
4	cloves garlic, finely chopped	4
1 tbsp	dried oregano leaves	15 mL
1 tsp	ground cumin	5 mL
½ tsp	salt	2 mL
½ tsp	cracked black peppercorns	2 mL
1	can (28 oz/796 mL) tomatoes, including juice, coarsely chopped	1
2 cups	cooked dried or canned red kidney beans, drained and rinsed	500 mL
2 cups	vegetable stock, divided	500 mL
2	dried ancho, mild New Mexico or guajillo chile peppers	2
2 cups	boiling water	500 mL
½ cup	chopped cilantro stems and leaves	125 mL
2 cups	corn kernels, thawed if frozen	500 mL
1	green bell pepper, diced	1
1	jalapeño pepper, seeded and diced, optional	1

1. In a skillet, heat oil over medium heat for 30 seconds. Add onions and celery and cook, stirring, until celery is softened, about 5 minutes. Add rice, garlic, oregano, cumin, salt and peppercorns and cook, stirring, for 1 minute. Add tomatoes with juice and bring to a boil. Transfer to slow cooker stoneware. Add beans and 1½ cups (375 mL) of the stock and stir well.

2. Place two clean tea towels, each folded in half (so you will have four layers) over top of stoneware. Cover and cook on Low for 8 hours or on High for 4 hours, until hot and bubbly.

3. Half an hour before recipe has finished cooking, in a heatproof bowl, soak chile peppers in boiling water for 30 minutes, weighing down with a cup to ensure they remain submerged. Drain, discarding soaking water and stems and chop coarsely. Transfer to a blender. Add remaining stock and cilantro. Purée.

4. Add chile mixture, corn, bell pepper and jalapeño pepper, if using, to stoneware and stir well. Cover and cook on High for 30 minutes, until pepper is tender and flavors meld.

Rice and Bulgur Pilaf

SERVES 6

Accompanied by a sliced tomato salad, shredded carrots in vinaigrette or a simple green salad, this tasty pilaf makes a nice weekday meal or an interesting side. It keeps warm in the slow cooker and is perfect for those evenings when everyone is coming and going at different times and can help themselves.

Make ahead

This dish can be partially prepared before it is cooked. Complete Step 2. Cover and refrigerate overnight. The next morning, soak the bulgur (Step 1) and continue with the recipe.

- **Works best in a large (minimum 5 quart) slow cooker**

1 cup	bulgur (see Tips, below)	250 mL
3 cups	boiling water	750 mL
1 tbsp	olive oil	15 mL
2	large leeks, white part only, cut in half lengthwise, cleaned and thinly sliced (see Tips, below)	2
2	stalks celery, diced	2
2	carrots, peeled and diced	2
4	cloves garlic, minced	4
1 tsp	dried thyme leaves, crumbled	5 mL
½ tsp	cracked black peppercorns	2 mL
1 cup	brown and wild rice mixture, rinsed (see Tips, below)	250 mL
¼ cup	finely chopped reconstituted sun-dried tomatoes	50 mL
2 cups	chicken or vegetable stock	500 mL

1. In a bowl, combine bulgur and boiling water. Set aside for 20 minutes, until water is absorbed.

2. In a large skillet, heat oil over medium heat. Add leeks, celery and carrots and cook, stirring, until carrots are softened, about 7 minutes. Add garlic, thyme and peppercorns and cook, stirring, for 1 minute. Add rice and toss to coat. Add sun-dried tomatoes and stir well. Add stock, stirring, and bring to a boil.

3. Transfer to slow cooker stoneware. Stir in soaked bulgur. Place a clean tea towel, folded in half (so you will have two layers), over top of stoneware to absorb moisture. Cover and cook on High for 3 hours or on Low for 6 hours, until liquid is absorbed and rice is tender to the bite.

TIPS
- Don't worry if the bulgur hasn't absorbed all the water by the time you are ready to add it to the rice. Any extra will be absorbed during cooking.
- To clean leeks: Fill a sink full of lukewarm water. Split the leeks in half lengthwise and submerge in water, swishing them around to remove all traces of dirt. Transfer to a colander and rinse under cold water.
- Mixtures of wild and several varieties of brown rice now come in packages. Use plain brown rice instead, or you can make your own by combining ½ cup (125 mL) of each.

Wild Rice with Mushrooms and Apricots

SERVES 4

This combination of wild and brown rice with dried apricots makes a tasty weeknight meal. Be sure to serve it with a good chutney alongside — tomato or spicy mango work very well. A grated carrot salad is a nice accompaniment.

Make ahead

This dish can be partially prepared before it is cooked. Complete Step 1. Cover and refrigerate overnight. The next morning, continue with the recipe.

- **Works in slow cookers from 3½ to 6 quarts**
- **Greased slow cooker stoneware**

1 tbsp	vegetable oil	15 mL
1	onion, chopped	1
4	stalks celery, diced	4
2	cloves garlic, minced	2
1 cup	wild rice and brown rice mixture, rinsed (see Tips, below)	250 mL
2 cups	vegetable stock	500 mL
1 tbsp	balsamic vinegar	15 mL
	Salt and freshly ground black pepper	
8 oz	portobello or cremini mushrooms, stems removed and diced	250 g
¼ cup	chopped dried apricots	50 mL
	Chutney	

1. In a skillet, heat oil over medium heat for 30 seconds. Add onion and celery and cook, stirring, until softened, about 5 minutes. Add garlic and rice and stir until coated. Add stock and balsamic vinegar and bring to a boil. Season to taste with salt and pepper. Transfer to prepared stoneware.

2. Stir in mushrooms and apricots. Place two clean tea towels, each folded in half (so you will have four layers), over top of slow cooker stoneware (see Tips, below). Cover and cook on Low for 7 to 8 hours or on High for 3½ to 4 hours, until rice is tender and liquid has been absorbed. Serve hot accompanied by your favorite fruit chutney.

TIPS
- You can purchase wild and brown rice mixtures in many supermarkets, or you can make your own by combining ½ cup (125 mL) of each.
- Accumulated moisture affects the consistency of the rice. The folded tea towels will absorb the moisture generated during cooking.

Barley and Sausage Risotto with Fennel

SERVES 6

Here's a tasty meal that is particularly suited to those days when schedules differ and family members arrive home for dinner at different times. The fennel adds a distinguishing note to an otherwise simple combination of flavors. All this meal needs is crusty rolls and a tossed green salad.

Make ahead

This dish can be partially prepared before it is cooked. Complete Step 1. Cover and refrigerate overnight. The next morning, continue with the recipe.

• **Works best in a large (minimum 5 quart) slow cooker**

1 tbsp	vegetable oil	15 mL
1 lb	mild Italian sausage, removed from casings	500 g
2	onions, chopped	2
1	bulb fennel, trimmed, cored and chopped (see Tips, below)	1
4	cloves garlic, finely chopped	4
2 tsp	dried Italian seasoning	10 mL
½ tsp	cracked black peppercorns	2 mL
2 cups	barley, rinsed (see Tips, below)	500 mL
1	can (28 oz/796 mL) tomatoes, including juice, coarsely chopped	1
3 cups	chicken or vegetable stock	750 mL

1. In a skillet, heat oil over medium heat for 30 seconds. Add sausage and cook, stirring, until no hint of pink remains, about 5 minutes. Drain all but 2 tbsp (25 mL) fat from pan. Add onions and fennel to pan and cook, stirring, until fennel just begins to soften, about 3 minutes. Add garlic, Italian seasoning and peppercorns and cook, stirring, for 1 minute. Add barley and toss until well coated. Add tomatoes with juice and bring to a boil. Transfer to stoneware. Stir in stock.

2. Cover and cook on Low for 8 hours or on High for 4 hours. Serve piping hot.

TIPS

• The fennel adds a pleasant slightly licorice taste that complements the flavors in the sausage but if you don't have it you can substitute 6 stalks of chopped celery.
• Use whole, pot or pearl barley when making this recipe.

Brown Rice and Beans with Cheese and Chiles

SERVES 6

Not only does this delicious casserole appeal to a wide variety of tastes, the combination of rice and beans creates a complete protein, making it particularly nutritious for vegetarians. Add a tossed salad and hot crusty rolls for a satisfying meal.

Make ahead

This dish can be assembled the night before it is cooked. Complete Step 1. Cover and refrigerate overnight. The next morning, continue with the recipe.

Variation

Substitute cranberry, Romano, pinto or red kidney beans for the black beans, if desired.

• Works in slow cookers from 3½ to 6 quarts

1 tbsp	vegetable oil	15 mL
1	onion, finely chopped	1
2	stalks celery, diced	2
¾ cup	long-grain brown rice	175 mL
½ tsp	salt	2 mL
½ tsp	cracked black peppercorns	2 mL
1	can (10 oz/284 mL) condensed cream of celery soup	1
1½ cups	vegetable stock	375 mL
2 cups	cooked dried or canned black beans, drained and rinsed (see Basic Beans, page 219)	500 mL
1	jalapeño pepper, finely chopped, optional	1
1	can (4½ oz/127 mL) mild green chiles, drained and chopped	1
2½ cups	shredded Cheddar cheese	625 mL

1. In a skillet, heat oil over medium heat for 30 seconds. Add onion and celery and cook, stirring, until softened, about 5 minutes. Add rice, salt and peppercorns and cook, stirring, for 1 minute. Add soup and stock and stir until smooth. Stir in beans and transfer to slow cooker stoneware.

2. Place two clean tea towels, each folded in half (so you will have four layers), over top of stoneware to absorb the accumulated moisture. Cover and cook on Low for 8 hours or on High for 4 hours, until hot and bubbly.

3. Remove tea towels. Add jalapeño pepper, if using, green chiles and Cheddar cheese. Cover and cook on High for 20 to 30 minutes, until cheese is melted and mixture is hot and bubbly.

TIPS
- Accumulated moisture affects the consistency of the rice. The tea towels will absorb the moisture generated during cooking.

Leek and Barley Risotto

SERVES 4 TO 6

In addition to being a tasty side dish, this tasty "risotto," makes an interesting centerpiece of a light meal, served with a salad and hot, crusty bread. In season, add some steamed yellow waxed beans, tossed with butter or butter substitute, lemon juice and finely chopped fresh dill.

Make ahead

This dish can be partially prepared the night before it is cooked. Complete Step 1. Cover and refrigerate overnight. The next morning, continue with the recipe.

- **Works in slow cookers from 3$\frac{1}{2}$ to 6 quarts**

1 tbsp	vegetable oil	15 mL
3	leeks, white part only, cleaned and thinly sliced (see Tips, below)	3
1 tsp	salt	5 mL
$\frac{1}{2}$ tsp	cracked black peppercorns	2 mL
2 cups	barley, rinsed (see Tips, below)	500 mL
1	can (28 oz/796 mL) tomatoes, including juice, coarsely chopped	1
3 cups	vegetable stock or water	750 mL
	Freshly grated Parmesan cheese, optional	

1. In a skillet, heat oil over medium heat for 30 seconds. Add leeks and cook, stirring, until softened, about 5 minutes. Add salt, peppercorns and barley and cook, stirring, for 1 minute. Add tomatoes with juice and stock and bring to a boil. Transfer to slow cooker stoneware.

2. Cover and cook on Low for 8 hours or on High for 4 hours, until barley is tender. Stir in Parmesan, if using, and serve piping hot.

TIPS

- To clean leeks: Fill sink full of lukewarm water. Split leeks in half lengthwise and submerge in water, swishing them around to remove all traces of dirt. Transfer to a colander and rinse under cold water.
- Use whole, pot or pearl barley in this recipe.

Leek Risotto

SERVES 4 TO 6

Serve this simple risotto as an accompaniment to a meat course, such as plain roast chicken or grilled veal chops. Accompanied by a tossed green salad, and some crusty rolls, it also makes a light weeknight meal.

● *Works in slow cookers from 3 1/2 to 6 quarts*

1 tbsp	olive oil	15 mL
3	leeks, white part with just a bit of green, cleaned and thinly sliced (see Tips, below)	3
2	cloves garlic, minced	2
1/2 tsp	cracked black peppercorns	2 mL
1 cup	Arborio rice	250 mL
1/2 cup	dry white wine (see Tips, below)	125 mL
2 1/2 cups	chicken or vegetable stock	625 mL
1/2 cup	freshly grated Parmesan cheese, optional	125 mL
1/4 cup	finely chopped parsley	50 mL

1. In a large skillet, heat oil over medium heat for 30 seconds. Add leeks and cook, stirring, until softened, about 5 minutes. Add garlic and peppercorns and cook, stirring, for 1 minute. Add rice and cook, stirring, until coated. Add white wine and stock and stir well. Transfer to slow cooker stoneware.

2. Place a clean tea towel, folded in half (so you will have two layers), over top of stoneware to absorb moisture. Cover and cook on Low for 4 hours or on High for 2 hours, until liquid is absorbed and rice is tender to the bite. Stir in Parmesan, if using, and parsley and serve.

> **TIPS**
> ● To clean leeks: Fill sink full of lukewarm water. Split leeks in half lengthwise and submerge in water, swishing them around to remove all traces of dirt. Transfer to a colander and rinse under cold water.
> ● If you prefer, use an additional 1/2 cup (125 mL) of stock instead of the wine.

Slow-Cooked Polenta

SERVES 6

Polenta, an extremely versatile dish from northern Italy, is basically cornmeal cooked in seasoned liquid. It is one of my favorite grains. Depending upon the method used, making polenta can be a laborious process. These slow-cooked versions produce excellent results with a minimum of effort.

Variation
Creamy Polenta
Substitute 2 cups (500 mL) milk or cream and $1\frac{1}{4}$ cups (300 mL) stock for the quantity of liquid above. If desired, stir in $\frac{1}{4}$ cup (50 mL) finely chopped fresh parsley and/or 2 tbsp (25 mL) freshly grated Parmesan cheese, after the cornmeal has been added to the liquid.

• **Works in slow cookers from $3\frac{1}{2}$ to 6 quarts (see Tip, below)**

$3\frac{3}{4}$ cups	vegetable stock or water	925 mL
1 tsp	salt	5 mL
$\frac{1}{4}$ tsp	freshly ground black pepper	1 mL
$1\frac{1}{4}$ cups	cornmeal, preferably stone-ground	300 mL

1. In a saucepan, bring stock, salt and pepper to a boil over medium heat. Add cornmeal in a thin stream, stirring constantly.

2. *Direct method:* Transfer mixture to prepared slow cooker stoneware (see Tip, below). Cover and cook on Low for $1\frac{1}{2}$ hours.

3. *Baking dish method:* Transfer mixture to prepared baking dish (see Tip, below). Cover with foil and secure with a string. Place dish in slow cooker stoneware and pour in enough boiling water to come 1 inch (2.5 cm) up the sides of the dish. Cover and cook on Low for $1\frac{1}{2}$ hours.

TIP
• You can cook polenta directly in the slow cooker stoneware or in a 6-cup (1.5 L) baking dish, lightly greased, depending upon your preference. If you are cooking directly in the stoneware, I recommend using a small (maximum $3\frac{1}{2}$ quart) slow cooker, lightly greased. If you are using a baking dish, you will need a large (minimum 5 quart) oval slow cooker.

Parsnip and Carrot Purée with Cumin

SERVES 8

The cumin adds a slightly exotic note to this traditional dish, which makes a great accompaniment to many foods.

Make ahead

Peel and cut parsnips and carrots. Cover and refrigerate overnight.

● **Works in slow cookers from 3$\frac{1}{2}$ to 6 quarts**

4 cups	peeled parsnips, cut into $\frac{1}{2}$-inch (1 cm) cubes	1 L
2 cups	thinly sliced peeled carrots	500 mL
1 tsp	cumin seeds, toasted and coarsely ground (see Tip, below)	5 mL
2 tbsp	butter or butter substitute	25 mL
1 tsp	granulated sugar	5 mL
$\frac{1}{2}$ tsp	salt	2 mL
$\frac{1}{4}$ tsp	freshly ground black pepper	1 mL
$\frac{1}{4}$ cup	water or vegetable stock	50 mL

1. In slow cooker stoneware, combine parsnips, carrots, toasted cumin, butter or butter substitute, sugar, salt, pepper and water. Cover and cook on Low for 8 to 10 hours or on High for 4 to 5 hours, until vegetables are tender.

2. Using a potato masher or a food processor or blender, mash or purée mixture until smooth. Serve immediately.

> **TIP**
> ● To toast cumin seeds: In a dry skillet over medium heat, toast cumin seeds, stirring, until fragrant and seeds just begin to brown, about 3 minutes. Immediately transfer to a spice grinder or mortar, or use the bottom of a measuring cup or wine bottle to coarsely grind.

Saffron-Scented Fennel Gratin

SERVES 8

Serve this flavorful gratin as a vegetable side — it makes a great accompaniment to roast chicken or beef — or as a main course sauce over mashed potatoes or polenta or even a white bean purée (see Tip, below).

Make ahead

This dish can be partially prepared before it is cooked. Complete Step 1. Cover and refrigerate overnight. The next morning, continue with the recipe.

- **Works in slow cookers from 3¹/₂ to 6 quarts**

1 tbsp	olive oil (approx.)	15 mL
3	bulbs fennel, trimmed, cored and thinly sliced on the vertical	3
2 cups	vegetable stock	500 mL
	Salt, optional	
	Freshly ground black pepper, optional	
¹/₂ tsp	saffron threads	2 mL
¹/₂ cup	coarsely grated Parmesan cheese	125 mL

1. In a skillet, heat oil over medium-high heat for 30 seconds. Add fennel, in batches, adding more oil as necessary, and cook, stirring, just until the fennel begins to brown, about 5 minutes per batch. Transfer to slow cooker stoneware and add stock. Season to taste with salt and pepper, if using.

2. Place a clean tea towel, folded in half (so you will have two layers), over top of stoneware to absorb moisture. Cover and cook on Low for 6 hours or on High for 3 hours, until fennel is tender.

3. Preheat broiler. Using a slotted spoon, transfer fennel to a heatproof serving dish and cover. Pour liquid from slow cooker into a saucepan and add saffron. Bring to a boil over medium heat and cook until reduced by half, about 6 minutes. Pour over fennel. Sprinkle with Parmesan and place under broiler until cheese is melted and brown.

TIP

- Easy White Bean Purée: Heat 1 tbsp (15 mL) olive oil in a skillet over medium heat for 30 seconds. Add ¹/₂ cup (125 mL) finely chopped parsley and 2 cloves minced garlic and cook, stirring, for 1 minute. Add 2 cups (500 mL) cooked dried or canned white kidney beans, drained and rinsed. Cook, mashing with a fork, until beans are heated through. Season to taste with salt and freshly ground black pepper.

Braised Sauerkraut

SERVES 8

If, like me, you're a fan of sauerkraut, there is nothing that does more to complement a pork roast. Many people think they don't like sauerkraut, but I'm sure it's because they have never tasted a good homemade version. One of the most important steps in using sauerkraut is to soak it well, overnight, in several changes of water to get rid of all the vinegar. When properly soaked, it is very smooth, like a well-flavored cabbage. This recipe, which I've adapted from Julia Child, is absolutely delicious. You'd be surprised at how many people request seconds.

Make ahead

This dish can be partially prepared before it is cooked. Complete Step 1. Cover and refrigerate bacon and vegetable mixtures separately for up to 2 days. When you're ready to cook, continue with the recipe.

- **Works in slow cookers from 3 ½ to 6 quarts**

5 cups	sauerkraut, soaked, drained and rinsed (see Tip, below)	1.25 L
8 oz	piece bacon, diced	250 g
1	onion, thinly sliced	1
2	carrots, peeled and diced	2
½ tsp	cracked black peppercorns	2 mL
1	bay leaf	1
1 cup	dry white wine	250 mL
1 cup	chicken stock	250 mL

1. In a skillet, cook bacon over medium heat, until browned. Using a slotted spoon, remove from pan and drain on paper towels. Set aside. Drain all but 2 tbsp (25 mL) fat from pan. Add onion and carrots to pan and cook, stirring, until carrots are softened, about 7 minutes. Add peppercorns and bay leaf and cook, stirring, for 1 minute.

2. Add drained sauerkraut and reserved bacon and toss well. Transfer to slow cooker stoneware. Add wine and chicken stock and stir well. Cover and cook on Low for 8 hours or on High for 4 hours, until hot and bubbly. Discard bay leaf.

TIP

- For best results, it's important to rinse sauerkraut thoroughly in several changes of water to reduce the bitter vinegar-taste. Soak it overnight in cold water, then soak and rinse twice more before adding to the recipe.

New Orleans Braised Onions

SERVES 8 TO 10

I call these New Orleans onions because I was inspired by an old Creole recipe for Spanish onions. In that version, the onions are braised in beef broth enhanced by the addition of liquor such as bourbon or port. After the onions are cooked, the cooking juices are reduced and herbs, such as capers or fresh thyme leaves, may be added to the concentrated sauce. In my opinion, this simplified version is every bit as tasty. This is a great dish to serve with roasted poultry or meat. If your guests like spice, pass hot pepper sauce at the table.

- **Works best in a large (minimum 5 quart) slow cooker**

2 to 3	large Spanish onions	2 to 3
6 to 9	whole cloves	6 to 9
½ tsp	salt	2 mL
½ tsp	cracked black peppercorns	2 mL
Pinch	ground thyme	Pinch
	Grated zest and juice of 1 orange	
½ cup	vegetable or beef stock	125 mL
	Finely chopped fresh parsley, optional	
	Hot pepper sauce, optional	

1. Stud onions with cloves. Place in slow cooker stoneware and sprinkle with salt, peppercorns, thyme and orange zest. Pour orange juice and stock over onions, cover and cook on Low for 8 hours or on High for 4 hours, until onions are tender.

2. Using a slotted spoon, transfer onions to a serving dish and keep warm in oven. Transfer liquid to a saucepan over medium heat. Cook until reduced by half.

3. When ready to serve, cut onions into quarters. Place on a deep platter and cover with sauce. Sprinkle with parsley, if desired, and pass the hot pepper sauce, if desired.

Potatoes and Artichokes

SERVES 6

If you like the combination of potatoes and artichokes, you'll love this dish. It's an unusual mixture of crispy potatoes and artichoke hearts in a flavorful gravy. It makes a superb accompaniment to roast lamb or grilled meats.

● **Works in slow cookers from 3¹/₂ to 6 quarts**

3	large potatoes (each about 8 oz/250 g)	3
¼ cup	olive oil	50 mL
4	cloves garlic, minced	4
2 tsp	dried Italian seasoning	10 mL
½ tsp	salt	2 mL
½ tsp	cracked black peppercorns	2 mL
1 tbsp	all-purpose flour	15 mL
¼ cup	dry white wine	50 mL
1 cup	vegetable or chicken stock	250 mL
1	can (14 oz/398 mL) artichokes, drained and quartered (about 6 artichoke hearts)	1
¼ cup	finely chopped parsley	50 mL

1. Cut potatoes in half lengthwise, then cut each half into 4 wedges. Pat dry.

2. In a skillet, heat oil over medium-high heat for 30 seconds. Add potatoes, in batches, and cook until they are nicely browned on all sides, about 7 minutes per batch. Using a slotted spoon, transfer to paper towels to drain. Drain all but 1 tbsp (15 mL) oil from pan.

3. Reduce heat to medium. Add garlic, Italian seasoning, salt and peppercorns to pan and cook, stirring, for 1 minute. Add flour and cook, stirring, for 1 minute. Add wine and stock and cook, stirring, until mixture comes to a boil and thickens, about 3 minutes. Stir in artichokes. Place potatoes in stoneware, add artichoke mixture and gently stir.

4. Cover and cook on Low for 8 hours or on High for 4 hours, until potatoes are tender. Serve immediately, garnished liberally with parsley.

Cheesy Butterbeans

SERVES 6 TO 8

Serve these tasty beans with grilled or roasted meat or add a salad and enjoy them as a light main course.

Make ahead

This dish can be partially prepared before it is cooked. Complete Step 1. Cover and refrigerate overnight. The next morning, continue with the recipe.

• **Works in slow cookers from 3½ to 6 quarts**

4 cups	cooked dried or frozen lima beans, thawed and drained, if frozen (see Basic Beans, page 219)	1 L
1	can (28 oz/796 mL) diced tomatoes, drained, ½ cup (125 mL) of the juice set aside (see Tips, page 34)	1
½ cup	chopped green onions	125 mL
1 tsp	salt	5 mL
	Freshly ground black pepper	
1	green bell pepper, chopped	1
1 cup	shredded old Cheddar cheese	250 mL

1. In slow cooker stoneware, combine beans, tomatoes, ½ cup (125 mL) tomato juice, green onions, salt and black pepper, to taste.

2. Cover and cook on Low for 6 hours or on High for 3 hours, until hot and bubbly. Stir in green pepper and cheese. Cover and cook on High for 20 minutes, until pepper is tender and cheese is melted.

Creamy Sweet Onions

SERVES 6

These luscious onions are the perfect finish to roast beef, chicken or even a grilled steak. They are delicious on their own but if you want to impress your guests, add the tasty topping.

Make ahead

This dish can be partially prepared before it is cooked. Complete Step 1. Cover and refrigerate for up to 2 days. When you're ready to cook, continue with the recipe.

• *Works in slow cookers from 3 1/2 to 6 quarts*

2 tbsp	butter	25 mL
3	sweet onions, such as Spanish, Vidalia or Texas Sweets, peeled and thinly sliced	3
1/2 tsp	salt	2 mL
1/2 tsp	cracked black peppercorns	2 mL
2 tbsp	all-purpose flour	25 mL
1/2 cup	vegetable or chicken stock	125 mL
1/4 cup	whipping (35%) cream	50 mL

Crumb Topping, optional

1 cup	dry bread crumbs	250 mL
1/2 cup	freshly grated Parmesan cheese, optional	125 mL
1 tsp	paprika	5 mL
1/4 tsp	salt	1 mL
	Freshly ground black pepper	
2 tbsp	melted butter	25 mL

1. In a large skillet, melt butter over medium heat. Add onions and cook, stirring, until softened, about 5 minutes. Add salt, peppercorns and flour and cook, stirring, for 1 minute. Add stock and bring to a boil. Transfer to slow cooker stoneware.

2. Cover and cook on Low for 6 hours or on High for 3 hours, until onions are tender. Stir in cream.

3. *Crumb Topping:* In a bowl, combine bread crumbs, Parmesan, if using, paprika, salt and pepper, to taste. Mix well. Add butter and stir to blend. Spread mixture evenly over onions. Cover, leaving lid slightly ajar to prevent accumulated moisture from dripping on the topping, and cook on High for 30 minutes, until cheese is melted and mixture is hot and bubbly.

Candied Sweet Potatoes

SERVES 6

These sweet potatoes are so delicious, I don't need an excuse to make them. My husband always has seconds.

• **Works in slow cookers from 3½ to 6 quarts**

3	sweet potatoes, peeled and cut into 1½-inch (4 cm) rounds	3
1 cup	packed brown sugar	250 mL
1 tsp	salt	5 mL
	Freshly ground black pepper	
2 tbsp	butter	25 mL
2 tbsp	orange marmalade	25 mL

1. In slow cooker stoneware, combine potatoes, brown sugar, salt and black pepper to taste. Stir well. Dot with butter.

2. Place a clean tea towel, folded in half (so you will have two layers), over top of stoneware to absorb moisture. Cover and cook on Low for 8 hours or on High for 4 hours, until potatoes are tender. Stir in marmalade. Cover and cook on High for 10 minutes, until melted.

Poire Williams Apples and Pears (page 286)

Desserts

Tapioca and Sweet Potato Pudding

SERVES 6 TO 8

I adapted this recipe from one in Andrew Chase's Asian Bistro Cookbook. It has great flavor and a particularly interesting texture with the large tapioca bubbles spread throughout. If you're feeling indulgent, add a dollop of whipped cream or a drizzle of soy creamer.

- **Works best in a small (3½ quart) slow cooker**
- **Greased slow cooker stoneware.**

½ cup	large tapioca pearls (see Tips, below)	125 mL
1	can (14 oz/398 mL) sweet potato or pumpkin purée (not pie filling) (see Tips, below)	1
1	can (14 oz/398 mL) coconut milk	1
2 cups	milk (see Tips, below)	500 mL
⅔ cup	Demerara or other evaporated cane juice sugar	150 mL
1 tsp	imitation coconut extract	5 mL
1 tsp	ground cinnamon	5 mL
½ tsp	freshly grated nutmeg	2 mL
	Toasted shredded coconut, optional	

1. In a bowl, combine tapioca pearls with water to cover. Stir well and set aside for 20 minutes. Drain, discarding liquid.

2. In prepared slow cooker stoneware, combine drained tapioca, sweet potato purée, coconut milk, milk, sugar, coconut extract, cinnamon and nutmeg.

3. Cover and cook on High for 3 hours, stirring once about halfway through the cooking time to ensure tapioca cooks evenly, until tapioca is tender. Stir well. Serve warm or transfer to a serving bowl and cover with plastic wrap to prevent a skin from forming and chill thoroughly. Garnish with toasted coconut, to taste, before serving.

TIPS
- Look for large tapioca pearls in Asian markets.
- If you can't find a 14-oz (398 mL) can of sweet potato purée, substitute 1¾ cups (425 mL) of puréed baked sweet potatoes or an equal quantity of canned pumpkin purée.
- If you are a vegan, substitute an additional can (14 oz/398 mL) of coconut milk for the milk and omit the coconut extract. Be aware that the saturated fat content will increase dramatically.
- The pudding will thicken as it rests.

Delectable Apple-Cranberry Coconut Crisp

SERVES 6 TO 8

I love to make this delicious dessert in the fall when apples and cranberries are in season. This version is a little tart, which suits my taste, but if you have a sweet tooth, add more sugar to the cranberry mixture. Great on its own, this is even better with whipped cream or a scoop of frozen yogurt or vanilla ice cream.

Variation

Apple-Coconut Crisp
Use 6 cups (1.5 L) of sliced apples total instead of the cranberries, reduce sugar to ¼ cup (50 mL) and use lemon juice rather than port wine.

- **Works best in a large (minimum 5 quart) slow cooker**
- **Lightly greased slow cooker stoneware**

4 cups	sliced, peeled apples	1 L
2 cups	cranberries, thawed if frozen	500 mL
½ cup	granulated sugar	125 mL
1 tbsp	cornstarch	15 mL
½ tsp	ground cinnamon	2 mL
2 tbsp	freshly squeezed lemon juice or port wine	25 mL
Coconut Topping		
½ cup	packed brown sugar	125 mL
½ cup	rolled oats	125 mL
¼ cup	flaked sweetened coconut	50 mL
¼ cup	butter	50 mL

1. In a bowl, combine apples, cranberries, sugar, cornstarch, cinnamon and lemon juice. Mix well and transfer to prepared stoneware.

2. *Coconut Topping:* In a separate bowl, combine brown sugar, rolled oats, coconut and butter. Using two forks or your fingers, combine until crumbly. Spread over apple mixture.

3. Place two clean tea towels, each folded in half (so you will have four layers), over top of stoneware. Cover and cook on High for 3 to 4 hours, until crisp is hot and bubbly. Serve with whipped cream or ice cream, if desired.

Rhubarb Betty

SERVES 6

There are many different variations on this traditional dessert, which is basically baked fruit with a seasoned topping. This version, which relies on bread crumbs for its starch component, is particularly simple and good. It works equally well with a rhubarb-strawberry combination or with apples. Serve with sweetened whipped cream or a non-dairy creamer or a vanilla ice.

Variations

Rhubarb-Strawberry Betty
Use 2 cups (500 mL) each of strawberries, quartered, and rhubarb, cut into 1-inch (2.5 cm) chunks. Reduce sugar to ³⁄₄ cup (175 mL) and omit cinnamon.

Apple Betty
Substitute peeled apple slices for rhubarb and the juice and zest of one lemon for the orange. Reduce sugar to ¹⁄₂ to ³⁄₄ cup (125 to 175 mL), depending on preference.

- **Works best in a small (3¹⁄₂ quart) slow cooker (see Tips, below)**
- **Lightly greased slow cooker stoneware**

¹⁄₃ cup	melted butter or olive oil	75 mL
2 cups	fresh bread crumbs (see Tips, below)	500 mL
4 cups	rhubarb, cut into 1-inch (2.5 cm) chunks	1 L
1 cup	granulated sugar	250 mL
1 tbsp	all-purpose flour	15 mL
1 tsp	ground cinnamon	5 mL
	Grated zest and juice of 1 orange	

1. In a mixing bowl, combine butter or olive oil and bread crumbs. Set aside.

2. In a separate bowl, combine rhubarb, sugar, flour and cinnamon.

3. In prepared slow cooker stoneware, layer one-third of the bread crumb mixture, then one-half of the rhubarb mixture. Repeat layers of bread crumbs and fruit, then finish with a layer of bread crumbs on top. Pour zest and orange juice over top. Cook on High for 3 to 4 hours, until bubbly and brown.

TIPS
- If you have a large oval cooker, double the quantity. Refrigerate leftovers and reheat.
- Fresh bread crumbs are far superior to the ready-made kind, which can be very dry. They are easily made in a food processor by removing the crust, if desired, cutting the bread into manageable chunks and then processing until the appropriate degree of fineness is achieved. Tightly covered, bread crumbs will keep for 2 or 3 days in the refrigerator.

Blackberry Peach Cobbler

SERVES 6

This recipe is an adaptation of one that appeared in Gourmet magazine. It's an absolutely mouth-watering dessert for late summer when these luscious fruits are at their peak. The advantage to making it in the slow cooker, rather than in the oven, is that you can be doing other things while it cooks to perfection.

- **Works best in a small (3½ quart) slow cooker**
- **Lightly greased slow cooker stoneware**

4	peaches, peeled and sliced (see Tip, below)	4
3 cups	blackberries (see Tip, below)	750 mL
1 tbsp	freshly squeezed lemon juice	15 mL
1 tbsp	cornstarch	15 mL
¾ cup	granulated sugar	175 mL
Topping		
1½ cups	all-purpose flour	375 mL
2 tsp	baking powder	10 mL
½ tsp	salt	2 mL
1 tsp	grated lemon zest	5 mL
½ cup	cold butter, cubed (1 inch/2.5 cm)	125 mL
½ cup	milk	125 mL

1. In prepared stoneware, combine peaches, blackberries, lemon juice, cornstarch and sugar. Stir well. Cover and Cook on Low for 4 hours or on High for 2 hours.

2. *Topping*: In a bowl, combine flour, baking powder, salt and lemon zest. Using your fingers or a pastry blender, cut in butter until mixture resembles coarse crumbs. Drizzle with milk and stir with a fork until a batter forms.

3. Drop batter by spoonfuls over hot fruit. Cover and cook on High for 1 hour, until a toothpick inserted in the center comes out clean.

TIP

- You can substitute 2 cans (each 14 oz/398 mL) sliced peaches, drained, for the fresh and use an equal quantity of frozen blackberries, thawed.

Poire Williams Apples and Pears

SERVES 8

I just love this combination of fruit baked in its own juices with sugar and a vanilla bean and finished with a dash of pear eau de vie. You won't believe this tastes as good as it does until you try it! With the addition of vanilla wafers you can serve this at even the most elegant dinner, as I have done.

Variation

Apples and Pears in Cointreau

Substitute 1 tbsp (15 mL) finely grated orange zest for the lemon zest and 2 tbsp (25 mL) Cointreau or other orange-flavored liqueur for the pear eau de vie.

• *Works in slow cookers from 3½ to 6 quarts*

4 cups	water	1 L
	Juice of half a lemon	
4	large firm pears, such as Bartlett or Bosc	4
4	Granny Smith apples	4
1½ cups	granulated sugar	375 mL
1 tbsp	finely grated lemon zest	15 mL
1	vanilla bean, split	1
2 tbsp	pear eau de vie	25 mL
	Chopped candied ginger, optional	
	Whipped cream, optional	

1. In a large bowl, combine water and lemon juice. Peel, core and quarter the pears and apples, dropping each piece into the lemon juice solution as it is prepared. (This will prevent the fruit from turning brown.)

2. In slow cooker stoneware, combine sugar, lemon zest and vanilla bean. Add drained prepared fruit and toss to evenly coat. Place a clean tea towel, folded in half (so you will have two layers), over top of stoneware. Cover and cook on High for 4 hours, until the liquid is syrupy and the fruit is tender but firm, gently stirring occasionally. Add eau de vie and ginger, if using. Discard vanilla bean. Serve warm with a dollop of cream, if using.

Cranberry Baked Apples

SERVES 6

Cranberries add an appealing kick to this delicious old-fashioned dessert that never goes out of style.

Variation

Granny's Baked Apples

For a simplified version of this recipe, eliminate the nuts and berries. Make a filling of $1/3$ cup (175 mL) packed brown sugar, $1/4$ cup (50 mL) melted butter and $1/2$ tsp (2 mL) ground cinnamon. Proceed as above.

• *Works best in a large (minimum 5 quart) slow cooker*

1/2 cup	chopped pecans	125 mL
1/2 cup	dried cranberries	125 mL
1/2 cup	packed brown or Demerara sugar	125 mL
1/4 cup	melted butter	50 mL
1/2 tsp	ground cinnamon	2 mL
6	apples, cored	6
1 cup	unsweetened apple juice	250 mL
	Table or whipped cream	

1. In a bowl, combine pecans, cranberries, brown sugar, butter and cinnamon. Using your fingers, pack filling into apples. Place in slow cooker stoneware, sprinkling extra filling over apples. Pour apple juice over top.

2. Cover and cook on Low for 6 hours or on High for 3 hours, until apples are tender. Transfer apples to serving dishes with a slotted spoon and spoon cooking juices over them. Pass the cream or top each apple with a dollop of whipped cream.

Irish Chocolate Tapioca Pudding

SERVES 6

In my opinion, there is nothing quite like tapioca pudding to conjure up memories of mother love. This version of that old favorite is delicious comfort food with a kick. Serve it with simple wafers, topped with a dollop of whipped cream and expect requests for seconds. Nothing gets better than this.

- **Large (minimum 5 quart) oval slow cooker**
- **Lightly greased 6-cup (1.5 L) baking dish**

¼ cup	tapioca pearls	50 mL
2½ cups	milk, divided	625 mL
6 oz	bittersweet or semisweet chocolate, broken into pieces	175 g
2	eggs	2
½ cup	granulated sugar	125 mL
¼ cup	Irish cream liqueur	50 mL
½ tsp	vanilla	2 mL
	Whipped cream	

1. In a bowl, combine tapioca pearls with water to cover. Stir well and set aside for 20 minutes. Drain, discarding liquid. Transfer to prepared dish.

2. Meanwhile, in a saucepan, heat 1 cup (250 mL) of the milk over low heat just until simmering. (Do not boil.) Remove from heat. Add chocolate and stir until melted. Pour into prepared dish and stir to combine.

3. In a blender, combine eggs, sugar, remaining 1½ cups (375 mL) of the milk, liqueur and vanilla. Blend until smooth. Add to prepared dish and stir well. Cover with foil and secure with string. Place dish in slow cooker stoneware and add enough boiling water to come 1 inch (2.5 cm) up the sides of dish. Cover and cook on High for 2½ to 3 hours, until a knife inserted in the pudding comes out clean. Stir well. Serve warm or cover and chill overnight. Top with a dollop of whipped cream.

Old-Fashioned Gingerbread

SERVES 6 TO 8

This delicious cake is wonderful with applesauce, stewed rhubarb, butterscotch sauce or a scoop of vanilla ice cream. Since I almost always have the ingredients on hand, I most often serve it with whipped cream flavored with candied ginger, which is usually available in the bulk food sections of supermarkets. Simply whip the cream and add finely chopped candied ginger, to taste. Expect requests for seconds.

- **Large (minimum 5 quart) oval slow cooker, if using baking pan**
- **Lightly greased baking pan or slow cooker stoneware (see Tip, below)**

1 cup	milk	250 mL
2 tsp	baking soda	10 mL
1 tbsp	ground ginger	15 mL
½ cup	butter	125 mL
½ cup	packed brown sugar	125 mL
1 cup	corn syrup	250 mL
2 cups	all-purpose flour	500 mL
1	egg, beaten	1
	Grated zest of 1 lemon	

1. In a saucepan, warm milk over low heat. Remove from heat. Stir in baking soda and ginger. Set aside.

2. In a large saucepan, melt butter over low heat. Add brown sugar and stir until dissolved. Add corn syrup and stir to combine.

3. Stir flour into syrup mixture, mixing well. Stir in egg, milk mixture and lemon zest, mixing to combine thoroughly. Pour into prepared pan and place in slow cooker or spread directly into prepared stoneware. Place two clean tea towels, each folded in half (so you will have four layers), over top of the stoneware. Cover and cook on High for 4 hours in a pan or 2 hours if directly in stoneware (see Tip, below) or until a toothpick inserted in the center of the cake comes out clean. Serve warm.

TIP

- One challenge with making cakes in a slow cooker is finding a baking pan that will fit. I make this recipe in a 5-quart slow cooker using a 6-cup (1.5 L) oval baking dish that measures 10¼ inches (26 cm) end to end. You can also bake this directly in the stoneware that fits a smaller slow cooker. However, the baking time will be significantly reduced. In that case, begin checking doneness at the 2-hour mark.

Pineapple Upside-Down Spice Cake

SERVES 6 TO 8

This recipe is an old favorite, remembered from my childhood. I still love it, topped with a big scoop of vanilla ice cream.

Variation

Peach Upside-Down Spice Cake

For the pineapple, substitute 6 peaches, sliced, or 2 (14 oz/ 398 mL) cans of peach slices, drained.

- **Works best in a large (minimum 5 quart) slow cooker**
- **Lightly greased slow cooker stoneware**

Fruit

¼ cup	melted butter	50 mL
½ cup	firmly packed brown sugar	125 mL
10	slices fresh pineapple or 1 can (19 oz/540 mL) sliced pineapple, drained	10

Cake

¾ cup	all-purpose flour	175 mL
1 tsp	baking powder	5 mL
¼ tsp	salt	1 mL
¼ cup	butter	50 mL
1 cup	granulated sugar	250 mL
1	egg	1
½ cup	milk	125 mL
1 tsp	ground cinnamon	5 mL
1 tsp	ground allspice	5 mL
½ tsp	ground cloves	2 mL
½ tsp	ground nutmeg	2 mL
1 tsp	vanilla	5 mL

1. In a small bowl, combine butter and brown sugar. Spread over bottom of prepared stoneware. Arrange pineapple on top.

2. *Cake*: In a bowl, combine flour, baking powder and salt. In a mixing bowl, using an electric mixer, if desired, cream butter and sugar until light and fluffy. Beat in egg. Add milk and flour mixture alternately, making three additions of flour and two of milk, beating well after each addition. Blend in cinnamon, allspice, cloves, nutmeg and vanilla. Pour mixture over pineapple slices.

3. Place two clean tea towels, each folded in half (so you will have four layers), over top of stoneware. Cover and cook on High for 3 hours or until a toothpick inserted in center of cake comes out clean. To serve, slice and invert on plate. Top with vanilla ice cream.

Plum Pudding

SERVES 8 TO 12

Here's a lightened up version of a traditional holiday favorite. Allow a week for the mixed pudding to soak in the refrigerator. I like to serve this warm with a simple lemon sauce or store-bought lemon curd, but if you're a traditionalist, hard sauce works well, too. Don't worry about leftovers. It reheats well and with a steaming cup of tea will take the chill off even the most blustery winter day.

- **Large (minimum 5 quart) oval slow cooker**
- **6-cup (1.5 L) lightly greased pudding basin, baking or soufflé dish**

1 cup	seedless raisins	250 mL
½ cup	finely chopped mixed candied fruit	125 mL
2 tbsp	chopped candied orange peel	25 mL
2 tbsp	chopped candied ginger	25 mL
	Finely grated zest of 1 orange	
	Finely grated zest of 1 lemon	
½ cup	brandy or dark rum (approx.)	125 mL
¾ cup	all-purpose flour	175 mL
¾ cup	fine dry white bread crumbs	175 mL
2 tbsp	ground toasted blanched almonds	25 mL
1 tsp	ground cinnamon	5 mL
¾ tsp	baking powder	4 mL
¼ tsp	freshly grated nutmeg	1 mL
¼ tsp	salt	1 mL
¾ cup	packed brown sugar	175 mL
½ cup	butter, softened	125 mL
2	eggs	2
2 tbsp	mild-flavored or fancy molasses	25 mL

1. In a bowl, combine raisins, candied fruit, orange peel, candied ginger and orange and lemon zests. Add brandy and stir well. Set aside for 1 hour.

2. In a separate bowl, mix together flour, bread crumbs, ground almonds, cinnamon, baking powder, nutmeg and salt. Set aside.

3. In a clean bowl, beat brown sugar and butter until creamy. Add eggs and molasses and beat until incorporated. Stir in soaked fruit mixture. Add flour mixture and mix just until blended. Spoon batter into prepared dish. Cover tightly with plastic wrap and let sit in refrigerator for a week, spooning additional brandy or rum over the top two or three times in 1 tbsp (15 mL) increments.

4. Remove plastic wrap. Cover with foil and secure with a string. Place dish in slow cooker stoneware and pour in enough boiling water to come 1 inch (2.5 cm) up the sides of the dish. Cover and cook on High for 4 hours, until a toothpick inserted in the center of the pudding comes out clean. Serve hot.

Oranges in Cointreau

SERVES 8

This delightfully different dessert is so easy to make, yet sumptuous enough to satisfy even the most sophisticated palate. It's delicious topped with whipped cream but I love to serve it as an oh-so-chic sundae, over vanilla ice cream or a complementary sorbet. Yum!

- **Works in slow cookers from 3¹⁄₂ to 6 quarts**

1 cup	granulated sugar, divided	250 mL
6	oranges, preferably organic, thinly sliced (¹⁄₄ inch/0.5 cm), seeds removed	6
1	cinnamon stick piece (2 inches/5 cm)	1
2 tbsp	Cointreau (see Tip, below)	25 mL

1. Sprinkle ¹⁄₄ cup (50 mL) of the sugar over the bottom of slow cooker stoneware. Arrange the orange slices on top in overlapping layers, burying the cinnamon stick in the center. Sprinkle remaining sugar evenly over the oranges. Place a clean tea towel, folded in half (so you will have two layers), over top of stoneware. Cover and cook on High for 4 hours, until the liquid is syrupy and the fruit is soft. Stir in Cointreau.

TIP
- If you prefer, substitute an equal quantity of any other orange-flavored liqueur, such as Triple Sec or Grand Marnier, for the Cointreau.

Rice Pudding with Cherries and Almonds

SERVES 6

This family favorite is delicious enough to serve at an elegant dinner party. Spoon into crystal goblets and serve warm or cold.

- **Works best in a small (3½ quart) slow cooker**
- **Lightly greased slow cooker stoneware**

¾ cup	granulated sugar	175 mL
½ cup	Arborio rice (see Tips, below)	125 mL
¼ cup	dried cherries (see Tips, below)	50 mL
2 tbsp	ground almonds	25 mL
1 tsp	grated lemon zest	5 mL
Pinch	salt	Pinch
4 cups	milk (see Tips, below)	1 L
2	eggs	2
1 tsp	almond extract	5 mL
	Toasted sliced almonds, optional	
	Whipped cream, optional	

1. In prepared slow cooker stoneware, mix together sugar, rice, cherries, almonds, lemon zest and salt.

2. In a large bowl, whisk together milk, eggs and almond extract, and stir into rice mixture. Cover and cook on High for 4 hours, until rice is tender and pudding is set. Serve warm or cover and chill. Garnish with toasted almonds and whipped cream, if desired.

TIPS
- Long-grain white rice can be successfully used in this recipe, but the pudding will not be as creamy as one made with Arborio rice.
- Use 1 cup (250 mL) fresh pitted cherries in place of the dried cherries, if desired. Or substitute an equal quantity of dried cranberries instead.
- For a richer pudding, use half milk and half cream.

Chocaberry Cheesecake

SERVES 8 TO 10

Here's a cheesecake to die for — a yummy white chocolate base, punctuated by luscious raspberries, resting on a rich chocolate crust. Even better, made in the slow cooker, it is virtually foolproof.

Make ahead

This cake is best made a day ahead and allowed to chill in the refrigerator overnight.

- **Large (minimum 5 quart) oval slow cooker**
- **7-inch (17.5 cm) 6-cup (1.5 L) soufflé dish, lined with greased heavy-duty foil, or 7-inch (17.5 cm) well-greased springform pan (see Tip, page 302)**

Crust

20	chocolate wafers	20
¼ cup	semisweet chocolate chips	50 mL
2 tbsp	granulated sugar	25 mL
2 tsp	melted butter	10 mL

Cheesecake

2	packages (each 8 oz/250 g) cream cheese, softened	2
½ cup	granulated sugar	125 mL
2	eggs	2
1 tsp	almond extract	5 mL
2 tbsp	amaretto liqueur, optional	25 mL
6 oz	white chocolate, chopped	175 g
¼ cup	whipping (35%) cream	50 mL
1 cup	raspberries, thawed if frozen	250 mL

1. *Crust:* In a food processor, combine chocolate wafers, chocolate chips and sugar. Process until fine. Add butter and pulse. Press mixture into the bottom of prepared dish. Place in freezer until ready to use.

2. *Cheesecake:* In a clean food processor, combine cream cheese with sugar and process until smooth. Add eggs, almond extract and amaretto, if using, and process until combined.

3. In a saucepan over low heat, combine white chocolate and whipping cream. Cook, stirring, until melted. Add to cheese mixture and process until smooth.

4. Arrange raspberries evenly over crust. Pour cheesecake mixture over top. Cover dish tightly with foil and secure with string.(If using a springform pan, see Tip, page 302). Place dish in slow cooker stoneware and pour in enough boiling water to come 1 inch (2.5 cm) up the sides of pan. Cover and cook on High for 3 to 4 hours or until edges are set and center is slightly jiggly. Chill thoroughly before serving.

Classic Flan

SERVES 6

To the French a flan is a fruit tart, often including a custard base, but I've always thought the Spanish laid claim to the term with their rich cold custards surrounded by bittersweet caramel. This version is simple to make and wonderful to eat.

- **Large (minimum 5 quart) oval slow cooker**
- **Lightly greased 4-cup (1L) baking dish**

1¾ cups	granulated sugar, divided	425 mL
¼ cup	water	50 mL
1 cup	table (18%) cream	250 mL
1	strip orange or lemon zest	1
1	cinnamon stick piece (2 inches/5 cm)	1
1 tsp	vanilla	5 mL
3	eggs	3
2	egg yolks	2

1. In a saucepan over medium heat, combine 1 cup (250 mL) of the sugar and water. Cook, stirring constantly, until sugar is dissolved and mixture comes to a boil. Stop stirring and continue to cook until golden brown, about 5 minutes. Working quickly, pour into prepared dish, tilting to distribute the syrup across the bottom and up the sides.

2. In a clean saucepan over medium heat, combine cream, orange zest, cinnamon stick, vanilla and remaining ¾ cup (175 mL) of the sugar. Heat just until it reaches the boiling point, then remove from heat and set aside.

3. In a bowl, whisk eggs and egg yolks until blended. Gradually add hot cream mixture, whisking constantly. Strain through a fine sieve into prepared baking dish. Cover with foil and secure with a string. Place dish in stoneware and add enough boiling water to come 1 inch (2.5 cm) up the side of the dish. Cover and cook on High for 3 hours, until a toothpick inserted in the center of the custard comes out clean. Chill thoroughly. To serve, run a sharp knife around the edge of the custard and invert onto a serving plate. Serve cold.

Buttermilk Lemon Sponge

SERVES 4 TO 6

Here's the perfect dessert: creamy yet light with just a hint of lemon. As it cooks, the egg whites separate into a "sponge" layer, leaving a velvety version of lemon curd on the bottom. Serve this warm with a mound of fresh berries on the side. Blueberries, raspberries, strawberries — whatever is in season — make an ideal finish.

- **Large (minimum 5 quart) oval slow cooker**
- **Greased 4-cup (1 L) baking dish**

½ cup	granulated sugar	125 mL
2	eggs, separated	2
⅔ cup	buttermilk	150 mL
1 tbsp	finely grated lemon zest	15 mL
3 tbsp	freshly squeezed lemon juice	45 mL
¼ cup	all purpose flour	50 mL
¼ tsp	salt	1 mL

1. In a mixing bowl, whisk sugar and egg yolks until smooth. Whisk in buttermilk and lemon zest and juice. Add flour and salt and whisk until blended.

2. In a separate bowl, beat egg whites until stiff. Gently fold into lemon mixture to make a smooth batter. Spoon into prepared dish. Cover with foil and secure with string. Place dish in slow cooker stoneware and pour in enough boiling water to come 1 inch (2.5 cm) up the sides of the dish. Cover and cook on High for 2½ hours, until a toothpick inserted in the center of the pudding comes out clean.

Lemon Cheesecake

SERVES 8 TO 10

The refreshing lemon taste combined with its rich cheese base makes this cake one of my favorites. Since almonds and lemons have a great affinity, I'm particularly fond of the Variation with almonds in the crust. In summer, I serve this with fresh blueberries.

Make ahead

This cake is best made a day ahead and allowed to chill in the refrigerator overnight.

Variation

Lemon Cheesecake with Crunchy Almond Crust

Reduce vanilla wafer crumbs to ½ cup (125 mL) and add ½ cup (125 mL) ground toasted blanched almonds. Increase sugar to ¼ cup (50 mL).

- **Works best in a large (minimum 5 quart) oval slow cooker**
- **7-inch (17.5 cm) 6-cup (1.5 L) soufflé dish, lined with greased heavy-duty foil, or 7-inch (17.5 cm) well-greased springform pan (see Tip, below)**

Crust

1 cup	vanilla wafer crumbs	250 mL
2 tbsp	granulated sugar	25 mL
Pinch	salt	Pinch
3 tbsp	melted butter	45 mL
1 tsp	grated lemon zest	5 mL
¼ tsp	vanilla	1 mL

Cheesecake

2	packages (each 8 oz/250 g) cream cheese, softened	2
¾ cup	granulated sugar	175 mL
2	eggs	2
½ cup	sour cream	125 mL
1 tsp	vanilla	5 mL
1 tsp	grated lemon zest	5 mL
¼ cup	freshly squeezed lemon juice	50 mL
Pinch	salt	Pinch

1. *Crust*: In a bowl, combine vanilla wafer crumbs, sugar, salt, butter, lemon zest and vanilla. Press the mixture into the bottom of prepared dish. Place in freezer until ready to use.

2. *Cheesecake*: In a food processor, combine cream cheese with sugar and process until smooth. Add eggs, sour cream, vanilla, lemon zest and juice and salt and process until smooth. Spoon mixture over crust. Cover dish tightly with foil and secure with string. Place dish in stoneware and pour in enough boiling water to come 1 inch (2.5 cm) up the sides of dish. Cover and cook on High for 3 to 4 hours, until edges are set and center is just slightly jiggly. Chill thoroughly before serving.

TIP

- If using a springform pan, ensure that water doesn't seep into the cake by wrapping the bottom of the pan in one large seamless piece of foil that extends up the sides and over the top. Cover the top with a single piece of foil that extends down the sides and secure with a string.

Steamed Strawberry Pudding

SERVES 4 TO 6

This remarkably light pudding-cake is a perfect dessert to make when fresh strawberries are in season and abundant. I think it's every bit as delicious as strawberry shortcake, with fewer calories and less fat.

Variation

Substitute blueberries or raspberries, in season. If using blueberries, substitute 1 tbsp (15 mL) freshly squeezed lemon juice for the balsamic vinegar when making the sauce.

- **Large (minimum 5 quart) oval slow cooker**
- **6-cup (1.5 L) lightly greased pudding basin, baking or soufflé dish**

Pudding

¼ cup	butter, softened	50 mL
¼ cup	granulated sugar	50 mL
4	eggs, separated	4
¾ cup	all-purpose flour	175 mL
2 cups	sliced strawberries	500 mL

Strawberry Sauce

¼ cup	granulated sugar	50 mL
¼ cup	water	50 mL
2 cups	strawberries	500 mL
1 tbsp	balsamic vinegar	15 mL

1. *Pudding:* In a bowl, cream butter and sugar until light and fluffy. Beat in egg yolks, one at a time. Gradually add flour, beating until combined. Gently fold in strawberries.

2. In a separate bowl, beat egg whites until stiff. Gently fold into strawberry mixture to make a smooth batter. Spoon into prepared dish. Cover with foil and secure with string or an elastic band. Place dish in slow cooker stoneware and pour in enough boiling water to come 1 inch (2.5 cm) up the sides of dish. Cover and cook on High for 2½ to 3 hours, until a toothpick inserted in center of cake comes out clean.

3. *Strawberry Sauce:* In a saucepan, combine sugar and water. Bring to a boil and cook for 1 minute. Add strawberries, return to a boil and cook for several minutes, until strawberries begin to lose their juice. Remove from heat and stir in balsamic vinegar. Spoon pudding into individual bowls and top with sauce.

TIP
- Substitute an equal quantity individually frozen, unsweetened berries, thawed, for the strawberries, if desired.

Marble Cheesecake

SERVES 8 TO 10

This is a rich and delicious cheesecake. The gingersnap crust and pumpkin-flavored base accented with chocolate is an irresistible combination.

Make ahead

This cake is best made a day ahead and allowed to chill in the refrigerator overnight.

- *Large (minimum 5 quart) oval slow cooker*
- *7-inch (17.5 cm) 6-cup (1.5 L) soufflé dish, lined with greased heavy-duty foil, or 7-inch (17.5 cm) well-greased springform pan (see Tip, page 302)*

Crust

1 cup	gingersnap cookie crumbs	250 mL
3 tbsp	packed brown sugar	45 mL
½ tsp	ground ginger	2 mL
3 tbsp	melted butter	45 mL

Cheesecake

2	packages (each 8 oz/250 g) cream cheese, softened	2
¾ cup	granulated sugar	175 mL
3	eggs	3
1 tsp	vanilla	5 mL
¼ tsp	each ground cinnamon, cloves and nutmeg	1 mL
½ cup	pumpkin purée (not pie filling)	125 mL
½ cup	whipping (35%) cream	125 mL
4 oz	semisweet or bittersweet chocolate, melted	125 g
	Chocolate curls	

1. *Crust*: In a bowl, mix together gingersnap crumbs, brown sugar and ginger. Add butter and mix to blend. Press mixture into the bottom of prepared dish. Place in freezer until ready to use.

2. *Cheesecake*: In a food processor, combine cream cheese with sugar and process until smooth. Add eggs, vanilla, cinnamon, cloves and nutmeg and process until combined. Add pumpkin and whipping cream and process until smooth. Pour mixture over crust. Pour chocolate over mixture, then, using a knife, swirl to marbleize. Cover dish tightly with foil and secure with string. (If using a springform pan, see Tip, page 302). Place dish in slow cooker stoneware and pour in enough boiling water to come 1 inch (2.5 cm) up the sides of dish. Cover and cook on High for 3 to 4 hours, until edges are set and center is slightly jiggly. Chill thoroughly before serving. Garnish with chocolate swirls.

> **TIP**
> - To melt chocolate: Grate the chocolate first by pulsing it in a food processor. Then melt in a double boiler over hot, not boiling, water, stirring constantly. This ensures that the chocolate doesn't "seize" and become grainy.

Coconut Pudding

SERVES 6

I like to serve this tasty dessert when fresh pineapple is in season. The combination of creamy coconut pudding and juicy pineapple is delectable.

- **Large (minimum 5 quart) oval slow cooker**
- **4-cup (1 L) lightly greased baking dish**

1	can (14 oz/398 mL) coconut milk	1
⅓ cup	packed brown sugar	75 mL
1 tbsp	grated lime zest	15 mL
1 tbsp	minced gingerroot	15 mL
1 cup	sweetened condensed milk	250 mL
3	eggs, beaten	3
½ cup	toasted shredded unsweetened coconut (see Tip, below)	125 mL

1. In a saucepan over medium heat, combine coconut milk, brown sugar, lime zest and gingerroot. Bring just to a boil. Remove from heat and stir in condensed milk. Let cool. Whisk in eggs. Strain through a fine sieve into prepared dish. Fold in coconut.

2. Cover with foil and secure with string. Place dish in slow cooker stoneware and pour in enough boiling water to come 1 inch (2.5 cm) up the sides of the dish. Cover and cook on High for 2½ to 3 hours, until a toothpick inserted in the center of the pudding comes out clean. Serve warm or chilled.

TIP
- To toast coconut: Spread coconut on a baking sheet and place in a preheated 350°F (180°C) oven for 7 to 8 minutes, stirring once or twice.

Cranberry-Red Currant Crumb Pudding

SERVES 6

Don't discard that slightly stale bread. Here is another great recipe for transforming leftover bread into a delicious dessert.

- **Large (minimum 5 quart) oval slow cooker**
- **6-cup (1.5 L) lightly greased pudding basin, baking or soufflé dish**

2 cups	milk	500 mL
¾ cup	granulated sugar	175 mL
2 tbsp	butter	25 mL
2 cups	fresh bread crumbs	500 mL
3	eggs	3
1 tsp	vanilla	5 mL
¼ tsp	salt	1 mL
¼ cup	dried cranberries or raisins	50 mL
2 tbsp	red currant jelly, stirred until smooth	25 mL

1. In a saucepan over medium heat, bring milk, sugar and butter to a boil, stirring, until butter melts. Remove from heat. Stir in bread crumbs.

2. In a bowl, beat eggs, vanilla and salt. Stir in cranberries, then ¼ cup (50 mL) of the bread crumb mixture. Add remaining bread crumb mixture and stir to blend.

3. Place red currant jelly in bottom of prepared dish. Add bread crumb mixture. Cover with foil and tie tightly with string. Place dish in slow cooker stoneware and pour in enough boiling water to come 1 inch (2.5 cm) up the sides of dish. Cover and cook on High for 2½ hours, until toothpick inserted in center of pudding comes out clean.

Old-Fashioned Rice Pudding

SERVES 6

This recipe is adapted from a nineteenth-century English recipe that describes the secret to a deliciously creamy pudding as "very slow and prolonged baking on the outer edges of the fire." Today, the slow cooker eliminates the need for "fire" and takes all the guesswork out of the task. It's also remarkably easy. Just mix the ingredients together and turn the cooker on — you don't even have to precook the rice. The results are absolutely delicious.

- **Works best in a small (3¹⁄₂ quart) slow cooker**
- **Lightly greased slow cooker stoneware**

³⁄₄ cup	long-grain rice	175 mL
3 cups	milk	750 mL
³⁄₄ cup	granulated sugar	175 mL
³⁄₄ tsp	ground cinnamon	4 mL
Pinch	salt	Pinch
¹⁄₃ cup	melted butter	75 mL
	Vanilla-flavored whipped cream	

1. In a colander, rinse rice thoroughly under cold water. Place in prepared stoneware. Add milk, sugar, cinnamon and salt. Stir to combine. Pour butter over rice mixture. Cover and cook on High for 4 hours, until rice has absorbed the liquid.

2. When ready to serve, spoon into individual dessert bowls and top with whipped cream flavored with vanilla.

Library and Archives Canada Cataloguing in Publication

Finlayson, Judith
    175 essential slow cooker classics / Judith Finlayson.

A collection of recipes, some already published in 150 best slow cooker recipes,
Delicious & dependable slow cooker recipes, and 125 best vegetarian slow cooker recipes.

ISBN-13: 978-0-7788-0143-6
ISBN-10: 0-7788-0143-8

1. Electric cookery, Slow. I. Title. II. Title: One hundred seventy-five essential slow cooker classics.

TX827.F555 2006   641.5'884   C2006-902493-6

Index

v = variation